The Drawing-Completion Test

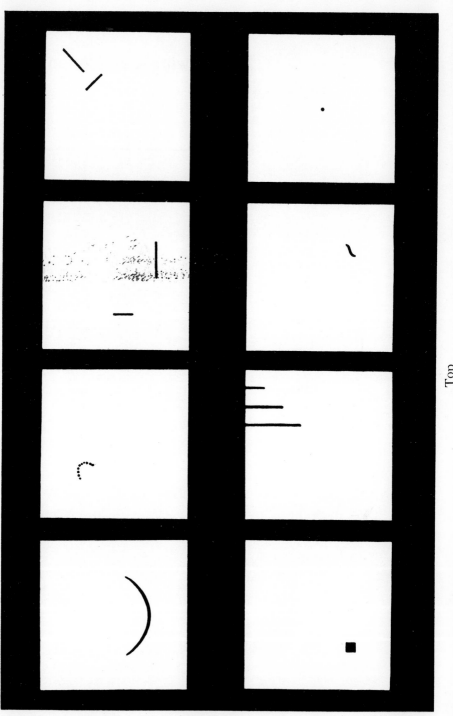

The Drawing-Completion Test

A Projective Technique for the
Investigation of Personality
Based on the Wartegg Test Blank

by G. Marian Kinget, Ph.D.
Staff Member, Counseling Center,
University of Chicago, Chicago, Ill.

foreword by Percival M. Symonds, Ph.D.
Professor of Education,
Columbia University, New York, N.Y.

GRUNE & STRATTON, INC.

New York   1952

First printing, February 1952
Second printing, December 1964

Copyright © 1952
Grune & Stratton, Inc.
381 Park Avenue South
New York, New York 10016

Printed in the U.S.A. (G-M)

Foreword

IN THE SUMMER of 1950, a visitor appeared in my class on expressive and projective techniques and left with me a manuscript which she wanted me to read. The manuscript was put aside until an appropriate time could be found for reading it and when I finally dipped into it, I discovered that here was not only another study which attempted to give an experimental basis for the interpretation of the projective elements in drawing but one which surpassed all of the previous attempts at such validation and provided for the first time really convincing validation data and an interpretation of the projective elements of drawing on satisfactory evidence.

The test which Miss Kinget has used resembles in method the well known Horn-Hellersberg test. However, the stimuli provided in the eight spaces in which to draw figures in Miss Kinget's test are based on an elaborate psychological analysis of their possible diagnostic significance. Historically, this test goes back to a psychological theory propounded by F. Sander at the University of Leipzig known as *Ganzheit Psychologie*. Sander attempted to study the impact of structure on experience by means of a fantasy test. This work was picked up by Ehrig Wartegg and the testing form which Miss Kinget employs in her study is Wartegg's form. Wartegg has given particular attention to providing adequate variety of form, location and structure of signs on the test sheet. These signs may be characterized by their unstructuredness which gives the subject the greatest possible freedom in conceiving and executing his drawing.

What impresses me in Miss Kinget's study is the criterion against which she determined the significance of each element of the drawings. Three hundred and eighty-three adults between the ages of 18 and 50 constituted her experimental group. She not only gave her test to each of these individuals but secured three types of validating data on them. Two of these types were in the nature of self-reports including a questionnaire and a forced choice test. The third was a rating scale whose content paralleled the questionnaire and forced choice test which was filled out by friends and acquaintances of her subjects who knew them well in everyday life. Armed with these data, Miss Kinget systematically reduced her validation material to workable categories and compared each of the elements which she analyzed from the drawing tests with the personality characteristics which are contained in the validation data. The result is an impressive analysis of the descriptive and diagnostic significance of the variables into which she has dissected the formal elements of drawing.

The latter part of the book discusses how the test can be used for clinical diagnosis.

I believe that this study makes a signal contribution to the difficult field of the projective significance of drawing. As workers in the field well know, the clinical use of projective materials has far outstripped the necessarily slower scientific validation of them. This study provides a model for such validation which can serve as a stimulus to other workers.

PERCIVAL M. SYMONDS, PH.D.

Acknowledgment

First and foremost, I wish to express my gratitude to Dr. J. Nuttin of the University of Louvain, who supervised the dissertation leading up to the present work. Much is owed to his constant interest, penetrating direction and the example of his work.

My warmest thanks are extended also to my professors in the United States, who by their interest and appreciation of the subject of this work contributed to its creation and made possible its publication.

In no lesser way do I feel indebted to the persons — friends, colleagues and students — who have given a great deal of their time and effort for the long and exacting work of computing and verifying the innumerable data involved in the research part of the work.

A special word of gratitude also goes to my American friends who undertook to correct the uncertain English of the first draft of the manuscript.

In addition to the intellectual profit obtained from the years of this study, the amount of interest and cooperation encountered has made it a unique social experience of lasting value.

G. MARIAN KINGET

Contents

Part Four: Illustrations and Commentary

Introduction

THE DRAWING-COMPLETION Test is a technique for the investigation of personality, using drawings obtained by means of the device shown on the frontispiece. This device presents a variety of small graphic elements, serving as a series of formal themes, which the subject is asked to develop in his own way. The drawings thus produced are then analyzed according to a number of criteria, referring to both form and content.

Since personality presents innumerable aspects and no technique is able to grasp them in their totality, let us first specify more precisely the diagnostic scope of this technique. Its primary aim is to explore the structure of personality in terms of what are often called "basic functions," such as emotion, imagination, dynamism, control, reality-function, encountered in all human beings but with different intensity and with different interrelations. This structure is not static but changeable in varying degrees, and it determines to a large extent the individual's behavior. Consequently, a technique which explores the *structure* of personality provides at the same time insights into its *functioning*, whether normal or abnormal. Indeed, when one or several components strongly dominate, the structure is unbalanced and the subject's functioning is defective. When his control function is overdeveloped, his behavior appears inhibited; when his imagination and ideation are excessively developed, his contact with reality and his social functioning may be impaired to the extent of suggesting serious disturbance.

Examining problems of pathology, however, was not the original aim of the technique; its extension to these problems is an outgrowth of the understanding of the basic structure of personality. In practice this outgrowth will become as important as, or more important than, the primary purpose, depending on whether the technique is used by the psychiatrist, the psychologist, the educator, the vocational counselor, the personnel director, or whoever is working in the field of applied psychology.

The choice of the drawing activity as a diagnostic medium is completely free from preoccupations concerning specific aptitudes or capacities. The products are considered only in their expressive and projective features, not in their artistic value. Control research has proved that these features are largely independent of artistic training.

The diagnostic value of drawings no longer needs to be demonstrated, as the extensive bibliography on the matter proves (2). Drawings yield data uniquely free from the many influences which distort verbal communication. Their "language" is almost completely independent of the misleading factors operating both consciously and unconsciously in the spoken or written word, for the communication transmitted by them is not recognized by the subject and thus escapes the vigilance of his mind. However, while this indirect language reflects the personality in a more reliable way, it is also more difficult to understand. Drawings are far from being an open book, even for those initiated into the understanding of human expression in general. Their diagnostic value is strictly dependent upon the examiner's ability to translate this specific language into common terms; and this ability is dependent primarily upon the amount of objective information available on the matter.

In spite of the early recognition that drawings received as diagnostic material, and despite their use on a large scale, relatively little systematic study of them has been made. This may be accounted for by the belief in the efficacy of general psychological knowledge for dealing with specific matters and by the fact that attention has long been directed exclusively to the *content* of the drawings. Interpretation of this aspect can proceed to an extent according to the rules applied to content in general, whether graphic, verbal or other. However, the extreme variety, the variability and the diagnostic malleability of content makes it an unsteady basis for diagnosis. An inner criterion for testing the meaning of the content of drawings is their *execution,* for the characteristics of execution are highly consistent. However, these more reliable characteristics do not present the immediate meaningfulness inherent to content, and it is especially in regard to these characteristics and their intertwining with various kinds of content that objective information is required.

Particularly suitable for systematic study of both projection and expression appearing in drawings is the device used in the test herein presented. This device was originated by Dr. Ehrig Wartegg (56) who, in his work *Gestaltung und Charakter,* presented an outline of characterologic typology by means of the same device, used in a manner considerably different from my own. Since the material reported in the work of Dr. Wartegg had not been the object of any known research, at the time I became acquainted with it (1943), I undertook to submit it to such a study. My initial goal was concerned only with the critical examination and objective verification of this material. The extensive research which this aim involved led beyond its proper scope, however, to a considerable increase in new insights, indications and hints. The material for a reorganization, differentiation and further development being thus largely acquired, I attempted, subsequently, to work the project into a serviceable tool for *individual diagnosis*. To this end, I investigated the diagnostic value of the *single* graphic elements—such as pressure, shading, covering—which, thus far, had been considered in *groups*. The significance of single elements is, obviously, not to be understood as unequivocal and invariable, this significance being largely dependent upon the ever-changing constellation of variables in which they appear. The indexes represented by graphic elements have, therefore, only a cue value, never that of a constant relation. However, when drawing material is broken down into a great number of characterstcs, and the cue value of each of them is duly assessed, the conclusions drawn may attain a surprising degree of validity. In such conditions, several related characteristics will be found in all drawings, whatever their kind, and will allow mutual checking of their cue value, thus making for largely verified conclusions.

The research underlying the conclusions presented here was carried out on a group of 383 "normal"—understood as functioning commonly—subjects. All these subjects were investigated by a number of techniques specially devised for the purpose of evaluating the drawings in terms of the concepts used by Wartegg. This multiple procedure yielded an average of about 500 information items per subject which served as criteria for establishing the conclusions here reported. In addition to the data obtained from this group, a large number of drawings has been studied for the purpose of clarifying specific points. The chief lines of this study are described in Part One, Chapter III.

The present account is conceived on a solely practical basis. From the original study it abstracts only material of immediate interest to the practitioner. It touches upon the more theoretical aspects only as necessary to enable the reader to locate the technique in its theoretical background, and to evaluate the methods of its construction (Part One, Chapters I, II, III).

The presentation of the diagnostic mechanism is strictly analytical, dealing separately with each graphic element in order to facilitate the use of this work for purposes of reference. The data thus presented should not, however, be used like the items in a dictionary—all with well-defined and invariable meanings. Not only is every element to be considered in the context of the whole drawing, as already mentioned, but the drawings are also to be examined with reference to fundamental data of the personality, such as age, sex, and level of education or occupation. Profitable use of the technique presupposes, therefore, thorough acquaintance with the totality of the matter here presented. Cursory reading or incidental reference cannot lead to satisfactory results in the application.

The Drawing-Completion Test presents a number of qualities which give it specific merit and justify its appearance in the already rather prolific field of projective techniques. Some of these qualities pertain directly to its value as a diagnostic instrument, others are practical, but no less important, since the actual usability of a test is largely dependent upon the latter. Among the first qualities is the fact that the test presents a combination of characteristics conducive to heightening the diagnostic value of both the subject's and the examiner's activity. To the subject it presents material that is almost completely unstructured. The graphic elements appearing on the blank are very simple and extremely few, and the space allotted for developing them is ample in comparison with their size. Thus, the subject is given vast possibilities for free association and expression. While the test shows so particularly unstructured a facet to the subject, it presents a highly structured one to the examiner, providing him with a considerable number of criteria for objective evaluation of the results. Indeed, the stimuli, in their simple materiality, have Gestalt qualities which are numerous, greatly varied and well defined. These Gestalt qualities fulfill a role comparable to the variables in experimental research and serve as criteria for the interpretation. In addition to the points of reference provided by the stimuli, a great number of criteria are identified in both the execution and the content of the drawings. Thus a multiple cross-checking and differentiation of the interpretation data is made possible.

Another merit of the test lies in the fact that the material used does not threaten the subject by the strangeness of its appearance or by its emotional implications, but rather appeals to him by its simple and neutral character.

The most important feature of the Drawing-Completion Test is, perhaps, its practical value in terms of time needed for the administration, scoring and interpretation, as well as for the examiner's initiation into its diagnostic mechanism. The administration takes none of the examiner's time. As to the interpretation, when use is made of the specially designed scoring and interpretation sheets which accompany the test blanks, the average time is less than an hour. This practical advantage is of great significance for, in view of the complexity and ambiguity of the data provided by projective methods, it is necessary to use several approaches in order to obtain a valid picture of personality. In practice, however, this multiple approach is prohibitive owing to the time-consuming efforts required, first, for acquiring insight into the diagnostic mechanism of most tests, and second, for applying them. These obstacles are overcome by the Drawing-Completion Test, making its use especially appropriate for checking, clarifying and completing the diagnosis obtained by means of other tests. Furthermore, it has appreciable qualities as a research tool, for, due to the numerous criteria which it provides, the reflection of the changes produced by therapeutic or other factors may easily be recognized.

Another advantage of the technique is its conduciveness to spontaneous verbal developments on the part of the subject. Although these developments are no indispensable part of the technique—since the conclusions here presented can be gained solely from the graphic data—such developments are valuable because of their role in reinforcing rapport and because of the significance of spontaneous communications for the ultimate diagnostic aim, complete understanding of the individual. It is well known that creative activity in general has a releasing and "opening" effect. In the present case, the subject is usually so surprised and often amused at what he has been able to make out of the insignificant, puzzling stimuli, that he feels inclined to continue verbally the flow of expression initiated by his drawings.

The Drawing-Completion Test, as here presented, obviously makes no claim to finality, the nature of projective techniques being one of incessant evolvement. The following account is intended primarily as an introduction into its basic mechanism and as an initiation to its use. Whatever additions or modifications further research may bring to the diagnostic part of this work, its analysis and description of phenomena is unlikely to undergo substantial changes; it offers, therefore, a workable basis, inviting further exploration. Meanwhile, the diagnostic potentialities and practical qualities of the technique will soon prove its use to be rewarding in various fields of applied psychology.

Part One:
Origin and Development
of the Drawing-Completion Test

I. The Blank

THE THEORETICAL and experimental background of the blank lies in Gestalt psychology, more precisely in the so-called *Ganzheit Psychologie* which developed at the University of Leipzig under the leadership of F. Krueger and F. Sander. According to "Ganzheit Psychologie" it is assumed that not only the *object* of experience but also the experiencing *subject* is to be conceived as a "structure." This structure is made up of a set of orientations and dispositions of a specific, dynamic nature which tend essentially toward "form-giving," that is, toward organizing whatever is afforded to experience. The supreme binding and all-pervading factor within the structure is emotion; it governs at any moment the configuration of the form-giving tendencies and determines the setting or significance of every element of experience.

Experience thus being, as it were, molded by the individual structure, it follows that experience necessarily bears the marks of that structure; it must, therefore, be possible to infer the characteristics of the latter from those of the former. In ordinary life situations this imprint of the personal structure on experience—as expressed in activity—is not easily recognizable because the material on which the activity is exerted lacks the necessary plasticity, or because the product of the activity has to conform to objective, prescribed standards. But in situations where the form-giving tendencies are freed from limiting factors attached to the material on which they operate, or to the goal which they have to achieve, the characteristics of the activity reveal the characteristics of the psychic structure.

In order to support these principles with experimental evidence, Sander (43) devised a technique which he called a *Phantasie Test*. In this test the subjects were confronted with material of the kind used in the Drawing-Completion Test, showing a certain number of irregularly disposed lines which were to be organized in a free manner. The products thus obtained manifested marked differences which reflected characteristic structural traits of the subjects. Sander considered his results only in their more obvious characteristics, both graphic and psychological, without submitting them to further analytical investigation

3

(see page 8). Since his goal was purely theoretical and not concerned with individual diagnosis, broad differences constituted sufficient evidence of the assumptions he wanted to verify.

The success of Sander's experiment induced another representative of the School of Leipzig, Ehrig Wartegg (53–56), to continue along the same line of investigation. To this end he originated the device used here.

He does not indicate whether his choice and combination of graphic elements, such as nature and number of the stimuli, dimensions of the drawing intuitive. As part of the present study I endeavored to discover the theoretical justification for the particular structure of the test blank and its constituent elements, such as nature and number of the stimuli, dimensions of the drawing spaces and form of the frames.

Information concerning the *qualitative variety of the stimuli* is found in the studies on nonrepresentational graphic expression, especially in the extensive studies by Krauss (27) and Hippius (20). In these experiments the subjects were asked to represent emotions (joy, anger, sadness), concepts (harmony, twilight), colors, materials (glass, gold) in mere line structures. The results showed that given lines and line structures implicitly function as symbols for given concepts, in other words, that concepts are apt to be translated into nonrepresentational figures. It appeared further that the implicit symbolism of lines is highly consistent and objective, the majority of subjects intuitively taking to similar types of lines and structures to represent the same concepts or topics. If, as proved by these experiments, lines and line structures possess symbolic value, it follows that the great variety of form, location and structure of the stimuli on the present test sheet may be considered as particularly fit for exploring a broad range of experience.

Variety in the stimuli used for eliciting the activity represents, however, only one of the requirements of a projective tool. Freedom of expression is another requirement, not easily compatible with the necessity for stimulus material. Generally the less material that is given the better, for the subject has more opportunity to imprint the mark of his own personality on the product. On the other hand there must be material enough to provide the necessary points of reference for a differentiated and objective treatment of the results. Completely free activity, drawing or other, while allowing full release of the associative activity, fails to offer a consistent basis for intercomparison and interpretation. The use of meaningless stimulus material greatly furthers free expression, such material being void of the directive influence exerted by meaningful or fairly structured material representing or suggesting definite objects and situations. However, even meaningless material may contain factors which limit or prohibit free projection, as appears from a study by Berger (7). Berger worked with Sander's device to try its fitness for examining vocational aptitudes. Like Wartegg, he modified the original material in accordance with his particular purpose. Thus, his blanks show the following characteristics: (a) the stimuli appearing within the rectangles present either three or four elements; (b) some of these elements are of a relatively large size; (c) some of them are complex, that is, are either broken lines or lines presenting a combination of straight and curved parts; (d) some elements are colored; (e) all of the elements are irregularly scattered over the drawing surface. The results of Berger's experimentation with these blanks showed, among other findings, that (1) the greater the number and the larger the constituent elements of the stimuli, the narrower the variation range of the responses; (2) the lower the individual "Gestalt value" of the stimuli and the greater the similarity of their elements the higher the integration (understood as meaningful organization into wholes) of the responses. The greater the individual value of the elements due to scatter, variety in color or in form, the lower the integration of the responses.*

In the light of the abovementioned results, Wartegg's modification of Sander's idea appears particularly felicitous. As can be seen from the blank reproduced herein, the stimuli are extremely few and most of them very small, two characteristics which make for broad variation of responses. Furthermore, the possibilities for constructing the stimuli into meaningful wholes appear to be high, for the individual Gestalt value of the stimuli and of their constituent elements is low; indeed, (a) their form is very simple, (b) their constituent elements are of a similar kind (the composed stimuli 3, 5 and 6 feature only straight elements; stimulus 7 only round elements); (c) the elements of the composed stimuli are not scattered over the surface but are grouped to form a unity (in this respect, see particularly stimuli 3, 5 and 7 which are practically always felt and treated as *one* stimulus).

From this it can be seen that in spite of the basic similarity and common origin of Wartegg's and Berger's blanks, the type used by the latter is far less suited to eliciting genuinely projective activity. This does not detract from the value of Berger's device for the purpose he pursued; on the contrary, since his purpose was to explore vocational aptitudes, presentation of problem situations of various degrees of difficulty was most appropriate.

In personality testing, however, any degree of difficulty hinders the freedom

*. . . Die Variationsbreite der Gestaltungs—anregungen der Vorlagen wird um so geringer, je zahlreicher und grösser (Formbestimmter) die Ausgangsfiguren sind . . . die Gefügtheit der Darstellungen wird um so inniger, je gestaltähnlicher die Einzelgebilde der Anordnung und je geringer der Eigenwert der Ausgangsfiguren ist. Die Gefügtheit wird umso lockerer, je starker die Vereinzelung der Stücke durch räumliches Auseinander, Verschiedenfarbigkeit und unterschiedliche Geformtheit ist (7, p. 536).

of expression and affects the diagnostic value of the results. Most important, in regard to the value of the material in question, seems to be the number of stimuli and their distribution within the field. Indeed, where several elements are used their arrangement over the drawing surface easily tends to show a definite configuration which influences the choice of the responses and reduces their variation range. The disposition of the elements within the field may be such that their organization into meaningful wholes is difficult to the point of becoming a function of intelligence. In both cases spontaneous projective activity is precluded and the material loses considerable value since the merit of a projective test rests largely on its selectivity, that is, its ability to elicit a great variety of answers, reflecting the individuality of the subject.

Another merit of the material here used is that it is void of threatening factors. Such factors may be present in words or images referring directly to aggression, sex, fear, depression, or they may arise from the strange and ambiguous character of the material. In such conditions the subject may feel hesitating, insecure, anxious—in brief, threatened—and is apt to present a more or less distorted image of himself.

The function and appropriateness of the shape and the size of the *enclosures* in which the stimuli are presented have been studied also. The role of the shape of the frame in which projective drawing is performed has been examined by Hippius (20). Her study demonstrates that even the most elementary geometric forms have an expressive value which may, to a certain extent, influence the choice of the subject matter. The general design of Hippius' experiment was similar to that followed by Harms (18) and Krausz. She gave her subjects a choice of sheets, showing various frames, and asked them to represent different concepts by nonobjective line structures, within the frame they considered best suited for each concept, and to motivate their choice of a frame. From these motivations it appeared that a considerable degree of agreement exists in the conception of appropriateness of certain forms in regard to framing certain contents. Simple geometric forms thus tend to possess a fairly definite symbolic value.

Hippius' study revealed further that the square and the rectangle possess a specific "frame" quality not found, for instance, in the circle, which tends to amalgamate itself with the object framed. Of all the forms presented the square was found most appropriate for framing any kind of subject matter, because it is practically free from limiting influences on the choice of content. Hence, the square may be considered particularly suited for projective drawing.

The *size* of the squares may appear at first too small for representing anything but very simple themes. The results obtained contradict this and prove that rather elaborate drawings may be made within this limited space.

Moreover, the smallness of the squares serves definite purposes. First, it assists the subject to focus his attention on a limited area, hence, on the stimulus; second, this size allows all the drawings to be viewed on one page and thus greatly facilitates the numerous comparisons involved in scoring and interpreting the results.

The intense black frame of the squares is also designed to favor the concentration of the subject's mind on the stimuli. The strong effect of contrast between frame and drawing surface sharply isolates the latter, emphasizes the stimuli, and thus furthers the reactive tendencies within the subject.

II. The Personality Schema

T HE CONCEPT of personality underlying the Drawing-Completion Test is an eclectic compound that meets the necessities of practice more than the requirements of theory.

The basic idea of the schema, like that of the test form, was derived from Sander. As mentioned, Sander attempted to prove experimentally that differences in the way people perceive and react to unstructured situations are representative of inter-individual differences of personality make-up. The results of his experiment showed three characteristic trends in the organization of the given material. Two of these trends represent primitive modes of organization and stand in sharp opposition to each other. The first merely connects the elements and results in meaningless, undifferentiated whole structures. The second organizes the material in several, mutually unrelated, often senseless part structures. In between these extreme forms of organization is a third mode which, through proper connection and completion of the elements, produces differentiated and meaningful wholes. On the basis of these results, Sander constructs a "typology" or classification of personality structures in which the types correspond to the above described modes of organization and which, in translation, can be called the *analytical A-type,* the *synthesizing S-type* and the *analytical-synthesizing AS-type.*

This typological division served as a starting point for the development of the personality schema devised by Wartegg. When the latter undertook to differentiate Sander's method of investigation into a "characterological typology" he started by increasing the psychological content of the above-mentioned, predominantly formal divisions. Thus, the S-type becomes the *vital-emotional type,* mainly determined by the unconscious and characterized by a predominance of emotion, imagination and driving power; the A-type corresponds to the *rational-volitional type* in whom perception, deliberation and control are strongly prevailing. The AS-type is called the *integrated type* who blends the characteristics of the two preceding types. The integrated type thus corresponds

8

to the balanced and productive personality, which shows a broad range of sensibility and reaction patterns.

Above this typological scheme—or better, next to it, for there is no direct development of one from the other—Wartegg devised a four-dimensional schema composed of the traditionally recognized basic functions: emotion, imagination, intellect and will.* He then split each of these functions into two more or less opposed characteristic aspects. This schema, formulated according to the way it is used here, is shown in table 1.

TABLE I. *Personality Schema*

Emotion	Outgoing
	Seclusive
Imagination	Combining
	Creative
Intellect	Practical
	Speculative
Activity	Dynamic
	Controlled

The content of these functions as outlined by Wartegg, and as completed and differentiated by myself, is as follows:

Emotion. The aspects of emotion, outgoing and seclusive, correspond approximately to what is called extraversion and introversion. The *outgoing* individual is oriented towards the external world and associates easily with people. He is generally amiable, cheerful, easy-going and free from tension, which facilitates his adjustment but also tends to make him emotionally a little flat. His attention and interests are versatile but fluctuating and often rather superficial, which constitutes a certain obstacle to his efficiency or achievements. The *seclusive* individual, on the other hand, is oriented not so much to the surrounding visible world as to the reflection of it within himself. He tends therefore to see things through the prism of his personal attitudes and biases. He is also very sensitive and overflows easily into over-sensitivity and depression. Consequently, he is prone to withdraw and to resort to a world of dreams, of speculation or spirituality. His experiences produce long-lasting effects on which he likes to reflect and tends to brood. He is inclined to develop conflicts and apprehensions and appears on the whole less fit for contentment than the emotionally outgoing individul, but on the other hand he often has something more personal, more "interesting" in his affective make-up.

*To conform with the tendency in contemporary psychology the term "activity" has been substituted here for the term "will."

Imagination. The *combining* type of imagination draws its material directly from the surroundings, organizes it according to objective standards and produces forms which fit into the world of sensorial experience. This kind of imagination is thus essentially based on perception and oriented towards visible reality. It may also present a fairly emotional undercurrent, as manifested in its products which often show an esthetic tendency, though of a conventional variety. The *creative* kind of imagination is characterized by the looseness of its contact with visible reality and by its preference for abstract constructs or for symbols of an emotional, philosophical or mystical sort. A touch of creative imagination is likely to enhance the personality and may be highly valuable in certain spheres of activity; however, a marked predominance of this kind of imagination is likely to be an obstacle to adjustment to ordinary life.

Intellect. The individual with *practical* intellect operates principally by perception and observation and is characterized by clear consciousness, orderly thinking and directness of expression which lend his personality a strictly matter-of-fact and positivistic quality. Whereas this type of intellectual make-up is oriented towards facts, concrete reality and inductive reasoning, the *speculative* type prefers principles to facts, reasoning to observation, and theory to practice. When this type is of above average intelligence he easily becomes highly sophisticated, likes to make fine distinctions and to devise vast theoretical systems. When he is of medium intelligence he presents a vaguely rationalistic, impractical and somewhat reality-estranged intellectual makeup.

Activity. The *dynamic* kind of activity includes all forms and degrees of driving energy, from mere mobility to impulsiveness. People who exhibit this kind of activity easily enter into new enterprises, are self-confident, daring and enthusiastic; they may be passionate or they may be irritable. They have a great amount of energy, which enables them to undertake many tasks at the same time. They often show a tendency toward asserting themselves, and their great drive toward action sometimes takes the form of pseudo-productivity and fussiness. The *controlled* type, on the other hand, is characterized by firmness of decision and consistency of behavior. He carefully plans his moves before he makes them and continues to reflect upon them afterwards. Because of the control and caution which he exerts he generally develops great accuracy and reliability, and because of his tenacity he achieves his goals in spite of obstacles. His attention is concentrated and he likes quietness and regularity. Therefore, his behavior appears consistent, uniform and calm. However, his concentration may develop into fixation, his tenacity into perseveration and his control into inhibition or compulsiveness.

The schema described above may have aroused various criticisms in the mind of the reader. Its structure and the concepts used may indeed be questioned from several angles. The "composition" of personality as presented in table 1 may be questioned with regard to the choice of the elements. Objections may be raised against considering them as "functions" and the content ascribed to the subdivisions of these functions may be called arbitrary.

These objections, although quite relevant in themselves, are concerned with issues of no immediate importance here. The primary problem of test construction, at the present time, is to find a workable basis for approaching the object of investigation. The aim of such a basis does not go beyond giving articulation and coherence to the entérprise, and although it uses concepts attached to certain schools it does not necessarily imply any commitment to these schools. Thus, a personality schema made up of a certain number of components or functions does not mean that personality is thought of as a "composite" of independent mechanisms. The word "function" applied to such complex groups of phenomena as intellect and activity is used only as a collective term referring to a number of observable—presumably specially interrelated—elements of behavior; in brief, they are *operational* concepts. The total concept of personality underlying the schema is obviously that of an indivisible unit, manifesting different aspects according to the stimuli and demands of the ever-changing situations. As for the bilateral subdivision of each of the four basic functions of the schema and the kind of aspects which they represent, they are indeed arbitrarily selected. Yet, the characteristics grouped under each of these subdivisions correspond to clusters of characteristics currently encountered in descriptions of personality.

In view of these considerations it seems that, from a theoretical point of view, the schema in question is altogether as justifiable as any other — to date necessarily tentative — schema. However, the value of the schema in the various practices of applied psychology, where the goal is almost always to gain information about the *individual* makeup of a person, may be seriously questioned. There is, indeed, little value in knowing that a person is more outgoing than seclusive or more controlled than dynamic, for such characteristics have too many modalities. Even definitions of the functions, like those described above, do not offer much help in practice, for their total content is not likely to be found within the same individual, each definition being more like a compound of several modalities. A person may be outgoing without being gay, easy-going or superficial; likewise, he may be seclusive without being sensitive, or he may be sensitive without tending to withdraw. The same is true in regard to *intellect* or *activity*. How is the hair-splitting rationalist to be distinguished from the constructively perspicacious mind, both of whom fall under the speculative pole of intellect? Similarly, how can the healthily controlled individual be recognized from the inhibited one and the latter from the perseverative type since all of these are classified under the same label?

Another practical drawback of the schema is the fact that the characteristics grouped under the poles of the various functions are not entirely mutually exclusive; except, perhaps, for the poles of *emotion*, these characteristics overlap to a noticeable extent. Indeed, several characteristics attributed respectively to practical intellect and to speculative intellect are compatible with one pole as well as with the other; a certain level of intellectual functioning even presupposes the characteristics of both poles. For instance, the productively speculative mind needs the basic contact with reality attributed specifically to the practical type of intellect; likewise, a high degree of healthy control requires the energetic impulse which predominates in the definition of dynamism.

From all this it follows that, unless there is a way of finding out what, in the individual case, is actually underneath the general labels, the scheme has only *typological* value, that is, it allows only summarization of a broad variety of phenomena. The clinical value of the schema is, therefore, essentially dependent upon the degree of differentiation achieved by the test; in other words, upon the number of correlations discovered between specific characteristics of personality and specific characteristics of the test results. When this is achieved a schema can be highly serviceable for organizing the material and for facilitating the work of tracing the individual characteristics; in brief it is useful as a frame for the individual picture to be inserted. Therefore, although the schema here used has no fundamental significance within the system, it has, at the present stage of development of the test, a practical value.

III. The Validation

A. The Problem

AS INDICATED earlier, the aim of the present work is essentially a practical one. Validation is not a strictly practical issue but it is so crucial in test construction that the chief lines and elements of this operation need to be presented.

Wartegg's work does not contain evidence of precise validation and thus fails to provide a basis for gaging its objective and practical value. His only reference to validation is a footnote (56, p. 129), giving the techniques against which the results of the drawing test were checked. One was a "story completion" test on given verbal themes, the other an "interpretation" test of non-objective designs. However, validating a new projective technique against other new projective techniques is a precarious procedure. Since projection material is ambiguous and plastic, the danger of "projecting" agreement among varying techniques is very real. Further criteria used in the initial approach were the typological systems of Kretschmer, Jaensch and Jung. These systems are extremely broad and inclusive, however, and their value as criteria is questionable. Wartegg alludes also to graphological, physiognomic and biographical sources as having served for verification of his conclusions. Such procedures may yield valuable material when handled by skilled specialists, but they do not offer an adequate, objective basis for validation of new techniques because they cannot be verified and quantified.

In order to elucidate the question of the validity of Wartegg's conclusions, I decided to apply the test to a large group of subjects and to compare its results with a well defined parallel criterion. However, that aim soon proved to present almost unsurmountable obstacles. First, Wartegg's definitions of (1) the *psychological functions* and (2) the *graphic characteristics* are scant and sometimes contradictory. Since clear knowledge of the scope of the terms involved is a prime requisite for verification of given relations, the incompleteness and obscurity of these basic data was a serious handicap. In an attempt to overcome it, a detailed analysis was made of the work in question; the elements

13

of definition spread throughout it were carefully traced, combined and completed into coherent wholes. Then, the drawings (illustrating *Gestaltung und Charakter*) of the subjects presenting identical or similar psychological traits were compared and analyzed in order to discover the graphic characteristics corresponding to these traits. Thus, through numerous cross-checking of psychological and graphic data a workable definition of the elements involved was finally achieved. Whenever contradictions or doubtful points arose, they were noted for subsequent clarification. The latter operation was carried out on drawings of well-known subjects chosen with reference to the particular point which needed examination.

After finding out exactly *what* was to be verified, the next step was to determine *how* to do it. Here arose the second and main difficulty: finding an adequate criterion for comparison. To this end a complete survey was made of the existing tests for the investigation of personality. The outcome of this survey showed, however, that none of these tests could serve as a criterion for examining the results of the drawing test, none of them approaching the personality from the point of view that Wartegg did. Some tests showed partial agreement with the schema used by him, but the corresponding parts were integrated in systems from which they could not be properly isolated. It appeared, consequently, that the sole possibility of determining the validity of Wartegg's work lay in the creation of a criterion *ad hoc*.

In view of the aforementioned obstacles it would, obviously, have been much simpler and easier to use the test form in a completely independent way, applying it to clearly differentiated clinical groups and studying its value for specifically psychiatric use. This procedure was rejected mainly because advancement in projective testing seems to be served better when a given approach is further verified, clarified and improved in the direction of practicability. Too many new devices or approaches are being tried without adequate investigation of the work that has already been done. Since the contribution of the individual, however great his efforts, is bound to remain very limited in a matter as complex as the investigation of personality, "chain work" seems in this field more fruitful than a profusion of creativity.

B. The Criterion

For this criterion to be adequate, the only feasible procedure was to work the content of the psychological functions, as sketched by Wartegg and completed by myself, into some kind of verbal test.

I was, of course, not unaware of the deficiencies of verbal techniques. However, if it is true that the limitations and pitfalls of such techniques are many, it is equally true that their nature is well known, which presents a considerable advantage in regard to the construction of new types. Moreover, whether a properly constructed verbal test is inferior to most projective tests is an open question. The fact is that the defects of the former can be demonstrated more easily and directly than those of the latter. The deficiencies of questionnaires, inventories and similar procedures are due, to a large extent, to hasty, defective construction and to misuse in the application, rather than to the principles underlying these techniques. It is evident that direct or "transparent" questioning of a subject on personality matters, without proper means of verification, can yield only unreliable results. However, when adequate precautions are taken against falsifying factors, the use of verbal techniques may be considered as justifiable as any other means. The shortcomings of such techniques can be largely overcome, although this requires an elaborate and impractical procedure. However, in view of the circumstances under which the present study had to be done, such a procedure was the only access to the problem.

The one adequate means for neutralizing the effect of subjectivity, inconsistency, inexactness and unreliability which may affect verbal information appears to lie in a multiplication and variation of the approach. At the present state of our knowledge it is, indeed, hard to conceive that one single technique could be made free of all the factors of error which may impair verbal communication. Consequently, a multiple criterion was constructed, consisting of a questionnaire, a forced-choice test and a rating scale, each of which was intended as a verifying and corrective factor for the others. The first two were presented to the subject himself, the last was given to one or several persons who knew the subject well and who were considered competent for passing judgment. The content of each test was chosen in such a way that it adhered strictly to the definitions of the personality components as described on pages 9–10. The results of these tests were consequently fit for close comparison.

The validity of these projects was not taken for granted or based merely on "armchair" procedure. Before being used as a criterion, each of them was built into an *objective technique,* according to regular methods of validation, as will appear from the following brief account of the construction of each of them.

1. The Questionnaire

The questionnaire was devised after the model of the Bernreuter Personality Inventory; that is, it was made up of a great number of interlocking questions presenting briefly sketched, concrete life situations.

The content of the questions was collected from different sources: existing questionnaires, publications on the matter, suggestions from colleagues and personal observations. The 154 questions thus gathered received preliminary validation by submission to five psychologists, duly informed about the project, whose task was to sift out those questions considered unfit for the proposed investigation. Thus numerous questions were modified and their total number reduced from 154 to 112, unanimously considered usable for diagnostic purposes.

The subsequent objective validation consisted of presenting the material thus selected to a group of 50 subjects, chosen as representative of the broader group on which verification of the drawing test would finally be carried out. The results obtained were then treated according to the "method of internal consistency," which, owing to the nature of the problem, was the only applicable method. After this operation* the number of questions was reduced to 72, all of which proved to have satisfactory diagnostic value.

In making up the final form the questions were arranged in such a way as to further the cooperation of the subject and to minimize possible sources of error which might result from the order of succession.† The procedure for answering was also changed. Instead of using the simple positive-negative ($+$ or $-$) the subject was given a choice of answers: $++$, $+$?, $-$, $- -$, which actually converted the questionnaire into a self-rating scale. The intensity-variation thus produced was taken into account in both the quantitative and the qualitative analysis of the results. The qualitative analysis consisted primarily of a search for "clusters" or "patterns" of response and constituted an important part of the treatment of the results. Such patterns emerge from the opposition between the answers given to certain sets of questions, and the answers given to other, contrary sets of questions. The intensity-differentiation resulting from the use of the five-step scale greatly facilitated the discovery and cross-checking of such patterns. The same qualitative analysis was applied to each of the other constituent techniques of the criterion, the cross-out test and the rating scale.

Below are examples of the kind of questions making up the questionnaire. The sample is taken from Emotion in its outgoing and seclusive aspects. (The translation is approximate.)

> Do you find it easy to start a conversation with strangers?
> Do you tend to forget a disappointment?
> Do you mind appearing before a large audience?
> Do you easily get used to a new environment, new people,
>   new ways of living?
> Do you dislike being alone for any length of time?

---

*Details of this operation are described in my unpublished thesis presented in 1948 at the University of Louvain, Belgium.

†For practical reasons of page spacing, six questions had to be left out of the list, which brought the final number to 66.

Do you prefer to express yourself by speaking or by writing?
Do you laugh easily?
Do you prefer to work alone? Or with other people?*
Do you often tell stories to children or jokes to your friends?
Do you like to give or organize parties?

2. The Forced-Choice Test

In this test the subjects were presented with a great number of independent words arranged in pairs and were asked to indicate their preference for one term of each pair by crossing out the other. The paired words were selected in such a manner that the choice made between them indicated subject's affinity with respect to the components of the personality schema. He was asked to consider the terms solely in themselves and regardless of their value for describing himself. In order that the choice between the terms might reflect personal preference rather than conventional standards, special care was devoted while forming the pairs to make both terms approximately equal in value-connotation. Crossing out one word was made obligatory for all of the pairs to avoid the considerable cutting down of data which frequently occurs when complete freedom is given.

An example of the kind of material making up the forced-choice test follows. The sample pertains to the Intellect function in its practical and speculative aspects.

clever—learned	philosophy—science
superficial—hairsplitting	ideal—fortune
techniques—principles	systematic—practical
exhibition—lecture	refined—easy
demonstration—definition	thinking—seeing
to invent—to use	to explain—to show
to speak—to write	to inquire—to reflect

The concepts pertaining to the same function obviously did not follow each other in immediate succession as in the above sample but were duly distributed among the concepts pertaining to the other functions so as to make the repetition and the general trend less apparent.

The purpose of this test was essentially to serve as an extension of the questionnaire. Since the validity as well as the reliability of a questionnaire depends to a great extent on the number of questions, it is essential to make it as long as practically possible. This practical possibility is limited mainly by the necessity of eliminating fatigue or boredom and of preventing the questionnaire from becoming "transparent." A maximum length is, therefore, relatively

*This type of question was answered by underlining one part.

quickly achieved. Extending the questionnaire must, consequently, be attempted by introducing a substitute or a variation of the procedure. Such variation presents, moreover, the advantage of approaching the subject from a different viewpoint, a procedure which always discloses new aspects of the personality.

The above-mentioned type of forced-choice test is particularly suited to serve as such an extension, because of the multiplicity of its elements and conciseness of its form. Another advantage of this type of test is that independent words lend themselves more to projection than do full sentences with definite meaning. Isolated words are less dependent upon accidental circumstances related to the subject's personal life than are concrete situations expressed in sentences.

Validation of the forced-choice test proceeded along exactly the same lines as described in relation to the questionnaire. The first operation was effected on 224 pairs of concepts; after intercomparison of the results, this number was reduced to 166. Further experimental validation of this material proved 99 pairs of the 166 to be fit for the proposed investigation.

3. The Rating Scale

The results yielded by the questionnaire and forced-choice test gave, strictly speaking, information on the subject's attitude with respect to the situations expressed in the questions, not on his actual behavior in these situations. However, when the subject has an average capacity of self-judgment, that is, has the necessary intelligence and maturity, and is ready to put this capacity at the disposal of the examiner, it may be assumed that his behavior will correspond, on the whole, to the answers given. This conformity of the answers with the behavior will be increased when the same questions are asked several times under different forms and their answers properly checked. However, in spite of all precautions, subjectivity and rationalization are not likely to be entirely eliminated, for a judgment is always a commitment of the self and the subject is confusedly aware of it.

For these reasons it was necessary to supplement the data obtained from the subject by information from other persons. To this end, a rating scale was devised, the content of which was focused on the same characteristics at which both questionnaire and forced-choice test were aiming. The procedures followed in the construction and validation of this additional test were the same as those used for the others, with the exception that the questions in the rating scale had a direct character, not a disguised one as those of the questionnaire. A few examples of questions used in the rating scale follow. (This sample pertains to the exploration of the poles of the Activity function, dynamism and control.)

Are his gait and movements relaxed and supple?
Is he persistent in his work: Does he go on to the end even under difficult circumstances?

Does he easily accept the decisions and opinions of others?
Is he moderate and conservative*
Does he appear self-assured?
Is he spontaneous and vivacious*
Is he capable of concentrated attention, observation or work for any
    length of time?
Is he ardent in games, discussion or activity?*
Can one depend upon his word?
Is he patient and tolerant?
Is he rather boisterous?
Does he appear vigorous and healthy?
Is he tidy and punctual?
Does he readily change his opinions and plans?
Does he offer tenacious resistance to difficulties?
Is he cautious and inclined to deliberate long?
Is he a "leader"?
Is he somewhat moody?

The rating scale, in its final form, consisted of 80 interlocking questions
which were to be answered on a five-step scale like the questionnaire. It was
given to persons (1) who knew the subject well in his every-day life and behavior; (2) who were not closely related to the subject, close relationships being
open to involuntary distorting of the information; (3) who presented certain
guarantees of ability to make judgments, guarantees which were estimated on the
basis of a certain acquaintance, on the part of these persons, with observing and
judging people. These three conditions could not always be found within one
and the same person; therefore, in a large number of cases the rating-scale was
given to two persons and, in a few cases, to three. Plotting of the results was
done on the basis of the agreement between the answers; where three judges
were consulted, agreement between two judges was considered as a sufficient
degree of reliability.

The total data (the maximum number was 506 per subject) provided by the
criterion were finally analyzed according to the components of the personality
schema and computed. In spite of the care taken, the constituent techniques presented the defects inherent in any single test. However, due combination of the
results represents about the optimum procedure practicable to date and may be
expected to provide appreciably valid information.

C. The Experiment

1. Experimental Group

The composition of this group was based on two considerations: (a) its
representative nature, requiring elimination of factors of error resulting from

*Crossing out one of the two characteristics is allowed.

the use of particular groups such as college students or males; (b) its homo-
geneity, requiring consideration of the significant differences in meaning
which projective material is apt to present, depending on whether it comes
from children or from adults.   Such differences also exist within the test
results of adults, for instance, between those of late adolescents and those of
middle-aged subjects, or between those of males and of females. Adjustments
must therefore be made in the interpretation. These adjustments are more or
less peripheral where adults are concerned, whereas the interpretation of children's drawings is likely to require basic changes. In order to heighten the
validity of the conclusions through the use of a relatively homogeneous research
group, it was decided to limit this group to either children or adults, and preference was finally given to adults because their personality is more consistent
and differentiated.*

The group finally selected was composed of adult subjects of both sexes,
various levels of age, educational background and occupation. This group
originally included over 400 subjects, but, owing to circumstances interfering
with the requirements for uniformity of the procedure, a certain number had
to be eliminated, which reduced the group to 383. This group fell within the
age limits of 18 and 50 years. By occupation, the subjects ranged from manual
laborers to students and professional men and women. In regard to education
and sex, the group presented the following distribution:

Education	Male Subjects	Female Subjects
Primary	73	67
Secondary	68	76
University	46	53
Totals	187	196

All of these 383 subjects were submitted to the complete plan of investigation, that is, to the threefold criterion and to the drawing test.

2. Validation Procedure

After the set of four tests had been applied and the results (answers
to verbal tests and graphic characteristics for drawing tests) quantified in
terms of intensity, the next step was reduction of the data to comparable
terms. To this end, the results of each individual with respect to the eight components of the personality schema in each of the four tests were converted into
deciles. Thus it was found, for instance, that the "dynamic activity" of subject
X fell in decile 3 according to the questionnaire, in decile 5 according to the

---

*The test blank has also been given to some 200 children (7 to 12 years old). The aim in
this was solely to gain some information on the differences in the products of children from
those of adults, regardless of their diagnostic implications.

forced-choice test, and in one of these or another decile for the rating scale. This conversion was indispensable for adequate comparison of the various results. After the material was thus made workable, an appropriate procedure for comparison between criterion and drawing test had to be determined.

The choice of such a procedure is largely dependent on the general approach of the test, that is, on the kind of schema used as a basis for investigation. The procedure to be followed in the present case was, therefore, bound to be somewhat different from current procedures. In the Drawing-Completion Test, where the components present a binary structure, that is, where one pole of each function stands in direct relation to the other pole, the problem is rather different from the one encountered, for instance, in intelligence tests or in personality tests which explore certain traits independently from other traits. In the latter cases the diagnostic problem is, generally, to determine the distribution of the examined traits among a large population and to situate the subject in regard to average values. This is not the aim of the D.-C. T., although it may become an aim at some later date. The purpose of this test — at the level of development presented at the time this validation was made — was to reveal the relative weight of the polar aspects of the four functions described earlier, that is, to indicate whether, for instance, a person is more outgoing than seclusive, more dynamic than controlled, and, approximately, how much more so. In view of this particular pattern of the diagnostic schema, the specific aim of the present validation was to find *the degree of agreement existing between criterion and drawing test with respect to the relative weight of the polar aspects of each function of the schema.*

Another problem involved in the comparison of the criterion and the drawing test was the fact that the three constituent tests of the criterion did not, in all cases, show complete agreement with one another. In view of this fact, three solutions could be considered: (a) comparison of the drawing test with each of the three tests separately; (b) comparison of the drawing test with the arithmetic mean of the results of the three tests; (c) comparison of the results of the drawing test with the main trends manifested in the other tests, that is, a comparison on the basis of the inner consistency of the result of all four tests.

After examination of these procedures it appeared that only the last one could be considered appropriate. Indeed, comparison of the drawing test with each of the other tests separately was not in line with the underlying concept of the multiple but "one" criterion, regarded as the only reliable formula. The second procedure, comparison with the arithmetic mean, had to be discarded also. Average values, indeed, flatten and neutralize the specific contribution of each of the tests of the criterion. Too many characteristic results are concealed by such values. The only adequate method for comparison proved, consequently, to be the method of inner consistency.

3. The Results

Comparison between criterion and drawing test was made separately for the male and for the female subjects. Such treatment was possible because the conversion into deciles had been done separately for each of the sexes. The results of this final operation, expressed in terms of percentages of agreement, were the following:

Functions*	Male Subjects	Female Subjects
Emotion	58.3	70
Intellect	70.1	73.7
Activity	58.9	70

The above results show two important characteristics: (1) the validity of the test—in its initial, *typological* form—is considerably lower for the male subjects than for the female (with respect to Emotion and Activity the results of the male group are definitely inconclusive); (2) for both groups the validity is lower for Emotion and Activity than for Intellect.

How are these results to be accounted for?

A partial explanation of the first point was suggested by certain observations made in the course of the operations carried out on the drawings. One of these concerned the fact that the drawings by females show, as a rule, a greater amount of both content and elaboration than those by males. Since the validity of a diagnosis is largely dependent upon the amount of material available, the conclusions concerning the female subjects, being based on more material, were almost bound to present a higher degree of validity. A similar observation was made in regard to the difference between the drawings of subjects with greatly different educational and occupational status. Uneducated or less educated subjects produce, on the whole, less subject matter than the more educated, who are familiar with the handling of paper and pencil. Since the male group included more manual laborers than the female group, it offered, consequently, less material and a weaker basis for diagnosis.

For the discrepancy between the validity of the test in regard to Emotion and Activity on the one hand, and Intellect on the other, no immediate explanation can be found. The greater validity of the test in regard to differences in the intellectual makeup of the subjects was surprising, because differences in the sphere of Emotion or Activity seem easier to recognize than in the apparently more subtle sphere of Intellect. On first sight this discrepancy appears even more surprising in view of the fact that the diagnosis of Emotion

*The data obtained for Imagination were not fit for quantitative comparison because several points had remained obscure with regard to this function. These data received, therefore, qualitative treatment only.

and Activity was based on a greater number of variables than that of the intellectual functions.

The unexpected character of this aspect of the results prompted an investigation of its causes. The outcome of this investigation pointed to the existence of certain systematic errors in the diagnostic schema, as it was conceived at that time. The results of the drawing test showed, indeed, a constant predominance of the *outgoing* pole of Emotion over the *seclusive*, and likewise, a predominance of the *dynamic* pole of Activity over the *controlled*. Further exploration revealed two factors of this disturbance. First, certain variables appeared to be unilaterally represented. For example, "Covering"* was considered in regard only to fullness, not to emptiness; account was taken of the "Originality"* of drawings, but not of (diagnostically important) "Popularity"* or commonness of occurrence. Second, and most important, the *frequency of incidence* of the variables correlated with one aspect of certain functions (the outgoing aspect of Emotion and the dynamic aspect of Activity) appeared to be considerably higher than the frequency of incidence of the variables correlated with the opposed aspects of these functions (seclusive Emotion and controlled Activity). The *number* of variables correlated with the first mentioned aspects was also greater. However, the number, as such, of the variables composing the basis for diagnosis was found not to have any significant bearing on the solidity of that basis.

In view of these factors a systematic predominance of certain aspects of the personality schema and consequently a lowering the degree of agreement between criterion and drawing test was bound to ensue.

D. Reorganization and Development of the Technique

As a result of the research sketched above, a great number of insights, observations and hunches had been accumulated. The major elements for reorganization and development of the technique thus being acquired, the remaining operations were undertaken as well. They consisted essentially of redistributing the graphic variables over the diagnostic schema and of introducing a number of new variables. Fitting these new variables within the schema required their diagnostic value to be tested. This operation was initially carried out in the same way in which the significance of *groups* of variables had been determined, that is, on the basis of the *global* results of the criterion. However, several of the new variables presenting finer distinctions than the initial ones, this procedure soon proved to be too gross, concealing important individual differences. To bring out these differences the criterion

*See below. Characteristics of Execution.

needed to be used in an analytical way. To this end, the items of each of the criterion tests were organized in clusters, considered representative for specific aspects of the personality components here examined. Thus it became possible to find out what, in the individual case, was the meaning of, for instance, "Control"—either inhibition, perseverance, or constructive control—or of "Seclusiveness"—withdrawal, anxiety, depression or introversion.

The separation of the criterion into clusters had required considerable work; it was deemed profitable to make a large use of the diagnostic pattern thus created within the criterion. Therefore, the analytical procedure, devised for examination of the meaning of a few variables, became extended to the complete list of variables, old as well as new. This resulted finally in a considerable differentiation and extension of the diagnostic value of the technique, raising it from the *typological* to the *individual* level.

The search for the meaning of the variables separately was greatly furthered by the intensity-differentiation brought within the results of the criterion by the use of the five step scale (++ , + , ? , — , ——.) Application of the test blank to 31 psychiatric patients and to a large number of other persons chosen because of certain marked features of their personality, also contributed to the clarification of certain diagnostic questions. The latter subjects were, however, not submitted to the criterion tests, but were considered solely in regard to either their psychiatric diagnosis or to certain of their commonly ascribed traits.

Save for a few exceptions, the following diagnostic presentation of the variables *separately* is not accompanied by quantitative data. In view of the variety of phenomena considered within each single variable, a statistical presentation is not feasible. Moreover, such a presentation would have no real meaning. A variable seldom or never appears in an identical form, whereas quantitative treatment requires practically identical material. Furthermore, the significance of the single variable is largely dependent on the *configuration* of variables into which it appears. Consequently, a quantitative presentation would offer precision, not scientific validity. Instead of aiming at such appearances, it was found preferable to indicate, for each variable, a number of qualitatively different *trends,* accompanied by the main elements of configuration by means of which the trend, present in a given case, can be recognized.

As appears from the above outline, the procedures used, however elaborate and lengthy, are far from realizing the scientific ideal of rigorous determination and treatment. However, they seem to represent the optimum procedure practicable to date. They maintain the diagnostic flexibility of the material and offer at the same time a variety of possibilities for meaningful integration of the elements.

Part Two:
The Diagnostic Mechanism

I. Administration

IN ITS PRESENT form, the test is suitable for administration to groups as well as to individuals, since the core of its diagnostic value lies in the *graphic* product, not in verbal associations with the latter or in other aspects of the activity. As a rule, individual administration will be more advantageous because of the direct contact between examiner and subject and because of the verbal developments which the test easily elicits. The latter, though independent of the test itself, naturally enrich the total personality picture of the subject.

The general administration procedure, whether the test is applied to individuals or to groups, differs very little. Material and instructions remain unchanged; only secondary aspects have to be adapted to the circumstances proper to each form of administration.

The testing room should be free, if possible, from wall decorations, objects that distract the attention or may influence the choice of subject matter. It is true that resorting to environment for inspiration is also revealing, but it lowers the projective value of the results. In group testing, care must be taken to prevent copying.

As a backing for the test form, a sheet of light cardboard should be used; never should the blank be placed directly over wood, metal or a tablecloth. This circumstance is not unimportant, for marked differences in hardness or softness of the backing result in differences in the apparent intensity of pressure which, in turn, affect evaluation of this important aspect of the execution.

The same considerations apply to the choice of the pencil, which should be neither too hard nor too soft, too sharp nor too blunt. Differences in hardness or sharpness produce differences in pressure and continuity of the line. They also determine to an extent the use of shading, and its structure, scrawled or smooth. The kind of pencil may even influence the choice of subject matter. A soft and rather blunt, smoothly gliding pencil may favor the representation of emotionally colored matter, whereas a hard one lends itself better to depicting matter-of-fact objects since it facilitates clear outline and precise structure,

27

which characterize such objects. The No. 2 pencil is particularly suited for this purpose for, besides its diagnostic "neutrality," it has the practical advantage of not smudging or blurring the drawings in their subsequent handling.

The pencil should also be equipped with an eraser. The initial procedure did not permit erasing, but further experience has proved that the diagnostic value of the drawings is raised by allowing the subject to erase. It is a well-known rule that projective techniques should be kept as free as possible from restrictions. With respect to erasing this rule is imperative, for when use of the eraser is not permitted every pencil stroke becomes final, causing the subject to deliberate longer over every move than he is naturally inclined to do; it actually blocks the reactions of certain subjects. Permission to erase allows more spontaneity in the choice of subject matter, since the subject may now try to depict whatever occurs to him as a suitable object. Such a procedure not only broadens the projective possibilities of the test but increases the validity of the interpretation because execution and content are likely to be more spontaneous. Moreover, considerable erasing is also significant in itself. As a form of behavior it evidences meticulousness, compulsiveness or indecisiveness. With respect to the object erased it may reveal a special concern for which the examiner should subsequently try to account. If the subject erases to such an extent that the blank or one square becomes unfit for completion, he may be given a second form.

As a matter of introduction, and to establish rapport, a few words should be said to reassure the subject about what he will be asked to do, and at the same time he may be asked whether he has any training or skill in drawing. Reassurance is especially necessary with the older subjects and with those who are less educated; it is generally useful because, in the minds of most people, drawing is closely associated with artistic talent, so that the subject tends to be upset at having to face a task that he cannot possibly fulfill to his credit. The examiner (indicated hereafter as E) might therefore start by asking casually whether the subject has any skill or training in drawing. If the subject (referred to as S) answers in the negative, E expresses satisfaction, pointing out that S preferably should not possess any artistic talent in regard to the little task he will be given. (This is true, for skillfully executed drawings are somewhat more difficult to interpret.)

On presentation of the test form E may say as follows: "On this form you see eight squares. Each of these squares contains little signs. These signs have no special meaning; they merely represent parts of drawings which you are asked to make in each of the squares. You may draw whatever you like and you may start with the sign you like best. You need not follow the order in which the squares are arranged, but I should like you to number your drawings in the order in which you make them. You may work as long as you wish and you may use the eraser. Do not, however, turn the sheet. This white part (E points to the white half of the sheet) must be the base of your drawings; that is, I must be able to view them properly while holding the sheet like this."

Depending on the attitude, education, or age of S, E may have to reassure him again: "Remember, this is not a test of drawing ability. I do not expect you to make artistic things. I am interested only in how you manage in your *own* way with this. So just do the best you can without worrying about your lack of training, and please don't forget to number your drawings."

E's presentation of the task may be met, on the part of S, by one of the following attitudes: the first is positive, matter-of-fact, relaxed and undramatic. The other two have marked emotional accent. One is enthusiastic and interested —S is amused with the idea and eager to try his hand on the task. The other is the exact opposite—he frowns, is reluctant, and pleads his inability and lack of imagination. In short, he tries to escape the task. This attitude is, however, rare, at least when E has been careful to establish proper rapport.

E should time the performance, for the amount of time spent in drawing is a prime factor in the interpretation. Timing should, however, be done in such a way that S is unaware of it, since visible measuring is especially disturbing in connection with projective work of this kind.

From the moment S is presented with the form, a phase of observation begins which is proper to testing situations in general. S's approach to and performance of a task being an important feature of his personality, such observation always yields valuable data. All manifestations of comfort, of discomfort, of zeal and speed or hesitancy should be noted, as well as S's copying nearby objects, his comments and remarks. E should permit S to interrupt his work and talk, but should not encourage this procedure, for prolonging the session often affects the results in an unfavorable way. Observation of the specific drawing behavior should concern only the easily observable aspects: erasure, preliminary sketching and planning—either on the test form directly, or on the backing—jumping from one drawing to another, or retouching of drawings already executed, viewing the product at a distance to see the over-all effect, etc. I have tried close and detailed observation of the drawing activity to various extents in the preliminary phase of my research, but cannot recommend this procedure. Such close surveillance cannot be done inconspicuously and is felt by S as a hindrance and a limitation of his freedom. Furthermore, such observation often results in a host of minute data which often remain unused, or encumber and dilute the specific results of the test.

An optimum test situation is one where E and S are seated in such a way that E has an easy view of S's activity while S does not have E directly in front of him. These conditions can be realized in a natural way when, for instance, S is seated at a separate table near the window or the light and slightly turned from E. It may happen that S seeks to escape observation by turning his back completely. Such behavior, however, is also revealing and is worth the loss of some other data. In sum, every circumstance which enhances S's feeling of freedom should be given priority. For this reason, it is important that E should himself be occupied during the drawing period, especially in cases where space limitations force the principals to sit opposite each other. Considering the fact that the average drawing time is about 20 minutes, although quite a few subjects take close to an hour and even more, such a working arrangement is profitable to E as well.

When S has finished, E asks him to explain, on the white half of the sheet, what each of the drawings represents. E does not make this request before S begins, for such a question would suggest that the drawings must represent something; that is, that they must be pictures. The word "pictures" should also be avoided in the instructions, because of its suggestive effect upon the content.

In case S has answered in the affirmative to E's earlier question about his having any drawing skill, E asks whether drawing is a hobby of his or the result of training. This information is very useful for the interpretation of the results, especially in regard to the Form level of the drawings (pp. 76–78). E may further inquire about the things S usually draws, so as to find out whether the possible greater perfection of certain drawings within the set is due to the fact that he has often made them or to some other reason. A profitable question is one that aims at finding out whether S has a leaning toward a given type or school of art, for this may throw some light on the choice of the content and especially on the manner of execution. If the drawings are very poor, E may ask S what he might have made out of the signs had he possessed the drawing ability—which S often pretends to be necessary for a satisfactory performance.

After the drawings are made and their titles written down, the administration of the test is, strictly speaking, terminated. However, profitable use should be made of the somewhat enlivening and expanding effect often produced by the performance type of test where the subject can directly see the results of his "puzzle-solving" efforts. As mentioned earlier, this verbal phase is no indispensable part of the technique, but it enriches considerably E's understanding of S and his products. S himself frequently initiates these verbal extensions, especially when he feels that he has been doing well on the drawings. If S fails to make any start, E may ask him how he happened upon the idea of each of the drawings. This question often elicits long answers, sometimes leading S to speak of things which to his mind may appear futile and irrelevant but which may, in fact, be quite revealing. It is often advisable for E to conduct this conversation in such a way that *the drawings and signs* appear as the focus of the discussion. Many an S, when becoming aware of the fact that he is overtly speaking about himself, tends to become self-conscious and to control or withhold comments which he might otherwise have expressed quite naturally.

The length and nature of this interview must be guided by S's general attitude; a talkative and cooperative S may even be asked to improvise some little "story" about the pictures. Such a question, on the other hand, may offend a serious-minded or matter-of-fact S and compromise the entire rapport. Although free association about the drawings may yield clinically valuable data, E should definitely refrain from prodding S to elaborate about what he may consider nothing but mere drawings. Many subjects regard such prodding as an annoyance and reject it as childish or "crazy." Moreover, many exploratory questions are too transparent for the intelligent and educated S. Furthermore, to seek motivation for every statement S makes by firing a "why" at him may affect him in a particularly irritating and painful manner. Again, the principle of the procedure must be a maximum of freedom for the projective or expressive activity. Therefore, E should refrain from noting verbatim the remarks and comments of S. Such a procedure is necessary in intelligence testing, where the verbalizations are scorable; in projective techniques it may interfere seriously with S's spontaneity and expansiveness. Therefore, the stream of his associations should be permitted to flow without interruption. It should be stimulated by genuine attention, encouraging remarks and pertinent questions. If some recording is considered necessary, it should be as inconspicuous as possible and only of a few key words serving as reminders for subsequent completion. When S seems to have "talked himself out," E may return to those key words and complete them, when possible with the help of S, asking casually, "What did you say this sign made you think of?" or "You said something like . . . about this drawing, didn't you?" in such a way that the significant elements of the conversation be retained in a reliable form for possible use.

In the case of group testing, this conversation should be replaced by the following questionnaire:

Did the signs make you think of anything else besides what you drew? If so, of what?

    Sign 1
    Sign 2
    Sign 3 and so forth

If you had been a skilled drawer what would you have made out of the signs?

> Sign 1
> Sign 2
> Sign 3 and so forth

Which drawings do you like best?
Which do you like least?
Which signs were easiest to complete?
Which were the most difficult?

II. Bases for Interpretation

THE MATERIAL discussed in the following chapters consists exclusively of the specific results of the test, that is, the drawings and their titles, considered solely in regard to the information obtained from the criterion tests. All other information provided by the comments or the behavior of the subjects, or by special knowledge about them, will be omitted. Only incidentally, for the purpose of illustrating some insufficiently explored potentialities of the test, will a given characteristic of the drawings be related to data derived from sources other than the criterion. Such limitation of the diagnostic basis necessarily results in limitation of the conclusions here reported. Therefore, these conclusions should not be regarded as a measure of the diagnostic potentialities of the test. It has happened not infrequently that people familiar with psychological expression in general or with a subject's life and personality successfully interpreted far beyond the level to which the following discussion is carried. However, although combination of data from various sources and the addition of the examiner's "intuitive" skill is valuable in clinical practice, it seems preferable, in presenting a new technique, to limit the discussion to the specific results of the technique rather than to dilute them with data for which no objective basis for evaluation is available. Improper combining of the results of a projective technique with information from other sources may end up in a reversal of the procedure: instead of getting information *out* of the test, the examiner projects meaning *into* it. The present study has especially endeavored to avoid such stretching of the interpretation. While the conclusions presented in it may be considered modest, at least they are—to a variable extent—objectively grounded.

The Drawing-Completion Test presents three different approaches to the study of the drawings. The first of these approaches considers the drawings in relation to the given stimuli or, more precisely, to qualities symbolized by the stimuli. A drawing is deemed appropriate to a given stimulus when it brings out one or more of these qualities. The appropriateness of the drawings may be greater or less and may vary from one stimulus to another. This aspect of the drawings, reflecting the affinity of the subject for the specific qualities of the stimuli, is indicated here as "Stimulus-Drawing Relation" and offers a first basis for exploring the structure of perception and affectivity.

The two other approaches examine the drawings as such, that is, (1) in their content, and (2) in their mode of execution.

A drawing, obviously, has content when it represents some visible part of the physical world, such as a house, a flower, a person or a scene, although a decorative design or a scribble has content also which, poor as it may be, places it in a particular category. Thus anything that might be said in answer to the question "What is drawn?" may be considered *content*. Since the content is a manifestation of free association, it lends insight into the predominant orientation of the subject's tendencies, interests and preoccupations. It constitutes the source of the *projective* data yielded by the test.

The diagnostic clues provided by content alone are not sufficient to allow for a reliable and differentiated interpretation. Many subjects, sometimes of widely different personality structure, draw the same things. This may be explained by several factors: a suggestive tendency of the stimuli to anticipate certain completions; the subject's proneness to reproduce objects of daily life; or the effect of seasonal events such as Christmas and Easter, when the drawings show an increased frequency of objects associated with these events.

The same content, however, always shows differences in execution. The same object may be represented in a relatively small or large size, may be vaguely sketched or sharply outlined, carefully or casually treated, shaded, fluent, rigid, etc. All these characteristics and many other answering the question "How is a thing drawn?" constitute the modal or formal aspects of the drawings and are considered here under the heading *execution*. The study of the execution, dealing with the *expressive* aspects of the results, aims at something even more fundamental than the subject's tendencies and interests. Through the numerous modal characteristics of a complex, yet free and easy task, it tries to discover the relatively permanent reaction pattern of the personality in terms of intensity, amplitude, flexibility, rigidity, firmness and other fairly consistent attitudes and behavior.

Both approaches, the projective and the expressive, are indispensable for achieving reliable and differentiated conclusions because of the mutual completion and the means of verification which each of these approaches provides for the other. For instance, when subject A draws flowers, children and landscapes, and when subject B draws athletes, wild animals and engines, these contents suggest that A is sensitive, kindhearted, sentimentally inclined; B, vigorous, aggressive and practically oriented. Such inferences are insufficiently grounded, however, for the content of drawings may be determined by superficial associations as well as by deeper impulses. But when A draws in light and softly curved lines, B with strong and bold strokes, then the diagnostic *possibility* suggested by the content of their drawings is immediately raised to the level of *probability*, which is the highest level of validity that conclusions based on projective-expressive material can reach.

Because of this threefold approach, the perceptive-associative, the associative-projective and the active-expressive, the final conclusions of the Drawing-Completion Test may be expected to yield an appreciable degree of objectivity.

A. Stimulus-Drawing Relation

The signs appearing on the test blank are intended to act as stimuli for both associative and graphic activity. They also constitute a means for objective treatment of the drawings, for they provide a series of invariables allowing for comparison and classification of the results of a large number of subjects. The specific and main value of the stimuli lies, however, in their diagnostic potentiality. Each of these stimuli has a particular "physiognomy"; in other words, it is expressive of a certain number of qualities inherent in the particular form and structure—the Gestalt—of each of them. This expressive value of the stimuli serves as a "resonator" for the sensibility of the subject; it is used as a means of exploring the way he perceives, feels and associates. The ability or inability of the subject to integrate these stimuli into drawings which bring out one or more of their physiognomic qualities, indicates his affinity for, or insensibility to, these qualities. Since the variety of stimuli is quite large, a wide range of qualities can be explored, and since some of the qualities expressed by each of them are common to several stimuli, the conclusions drawn on the basis of the above-mentioned affinity or insensibility can be verified by comparison. The set of stimuli thus makes the blank into a differentiated and reliable tool for studying the subject's perceptual and emotional structure.

The various qualities of each of the stimuli, as indicated by Wartegg and confirmed by the present study, are described below. This description is not derived from armchair procedures but is composed essentially on the basis of the spontaneous remarks, sometimes awkward but sometimes pithy, made by many subjects.

Stimulus 1, the dot, has the characteristics smallness, lightness, roundness, centrality. In itself this stimulus is unimposing and could easily be overlooked by the less perceptive or less sensitive subject. However, its exact central position lends it an importance which retains the attention and calls for acknowledgment.

Thus a tension arises between imagination and thinking, for the material insignificance of this stimulus must be combined with its functional importance in order to result in adequate completion.

Stimulus 2, the wavy line, suggests something lively, mobile, loose, fluttering, . growing or flowing. The qualities of this stimulus decidedly resist matter-of-fact treatment or technical use and require integration into something organic or dynamic.

Stimulus 3, the three vertical regularly increasing lines, expresses the qualities of rigidity, austerity, regularity, order and progression. These qualities may blend and produce complex impressions of dynamic organization, gradual development, methodical construction and similar concepts.

Stimulus 4, the black square, appears heavy, solid, massive, angular and static and evokes concrete materiality. While stimulus 3, in spite of its mechanical character, still shows something growing and dynamic, stimulus 4 is completely inorganic and inert. It also has a somber appearance, conducive to associations of a somewhat depressive or—in rare cases—threatening character.

Stimulus 5, the two opposed slanting lines, expresses predominantly the idea of conflict and dynamism. The position of the longer· line evokes something directed decidedly upwards, to which the shorter line shows frank opposition. The rigidity of the lines and their perpendicular relation also suggests construction or technical use.

Stimulus 6, the horizontal and vertical lines, has a strictly matter-of-fact, sober, rigid, dull and uninspiring aspect. At first sight it seems fit only for completion into simple geometric patterns or elementary objects. Experience shows, however, that this stimulus may be worked into a variety of interesting combinations. However, the off-center position of each of the lines makes their completion into a balanced whole a tough task requiring considerable planning activity.

Stimulus 7, the dotted half-circle, suggests something very fine, delicate round and supple that is at the same time appealing and a little puzzling because of its complex, beadlike structure. This structured aspect of the stimulus, together with its somewhat awkward location within the square, forces the selective activity of the mind and resists casual or crude treatment.

Stimulus 8, the broadly curved line, has the organic qualities of roundness and flexibility of stimulus 7, but whereas 7 has something irritating in its complexity and smallness, stimulus 8 appears restful, large, fluent, and easy to deal with. Its smooth curve readily suggests completion into organic subject matter, animate or inanimate, while its downward bending movement and location connote the idea of cover, shelter and protection. Its relatively large dimension also evokes expansion and vastness as proved by the frequent completion of this stimulus into natural phenomena such as rainbows or sunsets.

The stimuli can further be classified into two groups, according to the *organic* quality of some of them (1, 2, 7 and 8), or to the *technical-constructive* quality of the four remaining. These groups are also called the feminine and the masculine groups. As they are used here, these denominations do not refer to analytical symbolism but simply to the commonly accepted greater affinity of women for the organic-emotional sphere and that of men for material-technical things.

The diagnostic use made of the stimuli consists of examining the appropriateness of the drawings as responses to the specific qualities of the stimuli and of drawing tentative conclusions concerning the affinity or insensibility of the subject for these qualities. For instance, if the subject successfully completes the organic stimuli, he is said to have affinity for the world of life and nature, to be interested in it, and in harmony with it. What kind of living objects he prefers, what he likes especially in them, in what way he likes them, has to be deduced from more specific characteristics of the drawings than their sole over-all appropriateness to the kind of stimulus. On the contrary, if the subject completes the organic stimuli into inanimate, rigid and static objects, he is said to lack feeling for the organic world, to be estranged from it or in conflict with it, depending on other characteristics of the drawings. In the same way, if the subject completes the dynamic and technical stimulus 5 into a flaring flashlight, as in drawings C/5 and D/5,* he shows affinity for these qualities; he "resonates" to them, which suggests that he carries these qualities within himself. Conversely, if he work stimulus 5 into a flower he reveals effeminate, distorted sensibility, and a lack of firmness, determination and aggressiveness.

The affinity of the subject for the qualities of the stimuli is revealed not only by the content, by what is drawn, but also by the way it is drawn. If, for instance, the delicate stimulus 7 is treated in heavy lines, grossly covering the fine structure of this design, or if the dark and angular stimulus 4 is worked out in weak or curly lines, such treatment also evidences a lack of sensibility to the expressive value of the stimuli.

Another basis for examining the subject's receptivity for the qualities expressed by the stimuli is the order in which he makes the drawings. Since the subject is free to complete the stimuli according to his preference, the order of

* In these combinations of letters and figures, the letter refers to the set of drawings indicated by that letter, the figure corresponds to the number of the single drawing within the set. The single drawings are indicated, not in the order in which they are executed, but in the regular order of the squares, that is, starting with the central dot, continuing horizontally over the black square and ending with the semicircle.

succession of the drawings may be regarded as an indicator for his sensitivity to the specific physiognomy of the stimuli.

The subject's reaction to each of the stimuli may show various forms: (1) indifference; (2) adaptation; (3) emphasis.

Indifference may be more or less outspoken. Its crudest form is a complete negation of the stimulus, even in its mere function of stimulus. Either the square is left untouched or something appears irrelevantly next to the stimulus or inconsiderately over it. Such complete disregard for the stimulus is not due to the subject's misunderstanding of the task, as appears from questioning him, or from the adequate completion of certain stimuli within the set. A lesser degree of insensitivity is present when the specific quality of the stimulus is recognized to some extent but without its being integrated into the drawing as illustrated by X/4. A reaction not of indifference but of deficient sensitivity to the stimuli appears in drawings where the content is adapted to the qualities of the stimulus but where the execution is inappropriate.

Adaptation is achieved when both content and execution prove that the stimulus has been perceived not only in its physical dimensions but also in its symbolic value. In such drawings the individuality of the stimulus disappears and becomes absorbed into the whole.

Emphasis occurs where the qualities of the stimuli are brought out with particular sharpness and pregnancy in drawings showing a harmonious blend of content and execution.

Cues for the interpretation of the subject's reaction to each of the stimuli are given in table 2. This table is planned in such a way that the examiner can check the diagnostic tendency of the subject's reaction to every single stimulus, through comparison with the diagnostic implications of the reaction given to the stimuli, with either similar or opposed qualities. The two middle columns of this table indicate the trend of meaning of the subject's receptivity to the stimuli with *contrasting* qualities; the side columns give the meaning of his indifference to these stimuli. Thus, the diagnostic indications emerging from a given stimulus-drawing relation can be ascertained through (1) confirmation and (2) absence of contradiction within the other stimulus-drawing relations. For example, when stimulus 1 is adequately completed, the examiner, before making any inferences from this single phenomenon, must check whether a satisfactory response has also been given to the stimulus—or stimuli—whose appearance and expressive value is nearest to stimulus 1, in this case, 7. If the subject's responsiveness to 7 confirms his affinity for 1, then the broad diagnostic trend emerging from this coincidence needs further differentiation. Has the subject responded to the organic qualities of these stimuli (symbolized by their roundness) or to their mechanical qualities (exact centrality for 1; preciseness of structure and equality of the elements for 7)? If this question cannot be answered with satisfactory clearness on the basis of the indications contained in the completions of the stimuli in question, it can be gained from an examination of the responses given to the other stimuli. When such an examination shows that the other organic stimuli (2 and 8) have received highly satisfactory completions, whereas the mechanical stimuli (3 to 6 inclusive) appear less well integrated, it may be assumed that signs 1 and 7 were grasped predominantly in their organic qualities. Conversely, if the mechanical stimuli appear to be emphasized, the organic ones less accentuated or somewhat neglected, the opposite conclusion is justified. Another constellation of cues is given when, for instance, the completion of stimuli 1 and 7 gives unambiguous evidence of the fact that the subject has responded to their organic qualities, and the examiner tries to evaluate the strength of the emotionality revealed by this form of reaction. For this he turns again to the characteristics of the subject's reaction to the other stimuli. If 2 and 8 appear to have received outstanding treatment, the subject may be assumed to be deeply emotional. However, before concluding that his emotionality is overwhelming and out of balance with his intellectual-volitional functions, the examiner must check the responses given to the mechanical stimuli. If the responses to these stimuli are equally well adapted, emphasizing their specific qualities, then a richly endowed, well balanced personality may be assumed. On the contrary, if the affinity for the mechanical stimuli appears poorer than for the organic, the subject is likely to present a predominantly emotional make-up. Finally, if his responses to these stimuli reveal a degree of indifference so great that it forms a sharp contrast with the completions of the organic stimuli, suspicions of defective rational-volitional functioning and imbalanced structure are justified.

By means of such multiple comparison and cross-checking, the stimulus-drawing relation is capable of yielding appreciably verified and differentiated information.

—————————————————————— Table 2. – *Diagnostic Tendencies Implied in the*

INSENSIBILITY	AFFINITY

to the mechanical stimuli 3, 4, 5, 6

Unrealistic impractical attitude.	Masculine personality makeup.
Overwhelming emotional or esthetic tendencies.	Predominance of the conscious functions.
Effeminacy.	Matter-of-factness.

to the complex stimuli 3, 5, 6, 7

Intellectual flatness.	Organizational and constructive capacities.
Lack of dynamism.	Analytico-synthesizing intelligence.
Reduced activity.	Sharpness of attention.
	Ingeniousness. Efficiency.

to the straight stimuli 3, 5 and 6

Predominance of the unconscious.	Predominance of the intellectual and volitional functions.
Defective control.	Firmness. Earnest makeup.
Inconsistency.	(Compulsiveness.)

to the oriented signs 3 and 5

Weak self-assertiveness.	Strong vital drive.
Reserve.	Self-assurance.
Placidity.	Impetus.
(Inhibition.)	

to the dynamic stimuli 5

Quietness.	Alertness. Audaciousness.
Unostentatiousness.	Ambition. Competitiveness.
Conflict-avoidance.	Tendency to dominate.

to the small stimuli 1 and 7

Casualness.	Delicate sensibility.
Unperceptiveness.	Sense of details.
Aversion for trivia.	Meticulousness.
(Obtuseness.)	(Irritability. Susceptibility. Compulsiveness.)

The words between parentheses refer to diagnostic
cues which are applicable only in cases of particular

Stimulus-Drawing Relation and Order of Execution. ——————————

AFFINITY   INSENSIBILITY

to the organic stimuli 1, 2, 7, 8

Feminine personality make up.
Predominance of the
    visceral-emotional impulses.
Sensitivity.
Adaptability.

Severe emotional deficiency.
Life-estranged attitude.
Inhibition.

to the simple stimuli 1, 2, 4, 8

Natural, relaxed attitude.
Commonsense.

Complicatedness.
Tenseness.
Insecurity.

to the curved stimuli 2, 7 and 8

Smoothness.
Flexibility.
Life-relatedness.
Congeniality. Affectivity.

Rigidity.
Austerity.
Over-intellectuality.
(Hostility.)

to the loose stimuli 1 and 2

Liveliness.
Flexibility. Spontaneity.
When sign 1 is seen in its centrality:
    predominance of intellect over
    emotion.

Constraint.
Rigidity.
(Inhibition.)

to the static stimulus 4

Consistency.
Affinity for concrete reality.
When the sign is perceived in its
    darkness: anxiety.

Over-refined sensibility.
Instability.

to the large stimulus 8

Openness. Lack of constraint.
Warmth. Mildness.
(Easy-goingness.)

Problem indicator.
(Severe maladjustment. Inhibition.
    Repression.)

emphasis of the qualities of certain signs with
simultaneous rejection of the opposed signs.

B. Content of the Drawings

As appears from table 3, the content of the drawings comprises a large number of characteristics used here as criteria for the interpretation. Several of these characteristics show relationships in their nature or appearance. They have, as it were, a common denominator which allows their classification into a certain number of groups. These groups, in turn, share certain aspects which permit their integration into broader units.

The most fundamental distinction within content is based upon the degree of representational value of the drawings. Those drawings featuring objects— natural or man-made—of the outside world and recognizable by the onlooker without comments of the subjects are representational. Three classes can thus be distinguished which, passing from the nonrepresentational to the fully representational, are: (1) Scribblings; (2) Abstractions, and (3) Pictures.

TABLE 3.   *Classification of the Content Matter.*

General Characteristics	*Particular Characteristics*
Scribblings	Motor
	Esthetic
	Symbolic
Abstractions	Symmetrical Decorative
	Asymmetrical Decorative
	Technical
Pictures	
Realism	
Nature	Animate
	Physiognomy*
	Schematism
	Inanimate
	Atmosphere*
Objects	Utility
	Style*
	Ornaments
Fantasy	Fancy
	Phantasm
	Symbolism

* Characteristic of *modality* referring to the immediately preceding characteristic.

1. Scribblings

This type of response is made up of haphazard, disordered scrawlings, criss-cross lines or confused shadowy forms. Objectively regarded, Scribblings* are completely nonrepresentational, but comments from the subject may sometimes reveal that they are intended to represent something, or that a certain meaning is projected into them after they are produced. Thus Scribblings may have to be scored additionally for other criteria of content such as Animate Nature, Inanimate Nature, Movement or Symbolism. On the basis of such elements, or of the over-all appearance of the Scribblings, the following subdivisions have been established: *motor scribblings,* characterized by violent scrawls and wild criss-crossings (L/7; R/1; d.† 1) *esthetic scribblings,* which have a softer, less tormented, and sometimes graceful appearance (P/1; d. 3) *symbolic scribblings,* which denote a tendency toward objective organization and meaning.

. . .

Scribblings are a form of reaction showing considerable or complete disregard for the given stimuli and thus suggesting a deficiency or disturbance of the sensibility. They further evidence a largely indifferent attitude to the task and to the expectations of the examiner, which does not speak in favor of the subject's sociability or desire to live up to reasonable standards of productivity. The lack of meaning of such drawings further shows that the subject feels no need to communicate on an objectively understandable level; their lack of differentiation points to a tendency to abandon the activity and behavior to unconscious impulses rather than to plan and to deliberate; the complete absence of Reality content arouses suspicion about the subject's contact with reality and his ability to adjust to it and deal productively with it. This convergence of indications justifies the suspicion that Scribblings are symptomatic of maladjustment or disturbance.‡

Well adjusted, normal individuals seldom respond with Scribblings. Of the 384 subjects of the "normal" group, only four completed the entire set of

* Words indicating drawing characteristics will be capitalized whenever they refer to those characteristics as *criteria.*

†The letter d is used hereafter as an abbreviation for the word "drawing" whenever references are made to the single drawings, that is, those which do not belong to a given set and which are numbered from 1 to 136; dd is used to indicate the plural.

. . . This sign separates the descriptive from the interpretive part in the discussion of every criterion.

‡The conclusions described above are not to be extended to the automatic, more or less unconscious "doodling" activity which frequently occurs when the mind is occupied and the hand holds a pencil. Such free, playful or nervous activity is a reaction quite different from the Scribbling response produced in situations where the subject is confronted with a definite task.

signs with Scribblings or scribbling-like drawings; 16 subjects gave between two and four such responses. The subjects who produced nothing but Scribblings were known to have severe problems and a few showed schizophrenic tendencies. The others did not reveal any apparent signs of disturbance, but it must be borne in mind that the aim of the present study was not to disclose specific forms of disturbance. Among the 21 clinical cases here examined, one patient diagnosed as schizophrenic and mentally retarded answered with mere Scribblings. Two patients gave 3 Scribblings; two gave 4 and six gave 1 Scribbling-like drawing. This distribution of the Scribblings among the products of normal and abnormal subjects is in agreement with the findings reported in the literature on drawings of psychiatric patients (2), which also records a high incidence of this type of graphic expression.

Motor scribbles result from a sudden muscular discharge and indicate acute tension, deficient psychomotor control and a proneness to violent outbursts. The strong and undisciplined vitality underlying this kind of reaction is a continual threat to the subject's balance and social integration. Four subjects who gave several or all motor scribbles were hostile and revengeful individuals, known for their difficult, aggressive and unsocial character.

Esthetic scribbles are produced by subjects who are conditioned by imaginative-emotional factors to the extent of being inaccessible to common understanding and of appearing somehow out of place in ordinary reality. Intellectually these subjects may be highly endowed but their intelligence is often turned exclusively toward theoretical-esthetic matters and they look with contempt upon commonplace things and conventional standards. Esthetic scribblings, showing a great deal of light shading, are usually produced by passive, dreamy subjects who display a low level of consciousness and energy. When the shading is heavy, such drawings reveal a confused, grossly emotional nature.

Symbolic scribblings share the emotional significance of esthetic scribblings. In addition, they have a specific meaning which depends upon (1) the nature of the symbols represented and (2) the extent to which the object symbolized can be recognized in the scribbling. Adequate relationship between the object and its representation shows a certain degree of logical functioning. Complete discrepancy between object and representation points to disturbance of the logical or the reality function. When such discrepancy appears to exist, the product may certainly be considered a pathological symptom, not only because it is a scribble but because its content is autistic. As a rule the intelligibility of Scribblings is low, except for such themes as "confusion" (L/7); "whirlpool" (R/3); "nothingness," and the like. However, the negative character of these themes destroys the favorable effect of adequacy between concept and symbol.

In conclusion, Scribblings indicate disturbance of the inner balance. Subjects producing predominantly Scribblings or scribbling-like drawings (sets L, N, P, R) show excessive predominance of the biological, vital-emotional factors over the rational-controlling and orderly creative factors. Some among these subjects appear life-estranged; they like to dwell in a world of fantasy or obscure speculation and show little concern for reality, people, conventions and common usages. This taken together predisposes them toward isolation and singularity.

Scribbling is diagnostically the worst response that can be given to the present test. Its symptom-value is such that even one such drawing within a chart is sufficient to justify suspicion.

2. Abstraction

These drawings consist mainly of line structures of a decorative or intellectual kind. The decorative varieties of Abstractions must be differentiated according to the more or less conventional or original character of their patterns. Thus three categories can be distinguished:

Symmetrical Decorative Abstractions which present regular, static, often rigid geometric patterns (dd. 17 to 32);

Asymmetrical Decorative Abstractions presenting lines and surfaces arranged in a free, playful, original way (set O, set Q and dd. 5 to 8);

Technical Abstractions pertaining to all kinds of intellectual symbols, geometrical figures or technical devices (set W and dd. 9 to 16).

. . .

The general significance of Abstractions depends largely upon their number. The occurrence of one or two Abstractions within a set of drawings has no particular significance. Many subjects produce at least one such drawing and when it is a Technical Abstraction this occurrence is desirable, especially with male subjects. However, when a set of drawings features primarily or exclusively Abstractions the subject may be suspected of being either evasive or inhibited. When other indications contradict these tentative conclusions, defective integration of the subject within life or within himself is highly probable. This is especially true for the Decorative Abstractions. Subjects producing exclusively this kind of drawing show a disturbance of the intellectual-emotional balance. Such individuals do not completely participate in life; they do not fit in with common reality and do not want to fit in. They have highly personal views on many things, find their happiness in ways of their own and have difficulty understanding other people's motives.

When the designs are all of the same kind, entirely Symmetrical, Asymmetrical or Technical, such uniformity indicates a narrowing of the subject's experience and capacity for expression.

When a person projects meaning into his Abstractions—that is in the Decorative kind, the Technical kind having meaning per se—the above indications may have to be modified in a positive or a negative sense. If the projected meaning is objectively acceptable the drawing acquires a certain utility value or intellectual meaning. For instance, it is acceptable to call drawing 20 a pattern for floor-tiling, drawings 25 to 32 motifs for tapestry or embroidery. When the meaning is far-fetched and not recognizable, the above interpretations are aggravated because the gap between the subject's conceptions and common perception is broadened. Thus, strongly predominant or exclusive production of Abstraction always requires investigation and always proves to be revealing.

It may happen that the subject misunderstands the instructions and believes that only nonobjective patterns are expected as completions of the stimuli. Therefore, whenever the drawings consist exclusively of designs the examiner should find out whether there has been any misunderstanding of the task. In such an event, the examiner reminds the subject that every kind of drawing is permitted and gives him the test a second time, though not during the same session. When giving the instructions anew, the examiner must take care not to say: "Work the signs into something else," but rather, something like: "Try to work these signs once again into a set of drawings."

Misunderstanding the instructions rarely occurs since most of the subjects make certain of what is wanted by asking whether the drawings "must mean something or not," upon which the examiner invariably answers that the subject is completely free and that he may draw whatever comes to his mind. In case the test cannot be repeated, the results are not worthless, for "misunderstanding" is often as revealing of the subject as a deliberate preference for designs.

Symmetrical Decorative Abstractions

Scoring of Symmetrical Abstractions is based on the complexity and esthetic value of the patterns. In the case of flat, schematic, more geometrical than esthetic patterns (set Y) it is often difficult to decide whether they should be scored as Decorative or as Technical Abstractions. Such drawings are so poor that they belong actually under neither of these criteria. They are more like "escapes" of the task for they represent a mere continuation and repetition of the stimulus, not an actual completion in the sense of integration into a broader whole. In order to reflect the unprecise nature of such content matter, the drawing must be credited partially for Symmetry and partially for Technicality; for the latter because of its schematic appearance, for the former because of its esthetic aecent, which is incompatible with the objectivity and logical significance of Technical drawings.

Decorative drawings result from the combined activity of emotional and rational factors. The former determine the esthetic aspect, the latter command organization in regular, well-proportioned patterns. One of these aspects will generally be stressed, as in drawings 17 to 24 presenting a strictly logical-geometric organization, and drawings 25 to 32 exhibiting an esthetic-emotional character. The kind of emotion revealed through Symmetrical Abstractions is always of a controlled, sublimated or intellectualized nature. Symmetrical Abstractions, especially those showing emphasis on the geometrical disposition of the elements (drawings 17 to 24) rarely occur with spontaneous, demonstrative, vitally conditioned subjects.

Asymmetrical Decorative Abstractions

To this variety belong those drawings which exhibit a free play of line and mass, of light and shading. These patterns are often created "out of themselves" with no significant amount of planning. They may be harmonious and well integrated or they may lack such inner balance and spontaneous gracefulness. Some of these designs are original, others eccentric, still others incoherent.

• • •

Asymmetrical Abstractions, like the preceding variety, are highly symptomatic. This type of drawing is almost always produced by subjects who exhibit strong artistic leanings and who are affected by some form of inadequacy for which they try to "cover up" by adopting so-called personal, unconventional tastes. They also manifest marked deficiency of rational-volitional activity and are almost entirely governed by their impulses. The latter conclusion may be attenuated when this kind of design is executed with great care, as in sets O and G. In such cases, however, the emotional tendencies, expressed by free creation, conflict sharply with the almost compulsive need for precision and perfection evidenced by such a degree of carefulness.

For these reasons, the Asymmetrical Abstraction must be considered an unfavorable symptom. While Symmetry points only to a narrowing of the emotionality and a detachment from concrete reality, Asymmetry generally occurs with subjects who, upon closer examination, reveal some disturbance of an emotional nature.

Technical Abstractions

This concept refers to all subject matter that is characterized by its intellectual meaning or logical symbolism.

Examples of the variety found under this heading and enumerated in increasing order of logical structuring are: the schematic designs produced by merely repeating, continuing or connecting the stimuli; elementary geometrical forms; numerals and letters; signs; stereometric figures; mathematical or scientific symbols and formulas; plans, blueprints and maps.

Several examples are not purely logical-technical; such are: monograms, names (d. 16), words (d. 15) which convey an esthetic or emotional accent rather than a logical one; route signs, on the other hand, are more to be considered as Objects than as Abstractions. The scores for such drawings must consequently be distributed over the categories involved.

.   .   .

Technical drawings, despite their intellectual flavor, are no proof of capacity to deal with abstract matters or logical systems, especially the elementary technical drawings such as simple geometric forms, numerals or letters. Instead, this type of content matter provides insight into the relative importance of the rational and emotional factors within the personality. Predominance of Technicals suggests that the mental activities overbalance the emotional functions, but gives no indication as to the level on which this mental activity is performed. If the configuration of symptoms shows that emotionality is not lacking, a strong representation of Technicals within the chart points to deficient integration of reason and emotion.

When the technical drawing features logical mathematical content (W, D/7, d. 9), it may be considered as evidence of intellectual interest, though not necessarily of intellectual capacity. In fact, many highly intellectual subjects refrain from this sophisticated type of completion and produce simple content matter. Male subjects of average intelligence often show a liking for such proofs of intellectual concern.

Technicals, consequently, do not afford a reliable basis for appreciating the *level* of intelligence. They solely point to the importance of the intellectual factor in the structure of the subject's personality.

3. Pictures

This class is the largest and most varied and is completely representational. A distinction must be made between (1) Reality Pictures and (2) Fantasy Pictures, depending upon the degree of relationship between what is drawn and the objective world.

Realism in pictorial content includes all drawings which represent things from the tangible, physical world. This comprehensive group may be further subdivided into:

Nature, that is everything that has life quality, however elementary or however complex. This category is further differentiated into: *animate nature,* comprising all human and animal figures or parts of such figures, and *inanimate nature,* referring to everything else in the natural physical world—not only vegetation, but water, mountains, clouds, etc.

Objects, all man-made reality, comprising: *utilitarian objects* of all kinds, from a simple tool to a monumental construction, and *ornamental objects* found in interior decoration or belonging to personal apparel.

Fantasy in pictorial content applies to drawings whose elements are taken from the physical world but are combined into representations of things that do not actually exist or are not perceptible. The variety of motifs encountered in this group may be differentiated into:

Fancy. The fiction represented in the drawing has a wondrous and often pleasant character such as found in fairly tales and mythical matter.

Phantasm. The appearance or meaning of the content is somber, grim, or even gruesome. Deathheads, grotesque masks, devils or monsters are found in this group.

Symbolism. These drawings are intended as graphic representations of concepts, sentiments, or ideals, such as progress, faith, harmony, devotion.

A further series of drawing characteristics refers to *modalities* of the objects drawn. For instance, a human figure may be represented as walking or recumbent, the facial expression, pleasant or serious. Likewise, a landscape may be sunny and bright, or in twilight and somber; a building may be a skyscraper, a church, a country house. These characteristics of modality are the following:*

Physiognomy is everything in the drawing of the human figure that reveals something about the person represented: his age, profession, or character.

Schematism refers to oversimplified representation of Nature content.

Atmosphere pertains to the emotional quality indirectly expressed by the drawing, especially by landscapes or situations other than human scenes.

Style refers to specific, character-conveying elements in the representation of utilitarian objects.

Nature

Animate Nature

The most elementary manifestations of animate nature appear under the form of parts of the body, such as eyes (d. 8), mouths (d. 43) or disembodied heads, that is, heads without indication of neckline or torso (V/1, 2, d. 64). A

---

*Some authors classify these characteristics with the *formal* aspects of the drawings. However, since these characteristics inform us about modalities of the subject matter rather than the manner of execution, they will be considered here with the characteristics of *content.*

higher degree of life is achieved when human figures are represented to the full extent allowed by the drawing area as is the case with large heads (d. 34), busts (C/2), entire human or animal figures (C/7, dd. 45, 46, 52, 55).

This enumeration conforms to the line of increasing complexity, from the more primitive phenomena to the more complete and elaborate, adopted here as a rule for the presentation of the matter. However, the *amount* of life, in terms of parts or wholes or number of items is not the sole basis for quantitative evaluation. The vividness which adequate execution confers to a given content is also an important factor in the scoring. This enhancing effect of Execution upon Content results from a combination of formal characteristics, later to be scored separately but considered here in the Gestalt function of their interplay. The nature of these heightening factors varies widely according to the kind of subject matter. In the reality class of pictures it will be anything that increases the concrete and tangible quality of the object, such as clearness of outline, adequate pressure or three-dimensional organization. For each of the subgroups of the Reality class this enhancing effect will be achieved in different ways. In the Nature group it will be through movement, fluency of lines, supple and casual treatment. Objects, on the other hand, call for emphasis upon consistency and concreteness of appearance, achieved by strong and continuous lines, straight angles, precise organization, etc. Such optimum execution leads to higher scoring for drawings showing perhaps only one item of a given group than for drawings featuring several poorly executed items.

· · ·

Animate Nature is one of the most direct indexes of the subject's integration and adjustment as manifested by the present test. It is an expression of the vital character of his experience and of the life-relatedness of his behavior, that is, of his capacity to participate and identify with the organic world of growth and movement. Animate Nature is therefore a sign of healthy emotionality, of spontaneity and of flexibility.

Subjects who draw predominantly Animate Nature are sociable, versatile and active individuals. Most of them are more or less cheerful and vivacious, but some may be just quiet and relaxed. Such individuals are interested in life because of the variety of its forms and peculiarities, or they enjoy its colorfulness and excitement, or they simply have a vague feeling of greater relation to the world of animate things than to mere materiality or speculation.

When the human figure predominates among the Nature content, a capacity for direct contact and an eagerness for dealing with people may be assumed. Whether this capacity operates on the more primitive, aggressive and egocentric level of the instinct, or on the more differentiated and humanitarian level of the feelings, whether the subject is more sensitively attuned to positive or to negative experiences must be disclosed from the examination of other characteristics of the drawings, mainly Physiognomy and Atmosphere.

Exclusive or strongly predominant occurrence of Animate Nature combined, for example, with low Form Level, Fullness and Strong Lines, indicates an overwhelming, heavily sensuous vitality which makes the subject unfit for intellectual work or any activity beyond the sensorial level (set Z). Thus, the meaning of Animate Nature, however favorable its general tendency, is like that of every other variable, fluctuating and dependent on the nature and intensity of the other variables entering into the composition of a drawing.

Complete absence of Animate Nature is an important indicator of a negative kind. It generally corresponds either to a lack of contact and interest in living things, to an over-developed interest in abstract or mechanical things, to a lack of emotional receptivity and warmth, or to acute inhibition. When animal life is amply featured and human life is lacking, conflict within important spheres of human relations is almost certain to be present.

Physiognomy

Physiognomy has to do with all indexes contained in drawings of the human figure which inform the onlooker about who or what the portrayed figure is, about its sex, age, occupation and character. Physiognomy also applies to animal figures in so far as the characteristics proper or attributed to certain animals are expressed or emphasized in the drawings.

The quantitative evaluation of this variable is concerned solely with the *degree* or amount of physiognomic expression, regardless of the specific information it provides about the figures represented. This amount is often in direct proportion to the degree of elaboration of the drawings. Compare, in this respect, the difference in the amount of information contained in drawings C/2 and 7, dd. 36, 48, 52 on the one hand, and drawings R/2, V/2 and the faces of set Z, on the other. However, elaboration is not an indispensable condition for expressiveness. An original arrangement of elements, a slight accentuation of one or more, or a characteristic detail (dd. 40, 42, 58) may achieve the physiognomic effect as well as completeness and richness of detail. Hence, scoring of this criterion is dependent to an extent upon the acquaintance of the examiner with the range of physiognomic phenomena depictable considering the limitations imposed by the stimuli and reduced drawing area. As a cue to quantitative scoring, it could be mentioned that, for instance, a faint indication of sex or age will score ½ point, a marked degree of differentiation in this respect from 1 to 1½ points; physiognomic elements which provide information about the personality of the figure may range from 1½ to 2 points; combined with other indexes of clothing or activity, these characteristics may reach the highest score.

The specific, *qualitative* indications conveyed by physiognomic phenomena such as facial or postural expression, type of clothing and activity of the figures, are obviously far more important for disclosing the individuality of the subject than mere *amount* of Physiognomy. However, quantitative treatment for these modalities cannot be provided, the range of physiognomic variety being practically unlimited. Consideration of these aspects belongs therefore to the process of qualitative differentiation which follows the quantitative determination of the personality pattern.

The most general and almost unavoidable physiognomic element in drawings of the human figure is the *sex*, indicated either through the amount, length or style of the hair, the character of the features, or the clothing. If this elementary indication is absent, owing to extremely sketchy or schematic execution of the drawing, special notice should be taken of such ambiguous and impersonal representation. When several human figures are drawn, both sexes are generally represented. It is remarkable that, when only one figure appears in a set, it is practically always of the same sex as the subject (see G/7, S/2, T/8, U/8).

A further step in characterizing the human figure is the approximate *age*. In general, it is easy to recognize whether the drawing represents a child, an adolescent, an adult or an elderly person. Some subjects, not necessarily the most skillful drawers, happen to represent figures, especially faces, which allow for a much closer evaluation of the age and which quite often show a surprising agreement with the age level of the subject (S/2, F/8, K/3, dd. 33, 34, 35, 39), thus making the figure, when it is of the same sex as the subject, literally a self-portrait.

The *facial and postural expression of the figures* is a rich source of diagnostic data and may be considered directly revealing of the subject's personality. Special attention should therefore be paid to whether the facial expression is bright (d. 33), smiling, laughing, humorous (T/8), or serious (K/3), stern (d. 41), tense (d. 37), sad, angry, wretched, pensive or painful (d. 41). The posture should be examined as to whether it is upright and straight, expressing energy (d. 35), assurance, dynamism (d. 47), aggressiveness; further, whether the figure is sitting in comfort (T/4), bent by hard work (d. 45) or by a symbol of moral burden (d. 133); gracefully or indolently reclined (C/7), lying down on earth (N/8) and expressing something like complete abandon, passivity, fatigue, depression or any other feeling which has to be specified in function of the trends manifested in the complete set of drawings. The over-all appearance of the figure also is to be considered. Is it supple (d. 69) and easy-going, or conventional (d. 48) and stiff (d. 57)? Another aspect deserving attention is the activity performed by the figures. Are they in motion or immobile, playing (d. 69) or working (dd. 45 and 46), alone or with others? Examination of these various physiognomic indexes always yields significant material.

Diagnostic cues are also provided by the *clothing* of the figures or the *role* which they are playing. These elements indicate the social class or status, or the profession of the person represented. Beyond this merely external information, they generally also contain psychological indications. They may express character features such as the dignified appearance of the teacher, the self-sufficiency of the bourgeois, the authority and rigidity of the general. These features seldom reflect directly the personality of the subject himself but may be an expression of interest or concern about such social or psychological characteristics. Their meaning is not readily understandable, but the comments given by the subjects show that they are not without significance. However, since the present study is not made from the angle of depth psychology, nothing definite can be said about the meaning underlying such physiognomic aspects. It seems, however, that their function is somehow similar to the manifest content of dreams and is therefore highly specific.

Portraits and caricatures are a particular type of expression-conveying drawings. Portraits represent definite persons, mostly well-known personalities in the world of politics, of films or of sports, and aim generally at suggesting the symbolic value of these persons rather than their individual appearance. Caricatures may or may not aim at representing a particular individual; they differ from portraits by deliberate exaggerations, contrasts and distortions of features, tending to produce a humorous effect.

An important point in the study of the physiognomic aspects of the human figure is *absence* of certain organs or features, or *emphasis* upon them. Special notice should therefore be taken of eyes, mouths, noses and ears, of hair, beards and mustaches. Attention should also be directed to the presence, absence, or emphasis upon primary sexual characteristics. Absence of these characteristics is particularly significant in drawings of nudes, where sexual indications are relevant. Presence or emphasis in drawings of fully dressed persons where sex indications are less appropriate is equally noteworthy.

When fragmentary representation is not imposed by the limits of the drawing space, deliberate limitation of the human figure to a specific part of it is always revealing. Of course, this "cutting-off" may be justified by the nature of the figures represented, for example if the Venus de Milo or Hermes theme is used. However, it should be kept in mind that these themes may be disguised, although milder, forms of the same underlying factors which cause deliberate truncation. A striking example of "cutting-off" is given by drawing 63, where the abrupt section of the figure at the hipline is most unusual, especially in view of the ample amount of space available for the representation of a full figure.

Representations of *animals* may be almost as symptomatic as those of human figures. The kinds of animals, their over-all expression or the accentuation of certain features are to be considered. They may be of the domestic variety, cows, sheep, pigs, rabbits, chickens, or they may be so-called companions of man such as horses, dogs, cats, parrots; they may be wild animals such as lions, wolves, elephants, snakes, or common species, such as birds, insects, fishes. Their expression may be aggressive, docile, sweet, passive or watchful; their appearance vigorous, heavy, lively or supple. Often one will discover that the features portrayed into these figures fit in particularly well with other trends contained in the total set.

The objection is often raised that the physiognomic value of the drawings depends upon the drawing skill of the subject. This is true where the accuracy and esthetic perfection of the picture are concerned; it does not hold for the aspects considered here, namely, the suggestive effect resulting from a certain disposition, accentuation and treatment of the parts of a face or figure. In this elementary sense almost any drawing featuring Animate Nature has physiognomic value, unless it is extremely schematic. and even then it is not entirely devoid of expression (see illustrative material on Schematism, page 61). Thus, technical ability does not play any significant role; the drawings produced by a control group of fine arts students confirmed this fact. Somehow the subject finds the proper, though often crude, means to objectify what he has in mind or, as happens most frequently, he seems to be guided by subconscious associations which urge him to give his figures certain features rather than others. Interestingly enough, the subject is often unaware of the expression that he imprints upon his figures and unable to explain how it came about.

Recognizing the correct physiognomic expression requires a good deal of training of the examiner because the portrayals are, objectively, often imperfect and rather ambiguous. In any case, it is advisable to check this aspect of the drawing with the opinion of the subject.

●   ●   ●

The general diagnostic trend of Physiognomy consists of an accentuation and differentiation of the meaning implied in representations of Animate Nature. As for the specific indications manifested by the physiognomic elements, they are as manifold as those elements themselves and this almost infinite variety of modalities makes Physiognomy one of the main factors for individualization of the basic diagnostic picture.

Particularly interesting among the physiognomic drawings are the self-portraits. Literal self-portraits are figures of the same sex and same age level of the subject. Not infrequently these drawings bear a real resemblance to their authors, either because of some physical characteristic such as a particular hairdo, a mustache, baldness, or because of the disposition of the facial features or emphasis upon some of them, or because of the presence of elements such as musculature (dd. 35, 36, 41), wrinkles (d. 37), beauty spots and the like. Usually the subject is quite unaware of this resemblance and is unwilling to recognize himself in the awkwardly drawn figures. Striking examples of literal self-portraiture appear in drawings K/3, dd. 33, 34, 35, 37. Another example of remarkably accurate self-portraiture is found in set S/2 where the young subject, characterized by his good looks and particularly beautiful hair, has worked stimulus 2 into a hairlock. Such drawings are like the signature of the drawer and it is not unusual to find that people, when asked to recognize the drawings of a particular person among a number of sets, are able to do so on the basis of some vague resemblance of the figure to the person who drew it.

The frequency of such self-portraits make them appear as a natural and—judging from the variety of personalities who produce them—not unfavorable phenomenon. As far as this study goes, it does not seem as if these subjects are more self-centered or more concerned about their bodily self or their personality than those who don't produce such direct forms of projection. Only when these drawings feature obviously recognizable physical traits of the subject has a more than usual awareness or concern—positive or negative—about physical appearance been encountered.

The specific value of the self-portraits lies in the expressions which they exhibit and which are a highly reliable indicator of the subject's feelings and attitudes. As a portrayal of the inner self, the concept of self-portrait may be extended far beyond the literal portrait. In a very broad yet very substantial sense, every drawing, regardless of its content, may be considered a self-portrait. However, in order to avoid stretching this concept beyond its common meaning, its use is limited here to figures of the same sex as the subject, showing either physical resemblance or psychological likeness. The latter variety of self-portraits are perhaps the most interesting. Examples of these are found in drawings such as 43, with the enormous bared mouth, mustache and large nostrils expressing the subject's crude sensuality and aggressiveness; in drawing 38, the schematic cut-off head, where the absence of hair, and eyelashes, the thin faintly smiling mouth line, tiny nose line, and complete absence of adornment or sex indication reflect the ascetic character of the S's life and personality; in drawing 42, where the heart-shaped mouth, beauty spot and sidelong glance of coquetry is a self-portrait in the most real sense.

Marked differences in age level between the subject and his figures may be significant too. This discrepancy seems to reveal a tendency toward more independence and power, when the figures belong to an older age level, or toward more protection and care when the figures look younger. However, this inference, lacking the support of deeper personality data, needs verification. Considerable differences in age, though, appear suspect, unless they are due to an objectively grounded concern about children or older people. Children appear frequently in the drawings of female subjects, generally with those who have children or who are working with children, and among these mostly with the kind-hearted, caring, unsophisticated, often somewhat naive type of woman. Children occur very seldom in the drawings of male subjects. Among the 254 men who took the test, only 5 featured a child figure. Two had children themselves, one was a teacher. All but one belonged to the friendly, unassertive, rather unvirile type of male; one of them was unmarried, 32 years of age, a distinguished philosopher, who, unlike the others who drew older children, made an elaborate representation of an infant lying in a baby carriage. The highly unusual character of such a theme obviously stresses its significance for a deeper understanding of the subject. However, such indications can only serve as cues for exploration with other methods since they are not clearly communicable through the projective type of investigation. In any case, interpretation of this kind of content must be made with regard to the subject's status and occupation.

As significant as the "self-portrait" is the figure representing a person of the other sex, at least, when this figure is the only one in the complete set (which occurs fairly rarely): In such cases, the drawing points almost unmistakably to a particular concern about something expressed or symbolized by that figure. For instance, D/2, with its marked female characteristics, expresses the strong but healthy sexual interest which the subject overtly admits having. Another drawing, not reproduced here, made by a girl 20 years of age, representing an elderly male figure with an expression of concentrated thinking (very much like drawing 41), was a typical projection of this masculine, dominating, and over-serious-minded girl. Of course, depth interpretations of phenomena such as these and such as self-portraits will be more appropriate and more rewarding than the mere statistical approach.

A set of drawings often contains two, three or even more human figures. In such cases both sexes are generally represented. Several human figures all of the same sex as the subject appeared, in the present study, only in the products of a few immature young women. As for the adult male subjects, uniform portrayal of figures of the same sex was found only with two unmarried, morally very strict individuals. The incidence of human figures is, on the whole, less frequent in the drawings of males than in those of females, except when used as secondary elements of the picture as in drawings 91 and 134, in which form they appear quite frequently. The occurrence of a figure of the other sex together with one or more of the same sex as the subject's does not seem as significant as when it is the only human figure within the set. But absence of figures of the other sex in a set of drawings containing several figures of the subject's own sex, and vice versa, is most unusual and calls for closer investigation.

Certain details in the representation of the human or animal figure are as important as the over-all physiognomic expression. Among these, the shape and size of mouth and nose prove to be most revealing. Fullness or accentuation of these features, which are specifically sensual as opposed to the eyes and ears which have a more cognitive-intellectual character, are indicators of the sensuousness of the subject's experience and tendencies. This conclusion receives additional support from the insistence and pleasure which the subjects display at drawing or shading them, especially at emphasizing the curves of the lips (D/2, R/2, dd. 34, 40, 42, 43). Compare the accentuated nose and mouth features in the preceding examples with the same features appearing in the drawings of the more intellectualized or sublimated individuals—judging from their total products—who made drawings F/8, K/3–4, S/2, V/2.

More direct and specific indicators of sexual concern are the primary sexual characteristics featured in dressed or nude figures. Nonrepresentational esthetic creations such as the drawings of set O also appear to be inspired by erotic impulses. Whereas the sexual element expressed in dressed or nude figures appears to be on the whole normal and healthy—though in the nudes fairly marked or uninhibited—it seems to be much less favorable when manifested through abstract drawings. When drawings of that kind show a type of execution characterized by exclusive use of the curved line and excessive use of shading, as in set O, the conclusions are particularly unfavorable, emotional disturbance being almost certain.

The use made of stimulus 1 in drawings 53 and 123 also suggests a sensual streak. Whereas four other subjects used this stimulus as a navel in the human figure, drawing 123 was the only one to present this use in the animal figure. Remarkable with respect to these two drawings is the fact that they were made by intellectually prominent and highly controlled male subjects with idealistic aspirations. The contrast between the personality of the subjects and the particular flavor of their drawings is so marked that such solutions tend to suggest repression. On the other hand, the same use of 1 as in drawing 53 was made by a young art student whose attitude regarding sexual matters was not well known but for whom sexual repression was less likely. Although the basic concern underlying the production of this kind of subject matter is of a sexual order, its specific meaning, like that of most indexes, is ambivalent and may indicate compliance with, as well as denial of, the underlying tendencies.

Absence of sexual characteristics where their appearance is relevant points definitely in the direction of either deficient or repressed sexual concern. A similar interpretation holds for the vast majority of cases of "cutting-off." When subjects who show a tendency to negate their instinctive nature or to subordinate their vital urges to intellectual or spiritual aspirations represent human figures—which they seldom do—they often draw heads without any indication of the rest of the body (d. 38), or at least without anything more than a faint neckline (d. 64.). However, no absolute rules are applicable; the indication from the cut-off element may be contradicted or dominated by other physiognomic elements or by formal criteria such as pressure or form level. Thus drawing 40, although cut-off, is not representative for control and repression but, in view of the character of its features and execution, is expressive of crude sensuousness. Maladjusted subjects also have a tendency to cut off or leave out certain parts of the body. Drawing 63 representing a male figure cut off at the waist was produced by an over-controlled, sexually repressed and insecure young woman.

A less direct and outspoken but not necessarily less significant sign of sexual concern is the accentuation of secondary sexual characteristics. Such indirect signs are, in the male figure, mustaches, beards and sometimes also ties and pipes which are specifically masculine apparel; in the female figure, emphasis on hair but especially on eyelashes, eyebrows and beauty spots. Secondary male characteristics often receive great care and emphasis in drawings of subjects who are rather lacking in self-assertiveness and virility. Emphasis on secondary female characteristics, in drawings of women, does not appear to have this compensatory function but seems to be directly representative of the subject's concern and awareness of her physical appearance or attractiveness.

Accentuation or distortion of the features leading to caricatures is generally worth further investigation. When the caricatured figure does not represent a common stereotype it may be the expression of a genuinely facetious and playful mind, but it may also be a manifestation of the subject's more or less conscious disturbance about some defective or unbecoming physical trait. Such was apparently the explanation of a drawing representing an ugly face, ridiculously swinging on top of a long swan's neck, made by a young man with a marked tendency toward obesity. Other cases showed that caricatures may be inspired by an unconscious attitude of envy, contempt or irritation directed either toward a type of person or toward a definite individual.

The clothing element also may contribute to gaining insight into the subject's attitudes and preoccupations. The uniform, for instance, when occurring with male subjects, generally reveals ambition, an effective or ineffective forcefulness and a marked need for domination. Conversely, the uniform may be used to express hostility toward characteristics associated with the military costume. Which of these interpretations is to be adopted can generally be recognized from the way the military quality is featured. In the first case the pressure is often strong, the physiognomic expression grave and the execution careful (see C/2). In the other case, emphasis is on insignia, decorations or some caricatural features. When appearing in the drawings of female subjects, the uniform is likely to reveal a marked and immature concern about the other sex, especially if the drawing is detailed and executed with obvious pleasure. Other significant types of clothing are historical (S/5) or exotic garments (K/6). These occur mostly with imaginative and artistically inclined subjects with an urge for self-expansion and sometimes a tendency toward world adventure. Adorned women's dresses are produced almost solely by shallow, somehow primitive-minded, female subjects. Figures wearing hats occur sometimes in drawings of conventional, class-conscious individuals, unless they serve to express the subjects' mocking and rejecting attitude toward conventions. Buttons, pockets and buckles are indicative of a compulsive concern about trivia. These details of clothing may well be representative of deeper attitudes which could not, however, be adequately investigated in the present study.

The kind of activity performed by the human figure is generally very symptomatic of certain characteristic traits of the subject. Compare in this respect the emphasis on recreation displayed in G/7, T/4, 67, 69, 70, 91, the emphasis on work in drawings 45, 46, the social character of drawings 48, 122, 129, 134.

Animal content often functions as an expression of certain tendencies, desires or preoccupations. When animals appear in sets which are void of human content they are often an indicator of emotional reserve or repression, which may account for the subject's refraining to use a more direct form of expression by means of the human figure. More frequently, as already mentioned, absence of human elements with presence of animal items is indicative of a problem in regard to human relationships. Whatever the content of the complete set, the animals must be examined with respect to their kind, size, over-all expression or characteristic details. Small or young animals of the familiar domestic kind, such as cats, lambs, rabbits, puppies, chickens, birds, pigeons are depicted by subjects having the same kindhearted, ingenuous, simple kind of personality as those who feature children. This is particularly true when the indications emerging from such content are confirmed by a type of execution which make the animals look all round, sweet and unaggressive, like the animals appearing in set H. In this set, the predominance of small and familiar animals, the fluency and carefulness of the execution, the conventional and simple style of the entire product give evidence of the subject's good-natured, quiet, modest, gentle, unassuming and naive personality.

Large or wild animals, such as horses, cows, elephants, tigers, foxes, serpents which appear frequently as completions of organic stimuli are also likely to have specific diagnostic value. Their incidence is, however, not sufficiently high to point to definite psychological trends. The only general observation here made was that the bigger and more aggressive animals occur practically only with male subjects; birds of prey, or at least with large beaks, such as A/2, Q/4, d. 49 also appear almost solely with male subjects. However, this general trend presents exceptions: in drawing 50, sign 2 is worked into a beak and was, this time, produced by a woman, though a homely and unfeminine type. Serpents, snails and worms, which represent fairly common responses also, are produced predominantly by women. Cats occur with about equal frequency for women and men as a popular answer to stimuli 7 and 8, and sometimes to 1. The meaning of animal content obviously can not be strictly catalogued according to the species featured. All that can be said is that the respective frequency of incidence of children and of animals of certain kinds in the drawings of male and female subjects seems to provide a basis for estimating the masculinity or femininity of the subject.

More specific cues for interpretation can be gained from the expression conveyed by the activity, the posture and general execution of the animals. For example, the cat with the fairly sharp features in drawing 52, contemplating her little victim, and the cat in drawing H/8 suggest very different characters; the same is true for the bird in drawing A/2, flying with broadly spread wings over the ocean, and the bird in drawing 49, artificially seated on a perch as if it were stuffed. The perception and appreciation of the specific physiognomic value of Animate Nature, whether animal or human, is obviously subject to inter-individual variations among examiners. In most cases, however, a considerable degree of agreement is reached as far as the more obvious characteristics are concerned. Almost everyone will agree that drawing 53, the foaming bull, and drawing 54, the wolf with the wide open mouth, convey an impression of aggresiveness; further, that the leaping horse in drawing 55 expresses strength, willful tension or successful effort; that the little mouse in drawing 51 suggests conflicting feelings of temptation and apprehension; that the bird in drawing 50 has something awkward, heavy and plain, and that the indefinite kind of animal in drawing 56 has something creeping and lurking.

Certain authors maintain that the location of the figure within the drawing space and its position in relation to the onlooker is significant. In the setup of the present test the study of these aspects presents particular difficulties, the *location* of the figures being determined mainly by the position of the stimuli within the square. As for the *position* of figures, it is true that the stimuli may be completed into full-face as well as profile drawings. However, since many blanks feature more than one human figure it is difficult to make a general statement about the positional aspect, for the position given to the figure is likely to be tied up with the particular significance of the figure and hence to be very specific.

Schematism

By Schematism is meant a particular variety of Nature content, characterized by its rectilinear or geometric treatment. Oversketchy drawings or those featuring merely an outline also fall under this heading. For illustrations see drawings 57 through 64; L/2, the human figure in the cloud; M/5, the little dog; and d. 80, the stylized flower.

A special kind of schematic representation of the human figure is the "stickman" or "wire figure" (L/2; d. 57), which is often produced by subjects who have studied physical training, kinesthetics or fashion drawing, and who find it convenient and customary to draw in such a manner. Commercial artists also may show a professional inclination to the unusual, eye-catching technique of representing the human figure in a cubistic fashion (dd. 62, 60). Therefore, before drawing any conclusions, the examiner must investigate the possibility that some objective reason might account for this technique. In such cases Schematism loses, of course, all or part of its significance.

•   •   •

Schematism is a frankly unfavorable symptom, and even if it appears in only one drawing of a set it is suspect. Scoring for this criterion must always be high.

The failure to represent the characteristic roundness and organicity of living objects, which essentially constitutes Schematism, points almost with certainty to some vital-emotional disturbance. The authors of such drawings are generally people who have difficulty establishing smooth relationships, or whose attitude toward others is somehow lacking in genuineness, depth and warmth.

In addition to this general trend, common to the majority of the subjects who exhibit some form of Schematism, the specific meaning of this characteristic may be quite divergent. It may simply express a lack of directness and concreteness in the social approach of these individuals. Schematism may also signify a potential or actual incapacity to establish relationships on a mature level; or it may reveal an emotionally complicated, unconventional and even eccentric personality. It may also be indicative of contempt or hostility for people in general, or for the bodily self. All these meanings have been encountered in the schematic drawings collected here.

Inanimate Nature

This group of Nature pictures also covers a broad variety of phenomena. It extends from the isolated representation of a leaf, a cloud, water, a simple flower or a piece of fruit, through more elaborate drawings of branches, plants, bushes, to landscapes and seaviews. Here again not only the amount of vegetation or scenery counts in the scoring, but also the adequacy of execution and general presentation of the theme. Thus, a flower executed with a high degree of delicacy and fluency will score higher than a schematic tree or even a vaguely suggested landscape.

In relation to scoring Nature in its Animate and Inanimate forms, the question often arises as to how to deal with the greater or lesser amount of life items appearing in drawings featuring mainly Objects. Subjects often draw houses surrounded by trees, shrubs or grass; streets populated with tiny human figures, telephone poles with clouds in the background (A/3), interiors with flowers in vases or pots (E/6, d. 101), etc. In all these instances the life element is secondary, that is, it is not the proper object of the completion and can thus, as a rule, not score higher than the essential object. However, in certain instances, as in drawings T/3 and d. 122, Nature content over-balances the actual object into which the stimulus has been completed and must, therefore, be scored in conformity. Other examples of relatively high scoring of the life elements are drawings S/4 and T/6, where the addition of these elements is so unexpected and even irrelevant that it appears almost compulsive. The criteria for scoring such secondary elements are their amount, functional importance, and the approximate frequency with which they appear within certain, often featured themes. Thus, for instance, V-shaped birds constitute a common part of the conventional seascape and will therefore receive a low score. Since birds used as clothespins as in drawing T/6 are most unusual, their occurrence manifests an excessive need to animate and calls for a high score.

•   •   •

Inanimate Nature, as well as Animate Nature, expresses an emotionally conditioned attitude toward reality. However, each of these criteria points to a largely different kind of emotionality. As expressed by Animate Nature, the accent lies on the vital drive towards association, identification and dealing with people, whereas the emotionality manifested by Inanimate Nature is predominantly a form of sensibility, directed more to the universe at large than to living beings in particular. Animate Nature reveals a more direct and sensuous life-relatedness and an eagerness for pleasure and action. Inanimate Nature corresponds to a more diffuse, more delicate and more idealistic affectivity with sometimes a leaning towards contemplation or day-dreaming. The participation in life of the person who features predominantly landscapes and flowers is consequently less direct, less complete and vivid, and less conscious. He exhibits a more selective attitude, shows more definite preferences· and aversions and is, therefore, not as easy-going and generally not as popular as the individual who draws a great deal of Animate Nature. Inanimate Nature is also often encountered with sublimated, emotionally rich subjects.

A certain amount of Inanimate Nature is desirable in the drawings of practically every subject, the optimum amount varying with age and sex. While a primary requisite with younger people, it is not indispensable with older subjects, especially males. A touch of Inanimate Nature should always be present in the products of women of any age, since it is sign of sensibility and affectivity. Almost no amount of this content could be too large for these subjects, provided that abundance of Inanimate Nature is counter-balanced by a fair amount of Animate Nature and Objects. If the latter contents are strongly outweighed by Inanimate Nature the subject is likely to be oversensitive, sentimentally inclined and lacking common-sense which altogether make adjustment to everyday life precarious. For the male subject a slight amount of Inanimate Nature, as in B/8 and D/8, is minimal, but may be considered sufficient. Any significantly larger amount is not immediately favorable and must be interpreted in regard to the indexes of intellect and activity contained in the whole of the set. When, as in set A, the large amount of Inanimate Nature is balanced by a good deal of Objects, Movement and superior three-dimensional Organization, there is evidence of rich potentialities, definitely conditioned by emotion, but on the whole well integrated and efficiently expressed. In other cases, where Inanimate Nature does not receive as favorable a counterpart, it is likely to be an expression of emotional immaturity. The authors of such drawings are characterized either by sterile idealistic leanings or by an inappropriate affectivity, and on the whole by an inability to come to terms with life in its commonplace aspects. In the case of male subjects, it is a sign of inadequacy due to lowered aggressiveness and virility.

Inanimate Nature is always an indicator of a certain youthfulness of character; sometimes of immaturity. However, the maturity of the individual who likes to feature scenery, foliage and flowers is not the kind of maturity characterized by readiness to compromise or by considerable lowering of the sensibility. It corresponds rather to an ordering of the demands, a certain resistance to disturbing influences and an acceptance of things as they come, in spite of keen sensitivity to their emotional or moral value.

Atmosphere

This concept applies to a complex and subtle quality of the drawings fairly easily recognizable by the onlooker, and subject to agreement among examiners but particularly difficult to define in general terms.

The atmospheric quality of a picture results from a manner of presentation and execution which confers a certain over-all feeling quality or mood quality to the picture. This feeling quality may be of any kind, ranging over the full scale of emotions whether cheerful or sad, exuberant or dreamy, humorous or romantic, although the term as used here applies in particular to the finer emotions. Atmosphere pertains specifically to the modalities of Inanimate Nature but it is also found in certain human situations and scenes, in representations of objects and even sometimes in abstract drawings.

Perhaps the best way to illustrate what, in a drawing, makes for Atmosphere will be to refer to some examples. For Atmosphere as expressed in Inanimate Nature, see M/8, which achieves with a minimum means an effect of harmony and breadth, though perhaps of solitude; drawing 90, through its heavily shaded representation of a tiny village lost in the immensity of land and sky and caught within the span of a rainbow, suggests a vaguely sad or somber atmosphere; drawing 89, with its shining sun and tropical vegetation, expresses warmth and brightness. Drawing 95 appears snug and cheerful with its gently waving sea, fluttering flag, birds, and especially with the little fisherman leisurely smoking his pipe; compare this drawing with d. 96, representing the same theme but void of any life or movement and which, together with the slanted and sinking position of the boat, expresses a feeling of solitude and abandon. Another contrasting presentation of a theme is found in drawings 97 and 98, the former somber and tormented, the latter shining and cheerful. Compare further the seasonal atmosphere of the trees in drawings 85 to 88; also, the characteristic, qualitative differences of the flowers in drawings 73 through 80, lending real physiognomy and character to these inanimate things.

Examples of Atmosphere in pictures of Animate Nature, of Objects or in combinations of either of these with Inanimate Nature are found in the following drawings: K/7 and 8, youthful and fresh; C/7, with the shaded background and the glamour girl holding a champagne glass, expressing in an intense and refined way the erotic character of the picture; T/4 featuring humorously the "Bachelors sphere of Happiness" as the subject calls it; the unique character of drawing 122 ingenuously romantic, with its bird couple sheltered under an umbrella; d. 91 with the tiny figure fishing from a bridge; F/1 and d. 113 conveying the idea of a warm and friendly home. In the latter examples material objects gradually predominate over living ones. The latter are indeed not indispensable to create Atmosphere, as appears from drawings like F/4, suggestive of a pleasant gathering; F/3, G/3, M/7, and d. 102 all evoking study and art; d. 68 recalling the pleasures of mountain climbing; C/5 which, through its use of sharply contrasting light and shadow for the particular kind of theme, is intensily suggestive of crime and detective stories.

Some nonrepresentational drawings of the decorative type also denote a certain emotional quality which transcends the purely esthetic arrangement, as appears from set O. Atmosphere-pervaded drawings can even be found in the most intellectual and matter-of-fact category of content, Technical Abstraction, as proved by d. 15 with its unique combination of emotion and abstraction.

In view of the practically unlimited variety and nuances of the atmospheric element, this characteristic, like the other criteria of modality is scored only with respect to its intensity. Satisfactory evaluation of this intensity, which is essentially relative, again requires a certain acquaintance with the degree to which Atmosphere can be expressed in drawings produced within the conditions of the present test. However, no amount of training will result in really objective and strictly consistent evaluations of so subtle a matter as the one under discussion. In fact, such an evaluation is unachievable for any aspect of the drawings, but the personal equation is larger for certain characteristics, such as Atmosphere, than for others. The purpose of the six-step scale (or the three-step scale with split steps adopted here for practical reasons) is precisely to reduce these individual differences in the evaluation.

.   .   .

Atmosphere is a direct indicator of emotion. It serves essentially to differentiate the meaning of Inanimate Nature, and further, to reveal the emotional undertone implied in many other forms of content matter. As we saw earlier, Inanimate Nature may be indicative of divergent tendencies. It may be an expression of refined sensibility, of a certain immaturity, of emotional repression, of sublimation or of evasion in day-dreaming. Which of these meanings is the right one in the particular case must be decided mainly on the basis of the atmospheric quality of the drawings.

When the atmospheric quality of a picture is outspoken and unambiguous, it is one of the most reliable indexes which drawings are able to provide. Whereas absence of Atmosphere does not necessarily point to a lack of emotion, its presence never misleads. It shows whether a person is either cheerful, exuberant, affectionate, serene, depressive, dreamy, facetious, modest, naive, contemplative, whether his feelings tend to be diluted by over-intellectuality or whether they lean toward hackneyed sentimentality; whether he is longing for peace and solitude, for broader horizons, or whether he is contented with the familiar forms of experience, the security of the home and the pleasures of everyday life.

A few cues for disclosing more specific aspects of a person's emotionality are the following. Flowers, for instance, are generally produced by the gentle and sensitive, often modest and somewhat conventional, sometimes slightly naive type of person. Landscapes or seaviews with deep perspective are sometimes interpreted as manifestations of repressed or unconscious erotic longing or of an aspiration toward something indefinite characteristically encountered with adolescents. This interpretation could not be directly verified but the frequency of occurrence of such pictures among young people tends to confirm its validity. Vague or chaotic cloud structures of the kind illustrated by drawing 97 are always unfavorable. Subjects who give such responses are generally impractical, emotionally confused and intellectually inarticulate. Vague, far-away or sketchy landscapes or scenes such as drawings 90 and 93 are unfavorable also, judging from their regular occurrence with depressive or poorly adjusted subjects.

A favorable element in atmospheric drawings of landscapes is the presence of an original touch of animate or man-made reality. Such minor elements often provide the key to an understanding of the specific mood-quality of both the picture and its author. Note in this respect the effect of the pipe in the mouth of the tiny figure sitting in the boat of drawing 95 and compare it with drawing 96, also a seascape with a boat. Both pictures give evidence of emotionality, but in the first example the emotionality appears attenuated by the presence, in the picture, of an element bespeaking a realistic and humorous streak in the personality of its author. The same interpretation is illustrated by drawings 91 and 117, both representing a bridge with a certain emotional-esthetic value. Whereas d. 91 acquires a familiar and congenial touch through addition of the little human and animal figures, d. 117 appears more formal and cold, more expressive of artistic sensibility, cultural refinement and sense of harmony than of a simple, quiet and friendly make-up.

When appearing in settings such as interiors (E/6), cottages (A/5), curtain-trimmed windows (101) Atmosphere reveals a caring, mild and slightly conventional kind of emotionality. In drawings such as the latter, Atmosphere may be hard to distinguish from Style; the same is true for the blend of Atmosphere and Physiognomy in drawings such as C/7. In such cases the respective value of each element must be determined by examination of the complete set of drawings.

Objects

Utility

This category includes all man-made reality, except Ornaments, ranging from the smallest and simplest items, nails, cups, boxes, tools, to the largest and most complex, engines, bridges, buildings, etc.

Quantitative evaluation of this variety of content is based not only upon its amount, but also upon the size of the objects and their level of utility. The objects here encountered may indeed range from the merely utilitarian, plain and commonplace things (I/5, dd. 107, 108) to the more cultural, scientific and refined ones (B/5, F/3) and 4, G/3, M/7, dd. 102, 103). The plainness of commonplace items can even be accentuated when only parts of larger objects are represented, as in some drawings of set I, whose meager and crude character cannot be surpassed.

The matter-of-fact quality of an object may be modified by the effect of other factors. Stylistic elements may enhance an otherwise utilitarian object (compare dd. 115 and 116). The context into which an object is placed may also attenuate its matter-of-factness; compare A/5 and B/6, and see also d. 72 and especially d. 68, where the addition of a few more objects creates something which transcends the level of mere utility.

Depicting Objects, especially Utility objects, is indicative of concern about concrete and practical matters and, all other things being equal, is a sign of an uncomplicated, commonsense, sometimes a little earthy make-up. The degree to which this interpretation applies to a given individual is dependent mainly upon the amount of objects featured, their kind and size, and the way they are depicted.

A certain amount of Object content in the complete set is necessary to allow for the conclusion that a person is well adjusted and has a healthy sense of reality. Complete lack of Utility, as well as complete lack of Animate Nature, is always unfavorable for it suggests a defective integration of practical intellect or of emotion within the total structure of the personality. On the other hand, strongly predominant, almost exclusive production of Objects is equally unfavorable, since it reveals a unilateral interest in the world of material things and a narrowness of experience, especially emotional experience. These are the general trends, but the specific meaning of lack or abundance of Objects is dependent upon factors such as age, sex and occupation of the subject. Absence of Utility is more serious in the drawings of males than in those of females, more so in drawings of older adults than in those of younger and more so in the products of manual workers than in those of intellectuals or artists, and vice versa.

In regard to the kind of objects featured, two aspects must be considered; their level of utility and their size (reality size, that is, the size of the object itself and not that of the drawing). Merely utilitarian objects such as tools, household utensils and similar equipment when abundantly represented, that is, in about four to six drawings (set I), reflect a dull and unimaginative personality which may be either mediocre and grossly insensitive, or very modest and somewhat prosaic, depending upon other indications emerging from the whole of the drawings. The kind of objects depicted often reflects the subject's occupation, and reveals his interest in and adjustment to his professional life. Remarkable is the frequency of household articles, furniture, cottages and interiors in the drawings of the well-adjusted housewife, or the home-maker type of girl. Women who find no pleasure in household duties or whose interests are otherwise oriented very seldom produce this kind of object. The Utility items appearing in the drawings of manual workers are almost exclusively tools or simple technical devices; intellectuals draw pencils, books, desk lamps, scientific instruments or objects involving a good deal of organization, whether this organized character is brought out in the picture or not.

The size of the objects also contributes to the interpretation of Utility; subjects with meager intellectual or general resources and but little need for cultural expansion feature mainly objects of everyday use and of a size that can be handled easily. Evidently, one or even two such objects in an otherwise satisfactory set of drawings would not have the same significance. In these cases, such an ordinary item represents a touch of plain realism which is not undesirable in the mature personality and which may even be an asset for certain types of occupation. Large objects such as buildings, bridges, streets, gates and the like, especially when they are represented in the third dimension, indicate a resourceful and productive personality. Engines, machines, and weapons occur mostly with active and technically oriented individuals. Cars and small houses are very common responses which do not seem to bear any specific significance beyond that which is proper to Objects and to Populars in general.

Finally, the way in which the objects are depicted is of great interest. The same item may be featured in a largely varied fashion, giving the object a completely different physiognomy (d. 117 and d. 118). When utilitarian objects are drawn without any stylistic or ornamental concern this may be considered a sign of either simplicity, objectivity and a sense of essentials, or it may evidence a lack of sensitivity and emotional warmth. The first interpretation is more likely to be applicable when such treatment occurs with male subjects, the latter with female subjects; both meanings may, of course, be combined in the same case. The significance of depicting objects in a simple way or in an ornate manner depends also upon the kind of object drawn. Some objects are suited for one way and not for another; some are fit for either one. When commonplace objects are being given undue embellishing elements or context, this may indicate fussiness, artificiality, or childish emotionality. On the other hand, the elementary simplicity of d. 115 and d. 105 may reveal an excessively matter-of-fact, almost 'cold attitude. However, here again the sex of the subject has to be taken into account. When produced by an adult male, the above examples may be considered very satisfactory and indicative of an objective and practical mind with a clear sense for essentials; but when produced by females the bare simplicity of these drawings will reveal an over-practical mind, a rigid attitude and a deficient emotionality.

Style

This criterion refers to stylistic features of any kind, appearing in drawings of buildings, furniture and decorative objects. Style is to Objects what Physiognomy is to Animate Nature; it confers "character" to the objects, shows whether they have a cultural accent (E/2, F/6) or an industrial character (C/3, G/4); whether they are rural (M/6) or urban (d. 114); unassuming or impressive, fancy or conservative; friendly and warm (F/1, d. 113) or angular and cold but practical (B/6). Very often a subject who feels reluctant to picture human figures, allegedly because of his lack of drawing ability, will give to his objects the same characteristics which another subject will imprint upon faces. Therefore it can be said that, to a large extent, Style, Physiognomy and Atmosphere are expressions of the same tendencies but associated with different basic attitudes, such as those expressed by Animate Nature, Inanimate Nature, and Utility. As a result of these various combinations, the underlying tendencies are modified in their intensity and general nature.

Style, Atmosphere and Physiognomy may also blend in an almost inseparable way, as in drawing A/4 where the style indicated by the shape of the windows fits particularly well with the atmospheric effect produced by the skillfully variegated shading and the over-all peacefulness of the picture. In this picture, Style and Atmosphere are so interwoven that it is difficult to determine the respective value of each factor. Generally, this scoring difficulty can be resolved by examining the predominance of either factor in the entire set of drawings. The set under discussion, although presenting more elements of Style shows clearly a predominance of Atmosphere. In set E, on the other hand, Style prevails over Atmosphere. The same scoring rules which were laid down for the other criteria of modality are to be applied in scoring for Style. Thus only the quantitative aspect, that is, the greater or lesser intensity or amount of Style, is to be taken into account. This intensity may range from a faint tendency as shown in M/5 to the marked Style of drawing 114 and finally to its emphasized form as shown in drawing E/2. The more specific qualitative aspects of Style again must be retained for the process of differentiation and individualization which follows the outlining of the basic personality pattern.

●   ●   ●

Style, like Physiognomy and Atmosphere, is an indicator of emotionality. The specific nature of the emotionality revealed by Style is, however, significantly different from that expressed by the two other criteria. Whereas Physiognomy evidences a spontaneous and often sensuous form of emotionality, and Atmosphere expresses a kind of diffuse and somewhat sentimental orientation of the affect, Style is a sign of a favorably controlled, stable and often refined emotional make-up. Style appears thus as a mitigator of the basic intellectual trend implied in Utility. Because of the balancing effect which the emotional significance of Style produces on the matter-of-fact implications of Utility, Style must be considered a thoroughly favorable phenomenon.

Absence of Style points to either emotional deficiency, especially when Context is also lacking in the drawing, or to primitive and undifferentiated emotionality. However, soberness of treatment may be very positive and indicative of essential intellectual and practical qualities, when other indexes within the complete set of drawings compensate for the absence of Style and when the markedly matter of fact character of such drawings is justified by the sex, age, and occupation of the subject.

Undue emphasis on stylistic or decorative elements, on the other hand, occurs almost exclusively with emotionally immature subjects who exhibit a somewhat naive and self-satisfied attitude and often an unsubstantiated need for recognition.

The kind of Style featured yields, of course, more specific information than does the mere amount of Style. It reflects, in an often striking way, the orientation of the subject's ideals, desires and ambitions. An outstanding example of this may be found in A/4 and 5, the gothic cloister and the isolated mountain lodge manifesting the subject's known aspiration towards a life of peace and solitude. See further the inviting cottage F/1, which is a common response obtained from the home-maker or family-life type of woman; the old-style gate in drawing 119 and the exotic pergola in drawing F/6, both representative of the refined, esthetically oriented feelings of their authors.

Style within Objects, because of the intimate blend of the conscious functions of perception and organization with the more unconscious tendencies toward harmony and beauty, makes a fair basis for drawing conclusions about the stability of the subject's rational and emotional integration.

Ornaments

Under this heading are grouped all concrete objects serving the purpose of personal adornment, jewels, bows, ruffles, or that of interior decoration, vases, pictures, bric-a-brac. Ornaments are not to be confused with decorative patterns such as are considered under Abstraction. The former have an applied character and a definite function, whereas the latter are nonobjective designs. Some ornaments, as a bow in the hair or a feather in a hat, are commonly a part of the object they adorn. Others occur very infrequently as do bow ties, chains, and earrings and are therefore to be given a higher score. A certain acquaintance with the frequency of occurrence of these objects is necessary for adequate scoring.

. . .

Ornaments are, like Style, indicators of emotionality within personalities characterized by an outspoken orientation towards concrete reality. The specific significance of Ornaments is, however, less favorable than that of Style. Whereas Style corresponds to a formal decorative element incorporated in an object with utility value, Ornaments are decorative both in aspect and in function. In terms of underlying psychological trends this difference points to a lesser degree of rational-emotional integration within the person who features Ornaments. However, decorative objects have a reality value which is absent from the mere decorative patterns and are therefore fundamentally sound as long as the amount of such content matter within the set is limited.

The type of subject who produces Ornaments, especially personal or costume ornaments is in general averagely endowed, and characterized by a concern about trivia, appearances and social conformism. In the material underlying the present study, no subject with outstanding intellectual or social qualities produced this kind of subject matter. An exception must however be made in regard to the not infrequent completion of stimulus 7 into a necklace, this use of the stimulus being a most adequate response to its specific qualities. In the majority of other cases, personal ornaments do not seem to have very positive implications.

The specific significance of Ornaments varies largely according to whether they serve to adorn persons or objects, interiors and buildings. In the first case they seem to be an expression of narcissistic tendencies. When used for interior decoration they express a need for homey and pleasant surroundings, especially when they appear within a broader context as in E/6 and d. 101. Less favorable are isolated decorative objects, particularly when they have baroque, pretentious forms and are poorly executed.

Here again, the subject's sex and age must be taken into consideration before drawing definite conclusions. In the products of younger subjects a slight amount of Ornaments denotes a natural concern about beautifying things and is especially appropriate with female subjects, for whom it reveals a healthy awareness of the feminine role. However, any larger amount of Ornaments must be regarded a sign of emotional shallowness combined with either vanity or naivete. When occurring in the drawings of males, especially adults, it points to emotional immaturity or intellectual mediocrity. Abundance of Ornaments in the drawings of these subjects is suspect, for it seems to be an expression of emotional disturbance.

Fantasy

Fancy

The Fantasy pictures will be discussed in decreasing order of their relation with visible reality, thus proceeding from fancy-colored reality, over fairly-tale matter and mythical figures, to free-fancy products. *Fancy-colored reality* refers to content matter which, although belonging to reality, is not taken from the subject's direct personal experience, either because it is situated in the past, Antiquity, Middle Ages, or nearer past; or in far-away places, such as the Far West, the Far East, the jungle (S/7), the desert (M/1). *Fairy-tale matter* includes characters of popular legends such as Santa Claus and Easter bunnies, or figures and scenes from known fairy tales, such as Alice in Wonderland, Red Riding Hood, gnome stories. Since such themes are directly inspired by cultural factors, their reality value largely predominates over the Fantasy element. *Mythical figures* may be of two kinds. The first are known mythological figures such as Neptune (P/5), Minerva, or divinities such as Isis, Buddha and the like. They represent a blend of fancy and reality wherein either element may predominate. The others are personal creations of the subject, generally personifications of natural or supernatural forces such as appear in S/3. In these pictures the reality elements become quite secondary. *Free-fancy pictures* generally lack the cultural basis underlying most of the abovementioned varieties of fantasy drawings. Only the material elements are taken from reality, their presentation and combination being largely independent of direct perception or cultural influence. There is often not much difference between the content of Free Fancy and Phantasm. Differentiation between these varieties of Fantasy drawings is made on the basis of their emotional tone. Where the emotional tone is positive, that is, lively, cheerful and pleasant (T/2, 6, 7 and 8), it is considered under Fancy; where it is negative, depressive, frightening, or weird, it comes under Phantasm.

Free-fancy drawings may become so independent of reality as to almost emerge into the nonrepresentational kind of drawings. In such cases, both the idea and the presentation of the matter is unrealistic. An example of this is found in d. 124, titled "Musical Fish" representing a music staff carrying the head of a fish with a music note as a tail. Such drawings represent borderline phenomena between Pictures and Abstraction, and are consequently to be scored for both these criteria.

•   •   •

The representational character of the Fancy drawings bespeaks basic contact with reality and allows for favorable presumptions. This favorable trend may, however, be considerably modified, depending upon the proportion between the reality and fantasy elements represented. The significance of Fancy drawings receives further support from the positive emotional tone which characterizes them. However, only a limited amount of this kind of content matter within the same set can be considered sound.

A touch of Fantasy, as appears in Fancy-colored reality, points to a vivacious and healthy imagination and to an interest that extends beyond the immediate surroundings. Subjects who draw this kind of picture are generally versatile in their interests and often have a streak of romanticism or adventurousness. Some of the drawings here encountered have a lively and colorful character: harlequins, mandarins, napoleonic soldiers, gondolas. Others have an outspoken intellectual-cultural accent such as sphinxes, hieroglyphics, "Golden Fleece Orders." Among the subjects examined here the latter variety of drawings occurred only with those who, although they were not without education, did not belong to the higher intellectual level. This coincidence of modest educational level on the one hand, and display of erudition on the other, suggests the possible action of a compensatory factor. The grandiose titles which these drawings were often given supports the inference concerning unfulfilled intellectual ambitions or conflict with regard to educational status.

Fairy-tale matter, when limited to one, or at most two drawings (all Fantasy drawings are infrequent, except for Fancy-colored reality) evidences a youthful turn of mind which may enhance a personality provided there is evidence of a satisfactory rational and realistic basis. If the latter is absent, or if Fairy-tale matter exceeds the indicated maximum, its appearance ceases to be favorable, for it points to a loose contact with commonplace reality and a degree of imaginative activity not usually encountered in the mature adult.

The frequency of Mythical figures in the material here examined was so low that no general trends of meaning could be inferred. Of the five subjects who produced Mythical matter, three had borrowed their themes from known mythologies; two featured personal creations. All five displayed artistic and philosophical leanings. One of them, the author of set S with the divinities appearing in his symbolically meaningful drawings 3 and 6 was an original

young male with superior endowment, emotionally and esthetically very sensitive. At the time this subject took the test he was intensely preoccupied with
problems of a moral and metaphysical nature which are likely to account to
some extent for the particular content of his drawings.

Free Fancy, when it features animals performing human roles, seems to be
an expression of tendencies for which the life conditions of the subject do not
provide an outlet. Drawing 123 for instance, was made by a male, 34 years of
age, leading a kind of life in which there was no room for fun and frolic; 122
came from a girl of 18 isolated from male contacts. In set T, the amount of
fantasy displayed is in itself not a favorable indication, for it points to an
immature, over-playful and unsufficiently matter-of-fact sort of person. The
far-fetched, almost bizarre character of drawings 6 and 8 of this set, suggests an
over-productive imagination and a somewhat peculiar emotional make-up.
Free Fancy of the kind appearing in d. 124 occurs rarely, and then only with
artistic and strongly emotional individuals. Such drawings have a subjective
and abstruse character which could not be properly investigated by the methods
here used but which, due to their subjectivity, do not seem to have positive
implications. As far as this study goes such drawings never occurred in the
products of well-integrated individuals.

Phantasm

These drawings are characterized by their extreme remoteness from visible
reality and by their negative emotional accent. They not only distort or ignore
the forms of reality, but also lack the cultural influence reflected by most of the
other Fantasy products. Typical themes encountered here are grotesque and
fabulous creatures (N/7, d. 128), monsters, dragons, devils, ghosts, fauns, scenes
of ruin, catastrophe and tragedy. The human or animal figures have an incon-
gruous, queer, weird and sometimes gruesome character which distinguishes
them from caricatures (d. 125, 127). Less spectacular, but even more removed
from reality are the semi-representational drawings featuring criss-cross structures with eyes, mouths, or faces scattered over the open spaces or with complex
outlines suggestive of human forms as in drawing Q/7. Certain schematic
figures such as drawing L/2 also have a note of Phantasm. Sets N and O bear
a peculiar accent which relates them to Phantasms and must be scored
accordingly.

•   •   •

Phantasms represent a definite exception to the generally favorable implications of the Picture drawings. The extreme looseness of their connection with
common reality, together with their threatening and uncanny appearance, makes
them readily suspect. Outspokenly fantastic drawings, or sets featuring an

almost compulsive repetition of lurking eyes or ugly grinning faces (Z/1, 2, 4 and 8) are always indicative of serious disturbance of the personality. Set Z was made by a schizophrenic boy of 18; drawings 27, 125 and 126, from the same set, came from an acutely repressed, anxious and compulsive individual. Phantasm-tinged products like set Q and set N came from subjects with severe problems of adjustment, involving anxiety, hostility and depression. Certain life-estranged individuals with a visionary streak also show Phantasm-elements in their drawings. Sometimes these drawings are directly projective such as L/2, where the "stick-man" flying to his cloud castle depicts the subject's social inadequacy and her desire to withdraw from the world. Sets N and Q, which were produced by professional artists, are obviously influenced by modern art trends. However, this fact does not attenuate the significance of such drawings to any considerable extent. The preference for this mode of expression is as symptomatic as the particular mode itself. The influence of art training may manifest itself in many ways, not necessarily through nonrepresentational themes. Of the 19 other artists who formed the control group of skilled drawers, none exhibited this kind of drawings; neither did any of them show the severe problems of the two subjects in question.

Symbolism

As used here the term Symbolism refers to representations of values, ideas and ideals, not to the intellectual or mathematical signs considered under Abstraction.

The symbolic drawing must be examined from two angles (1) the kind of values or ideas represented and (2) the media used for representing them, that is, signs, line structures, or objects. The first of these approaches provides cues to the subject's moral and philosophical orientation, his preoccupations and aspirations; the latter informs about his intellectual make-up, and especially his contact with concrete reality.

The signs most commonly encountered in the symbolic kind of subject matter are: crosses (U/3 and 6); "Victory V's" (U/2 and 4); national or political emblems (V/3 and 8); the latter may also be represented as Objects (d. 134). Object-bound symbols of the conventional kind are badges, arms, flags, rosaries, prayer books, keys, scales (d. 136) hearts (V/5) altars, scaffolds, cemeteries, Madonnas (K/3). Examples of personal creations among the object-bound symbols are d. 129 "Harmony of all Peoples" (made by a young woman with strong concern about racial problems); d. 130 "Conception of the Structure of the World"; d. 131 "Civilization 1940-1945"; d. 133 "Mankind Carrying its Cross"; d. 135 "The Drive of Man toward Power."

A symbolic connotation or even a basically symbolic meaning can some-times be contained in drawings which are not consciously intended as symbolic, such as drawing E/1 "Straight to the Goal" expressing the subject's alertness to central goals and her willful determination toward reaching them. Such im-plicit Symbolism may be much more revealing of the personality than explicit Symbolism expressed through conventional signs and objects like national and religious emblems. The latter are often superficial associations with objects and ideas of the subject's surroundings rather than manifestations of his deeper attitudes and aspirations.

. . .

Symbolic drawings are generally directly revealing of basic elements of the personality such as its values, goals and issues of deep concern.

The conventional kind of symbolic signs and objects are least significant although they always indicate some relation to or concern with the ideas or values represented. Religious symbols, for instance, even simple crosses, rarely appear with nonreligious individuals, nor are emblems of transcendent values featured by individuals concerned solely with material values, save for rare exceptions. Symbolic themes of personal creation such as dd. 130, 131, 132 and 135 obviously are expressive of the subject's moral make-up and his vision of human problems. Such drawings reveal the capacity to transcend the immediate conditions of time and place, and to grasp meanings rather than recording mere facts and events. Although the appearance of one, or at the most two such draw-ings in a set may be indicative of outstanding potentialities, any larger amount is likely to point to defective adjustment to the ordinary demands of life and society. Abundance of symbolic content occurs only with subjects who show an exces-sively metaphysical orientation, or with pseudo-thinkers who like to indulge in obscure and sterile speculations.

Symbolism expressed through objects, animate, inanimate or simply ma-terial, is sounder than Symbolism expressed through line structures and signs. The former suggest a satisfactory integration of speculative and practical in-tellect; the latter are abstract in both theme and mode of expression which allows the suspicion that the subject's intellectual balance and general integra-tion are precarious.

C. Execution

Form Level

The examination of the formal aspects of the drawings begins with a complex characteristic encompassing a number of elements which will be treated later under separate headings. Logically this complex characteristic should be considered after the reader has become acquainted with its constitutive aspects, but since discussion of the latter involves frequent reference to this broader concept, it is introduced first.

Form level is a concept hard to define because of its fluid character which makes it something different in every single case. It corresponds essentially to the effect of a combination of characteristics which determine the quality of a drawing. High Form level is not to be confused with trained skill or craftsmanship. It is more like a genuine mastery of the pencil, not independent of acquired psychomotor control of the hand, but largely independent of actual labor. High Form level can be achieved through a variety of means; however, a few characteristics seem always to be present. One of them is the *quality of the line.* Another one is the *harmony between content and execution,* that is, the appropriateness of a certain type of execution to a given content. Still another constant element of high Form level is the over-all *"character"* of the

TABLE 4 — *Classification of the Formal Characteristics.*

Form Level

Line	Pressure	Strong — Soft — Reinforced
	Type	Straight — Curved
	Stroke	Continuous — Discontinuous
Covering		Scant — Full
		Expanded — Constricted
Shading		Dark — Light
Composition		Wholes — Parts
		Context — Isolation
		Detail — Organization
		Closure — Orientation
		Repetition — Variety
		Carefulness — Casualness
		Movement
		Originality — Popularity
		Clearness — Vagueness
		Consistency — Inconsistency

The underlined characteristics do not receive quantitative evaluation.

drawing. The latter quality may result from a casual treatment as well as from a highly careful one, from simplicity of composition as well as from sophistication, or from anything that lends a note of distinction or originality to the execution of a drawing.

As used here, the concept of Form level does not correspond to the same concept used in the Rorschach technique, where it signifies mainly sharpness and accuracy of form. In the present test, sharpness and accuracy of representation are not sufficient to qualify for high Form level. Drawings 43 and 45, though clear and accurately featured, are nevertheless to be considered of a poor Form level, whereas drawings 90, 124 and 129, though lacking in sharpness of outline and differentiation of composition, must be assigned a high Form level because of the personal touch of their treatment, their elegant casualness and firmness of stroke.

Since Form level is determined to a significant extent by the neuromuscular control of the hand, it follows that occupation and the specific training of the subject must be taken into account in evaluating this variable. Furthermore, since Form level includes a subtle esthetic element, it is also dependent, to an extent, upon educational factors. However, the absence of these factors manifests stronger and more consistent effects than their presence; drawings of subjects who are not accustomed to handling a pencil, who have no artistic training and no cultural refinement, generally present a low Form level, whereas drawings of subjects who have any or all of these characteristics do not necessarily achieve high Form level. Cases showing a reversal of this relation have, obviously, increased significance. The value of Form level must also be checked against drawing time and amount of erasing. The higher these two aspects of the performance, the lower the significance of Form level.

No quantitative evaluation is made of this aspect of the drawings. As will appear from the following discussion, Form level serves more as a point from which to view a number of other criteria, than as a direct basis for interpretation.

•   •   •

When understood as defined above, and not as resulting mainly from painstaking efforts, the Form level of a drawing offers a basic contribution for evaluating the personality in terms of general endowment, especially social and emotional endowment. Subjects whose drawings show a genuinely high Form level are generally characterized by a natural ease, versatility, a striving toward satisfaction rather than toward profit and success, and the ability to achieve their goals with a certain facility. High Form level is seldom encountered among tense, unbalanced or disturbed individuals. However, Form level does not, any more than other single variable, offer a sufficient basis for definite conclusions. It is one cue among the many and its diagnostic tendency has to be checked against the number and intensity of the variables with which it occurs.

The Line

As shown in table 4, the line presents a number of characteristics related to its *intensity, type* (straight or curved) and *quality*.

These characteristics prove to be very consistent because they are determined primarily by biophysiological factors, operating at an unconscious level and, therefore, not easily affected by fortuitous factors or by conscious control.

Intensity

The intensity, resulting from differences in pressure, varies between the extremes of very strong and very light. The gradations between these extremes are of course continuous, but for practical reasons a few levels of intensity are selected for reference and given a specific name. Whenever it is possible these points of reference are presented in sets of three so as to match the three-point scoring scale and thus to indicate the approximate score. As mentioned earlier the intensity of the line is influenced considerably by technical factors such as hardness or softness of pencil, and backing of the sheet. It is always necessary, therefore, to use medium hard pencils and firm desk pads.

Strong Varieties of Intensity

Strong lines are characterized by their darkness and deep imprint, visible especially on the back of the sheet. Gradations of this kind of intensity extend from the *moderately strong* through the *markedly strong* to the *excessively strong* somewhat greasy line. The latter degree of intensity can hardly be produced by the number 2 pencil without *Reinforcement*, that is, without strengthening the line by repeatedly going over it.

Strong lines are not necessarily sure and continuous lines; drawings U/6, Z/3, dd. 11 and 126, for instance, show strong but awkwardly groping and broken lines. Intensity and quality are thus independent of each other except for the extreme values, that is, the extremely strong and the extremely weak lines which seldom occur with quality.

·   ·   ·

Strong lines, like most expressive phenomena, may have different meanings depending upon the configuration of elements into which they appear. A constant fact, however, about strong lines is that they always reveal the presence of a strong vital drive or constitutional strength which the subject has available or which he discharges into action. This vital drive may or may not be accompanied by mental energy and capacity. When strong lines are accompanied by indexes of mental capacity such as highly appropriate use of the stimuli, high level of Organization and good quality of the Originals, this combination reveals almost unmistakably a rich, ambitious, often enthusiastic and generally productive personality. The activity of such a person is then determined by a spontaneous urge for effective action and self-expansion rather than by external conditions or necessities. Strong pressure not accompanied by these characteristics points either to a lack of mental resources or to overpowering of the intellectual and more delicate emotional mechanisms by primitive vitality.

Another constant fact about strong pressure is its value as an indicator of deep emotionality. Such emotionality is characterized by an intensity approaching heaviness; by a warmth that is more like passion than like congeniality; in brief by an emotional attitude which seems to emerge from biological urges rather than from properly affective tendencies. This emotionality may exert an enhancing role when it is well balanced in the total economy of drives and functions. However, when it attains a degree such as expressed by marked or excessive pressure it is likely to interfere with a person's inner balance or social functioning.

A somewhat less constant, but nevertheless frequent, cue contained in strong pressure is its significance with regard to certain aspects of the subject's relation to concrete reality. A person's interest may be focused on material reality because circumstances have denied him access to the intellectual or esthetic spheres. But he may also have a genuine preference for material values. The stronger the intensity of the line, the stronger, generally, the subject's interest in tangible objects. This is true especially when markedly strong pressure occurs with Utility content.

One of the major criteria for disclosing the specific and full meaning of intensity, is Form level. The following combinations of Intensity and Form level indicate certain psychological trends which are frequently encountered in those combinations.

Strong intensity + high Form level is generally indicative of efficiency because it requires an optimum balance between the driving and the controlling forces. The subject whose drawings exhibit these characteristics is likely to have both initiative and endurance. However, when the subject is known to have a particularly strong vitality, the combination of strong pressure with high form level may reveal over-control and compulsiveness, especially when straight lines are predominant or when the drawings are executed with great care (Sets B and M).

Strong intensity + medium Form level, especially when accompanied by a fair amount of curves constitutes a favorable combination, indicating dynamism, self-assurance, spontaneity and easiness in dealing with practical and social matters (Set D).

Strong intensity + poor Form level occurs with subjects whose driving and controlling forces are out of balance. Such subjects have difficulty concentrating or persevering in either thought or action. They may be efficient but only in matters where audaciousness, quick decision and a certain ruthlessness are required. Despite their lack of smoothness and considerateness, these individuals often associate easily with people, though always on a lower emotional basis, for they are not likely to appreciate the more refined aspects of human relationships.

The above indications are applicable in particular to moderately strong or slightly stronger lines. When the intensity is or tends to be excessive, the diagnostic trend shifts to less positive meanings.

Excessive intensity + high Form level is seldom encountered. When it occurs it points to a degree of control that may be effective but is achieved at the price of violent emotional tension. This combination appears only with extremely tenacious, high strung and often immoderately ambitious individuals.

Excessive intensity + poor Form level especially when accompanied by Full Coverage is an expression of impulsiveness, of a tendency to dominate and to destroy whatever obstacles interfere with action (Set R). It may also be a sign of gross and infantile emotionality. When this combination of intensity and form level is accompanied by exclusively material content, as in set I, it evidences, besides the above mentioned trends, a primitive and inert nature, crudely earth-bound, and incapable of intellectual or emotional expansion.

Summarizing the main trends emerging from the above discussion it appears that, all other things being equal, the moderately strong intensities of pressure are readily favorable. The higher the form level with which they occur, the higher the probability for a productive blend of dynamism and control; on the other hand, the lower the form level the lower the probability for effective control of the impulses and for smoothness of behavior. Excessive degrees of pressure are almost always unfavorable, revealing a degree of vitality which constantly threatens the subject's balance and adjustment. The subjects exhibiting this intensity of pressure are generally prone to violent outbursts and often manifest crushing self-assertion and ruthless aggressiveness; they are emotional extremists who passionately love or passionately hate. When they occasionally achieve a high degree of control as expressed by high form level it is at the expense of a disturbing amount of effort.

Soft Varieties of Intensity

The gradation of the soft lines ranges from the *moderately soft*, through the *delicate* line to the extremely *weak* and faint line. The first is agreeably clear and therefore appropriate to all types of subject matter. The delicate line has a subtle, somewhat dematerialized appearance which is particularly fit for enhancing the feeling-quality of atmospheric, or symbolic drawings but which is inadequate for representing tangible objects. The weak line is an indistinct, pale and inexpressive line that is hardly appropriate to any type of content.

·   ·   ·

The significance of the soft varieties of Intensity is somewhat more ambiguous than that of the strong ones. Whereas strong pressure is invariably indicative of strong vitality, soft pressure does not readily indicate the contrary. It may be an expression of lesser drive and potential energy, or it may be an effect of differentiated or controled energy. The majority of the subjects belonging to intellectual or nonmanual professions draw moderately soft lines whereas almost all of the laborers show strong intensities. While it is not likely that the amount of vital energy of intellectuals is necessarily lower than that of laborers, its use requires generally greater differentiation and often more control. Instead of remaining in its primitive form, as expressed by muscular activity, the vitality of the intellectuals becomes patterned by the mental mechanisms. There is an increase in complexity of the reactions and a simultaneous decrease in amplitude and force. In terms of drawing characteristics this phenomenon is manifested by a lower intensity of pressure and by either a higher form level or a quicker and more adequate integration of the stimuli.

On the biological level, soft pressure thus may or may not signify lower vitality and drive. On the psychological level it is indicative of either the intellectual or the emotional makeup of the subject. In the first case, soft pressure corresponds to a strongly pronounced orientation of a person's interest towards intellectual or spiritual matters, to an abstract and detached attitude, with the positive or negative effects which this may entail for the personality. In the second class it points to either a refined sensibility, to a lack of emotional warmth, to submissive tendencies or to depression. Which of these explanations is appropriate in the particular case must be inferred on the basis of other elements contained in the drawings.

When the usual relation between intensity of pressure and type of occupation is reversed, the abovementioned trends of meaning are considerably strengthened. In such cases, strong pressure reveals either an excessive degree of vitality, ambition and self-assertiveness, or a markedly deficient control, depending on form level and coverage of the drawings. Weak pressure, in this unusual combination would almost unmistakably reveal defective adjustment due to strong inhibitions or to feelings of inferiority.

Soft intensity + *high Form level* suggests a harmonious integration of the vital and mental mechanisms with a predominance of the latter. When the subject is known to have a strong vitality it may be assumed that his basic energy is used productively on the intellectual level and that his controlling forces operate in a positive way, in the sense of discipline, not of inhibition. When the subject is of medium or lower vitality he is generally a smooth, unassertive person with delicate sensibility.

Soft intensity + poor Form level appears with subjects who are unaggressive, unimaginative and emotionally rather dull or with those who, although they may be gifted and efficient, are unenthusiastic and somewhat apathetic.

Whereas moderately soft pressure has in general a positive value, delicate pressure is not unequivocally favorable. In whatever combination such light intensity of pressure appears, it is somewhat suspect. Its meaning is not necessarily improved through high form level, for whenever extreme values of intensity and form level appear together, that is, when either excessively strong or weak pressure is combined with either high or poor form level, disturbance is likely to be present. With strong intensity this disturbance will be either of an impulsive or a compulsive nature, depending on the accompanying low or high form level; with light intensity it will reveal either intellectual overdevelopment and alienation of the vital needs, or depression and feelings of inferiority.

Delicate intensity + high Form level is often encountered in subjects who are emotionally rich and intellectually productive but precariously adjusted to ordinary life conditions. Such individuals easily become over-refined and oversensitive.

Delicate intensity + low Form level occurs generally with withdrawn, overmodest, often insecure individuals who may be adjusted to small familiar groups and efficient in limited areas but who are emotionally and intellectually rather flat. This combination of characteristics may also appear with otherwise well endowed, but deeply depressed subjects.

The negative trends expressed by delicate pressure may be largely attenuated by the content, especially by Animate Nature, in which case the above combinations are likely to indicate a kind, considerate, modest and smooth emotional makeup.

Weak intensity is always unfavorable, whatever the context in which it appears. When it is not the effect of organic disturbance or of constitutional apathy, it is a sign of anxiety, inhibition, withdrawal or depression. Weak pressure is generally accompanied by poor form level. When it occurs with high form level it is an unmistakable sign of neurotic over-refinement.

The study of Intensity is particularly interesting when objective data such as biometric indexes and I. Q. or comparable aptitude records are available. Such data provide important information regarding basic components of the personality but they fail to inform about the actual functioning of these components in terms of drive, efficiency and consistency of the activity. In other words, such data do not reveal whether the vital and intellectual energies operate more or less independently or whether they blend smoothly and productively. A person's intelligence may work with the consistency that characterizes his vitality, or it may work independently of that vitality in a sporadic unreliable way; his vitality may tend to exhaust itself in either external activity or cerebrality or it may be distributed more or less evenly over both muscular and intellectual mechanisms. The correct study of Intensity as related to other characteristics, especially to Form level, provides a means of gaining insights into the degree of integration of these basic components of personality.

Reinforcement

The reinforced line is not to be confused with the line composed of a great many superposed short strokes, which is a very commonly used technique of tracing. Reinforcement refers to a duplication or multiplication of the same line over its entire length, (R/1, 7 and 8; d. 106). The repetition of the contour is not always as clearly visible as in these examples; the lines may blend into one consolidated gross line as in dd. 11 and 15.

Reinforcement may occur throughout the chart as a consistent characteristic of the subject's way of drawing, or only an occasional characteristic in the single drawing.

                                        •   •   •

When Reinforcement is only occasional it may be motivated by the greater difficulty of representing certain parts of the objects drawn, because they involve either curves or complexities of organization. When such objective explanations are not plausible, Reinforcement may reveal preoccupations with the reinforced object or that which it symbolizes. The present study not being oriented towards depth exploration, this interpretation could not be properly verified, but the aforementioned trend tended to be confirmed, at least when occurring with Animate Nature.

When appearing as a constant characteristic, Reinforcement is a negative sign. Such persistent and somehow obsessive repetition of the initial movement points to a lack of spontaneity and a need for constant revision of the behavior. This, in turn, suggests a basic insecurity or anxiety and a need to cover up for it. Whatever the explanation of this way of drawing in the particular case, it occurs mostly with subjects who manifest evident signs of maladjustment.

The meaning of Reinforcement varies further depending upon the intensity of the line. With weak lines, reinforcement appears always to be a sign of insecurity and when combined with over-careful execution, to be indicative of obsessive-compulsive tendencies. With strong pressure it reveals a tendency toward perserveration and to mental or emotional fixation. However, the interpretation of Reinforcement, as well as that of Intensity, requires consideration of the subject's occupation. Manual workers, for instance, tend to reinforce their lines strongly. Reinforced outlines give the drawings a kind of tangible quality which those subjects feel a need to objectify. With intellectual subjects, however, marked reinforcement seems highly symptomatic of disturbance, the severity of which is likely to be suggested by the amount of reinforcement.

Type of Line

Straight

This line may be perfectly straight, as if traced with a ruler, or awkward and poor. The quality of the straight line is not without importance; however, it receives due consideration under Carefulness. In scoring the line for Straightness, only its approximate amount within the drawing is to be taken into account. Straight lines may score particularly high when they take the place naturally required by curved lines, as in stylizations and schematizations, or when they are used for completing the organic stimuli, especially 3, 7 and 8.

. . .

The Type of line is one of the most valid indexes provided by graphic material, for like Intensity it is, to a large extent, determined by the physiological condition of the subject. Straightness or Curvedness is largely the effect of neuromuscular factors which determine the subject's state of relaxation or of tenseness.

The straight line predominates in the drawings of subjects characterized by sharpness of attention and perception, general alertness and rational-volitional functioning. A certain amount of straight lines is necessary for any set of drawings to be indicative of the subject's basic integration. Absence of straight lines—or rather excessive scarcity, complete absence not being likely to occur in view of the given stimuli — always points to some disturbance of will functions in the sense of a lack of determination, consistency, or capacity to deal successfully with difficulties. On the other hand, excessive predominance of the straight line often reveals rigidity, intransigeance and even hardness or, at least, a limited capacity for establishing smooth and pleasant relationships. These indications are especially reliable when the subject forces the organic stimuli into straight line structures.

Straight lines + high Form level are indicative of constructive, efficient control with, however, a predisposition towards inflexibility and compulsiveness. When the straight lines strongly predominate and a noticeable amount of Carefulness enters the product, compulsive predispositions are practically certain to be present. When Nature is scarcely represented in this combination, neurotic tendencies may be suspected.

Straight lines + poor Form level is generally encountered with insensitive, somewhat tough, individuals. When occurring with Weak pressure, this combination indicates an aloof and life-estranged attitude, lacking warmth and enthusiasm. With Strong pressure it suggests a hard, aggressive and domineering nature. When the drawings present sharp angles, criss-crossings and a chaotic aspect, as in set L, overt hostility and acute conflict are certain to exist.

Curved

The curved line, especially the supple, free-flowing line, results from a relaxed muscular tonus. When appearing in perfectly featured circles (B/2), spirals or arches on which the subject has spent painstaking effort, the curved line, obviously, is due more to muscular control than to relaxation.

A clue to the qualitative evaluation of curves may be found in the following examples. In Set N the curves are poor, inert, awkwardly bent, in Set D they show more flexibility, in Set Q they are graceful and fluent. As for the harmoniously curling lines of Set O they represent the curved line at its best.

The curved line, like the straight line, scores particularly high when inappropriate use is made of it, that is, when it is used for completing the mechanical stimuli.

Curved lines are one of the surest indicators of emotionality, of flexibility, of capacity for adjustment and identification. The organic roundness, the movement and suppleness of this type of line is, as it were, a direct expression of the subject's life-relatedness.

Curved lines + high Form level indicates emotional refinement and an adaptable, uncomplicated nature.

Curved lines + poor Form level, especially when accompanied by Strong Lines, appears in subjects with overwhelming vital-emotional makeup.

Broadly expanding, fluent lines suggest breadth and comprehensiveness of the feelings. Subjects producing such lines generally exhibit a tendency toward openness, liberality and benevolence.

Excessive use of the curved line, combined with nonrepresentational content, points to defective control, sensuous excitability and manic tendencies.

Absence or very scant use of curves is even more serious, for it is a sign of extreme rigidity, emotional as well as intellectual, and occurs generally with withdrawn, indifferent or hostile individuals. When young subjects are incapable of expressing themselves through fluent lines, emotional disturbance is likely to be present. When scant use of Curves occurs with subjects of a relatively more advanced age, or with manual workers, its significance is attenuated, a lowering of the need for vital-emotional expression being usual with these subjects.

The Stroke

Continuity and Discontinuity

A line may be drawn in long, continuous drafts, or in short strokes more or less overlapping or showing slight interruptions. *Continuity* of line is not to be understood as completeness of outline. An outline may be incomplete, yet executed in continuous strokes, and vice-versa. Certain lines are apparently continuous, although in fact they result from a carefully overlapping of short strokes. These apparently continuous lines are one form of *Discontinuity*. Another, obvious form, presents a splinter-like or hairy composition showing many and pronounced off-shoots. The worst form of Discontinuity is the interrupted, broken line. In evaluating the degree of Discontinuity, both the importance of the breaks and their approximate number must be examined. As for the apparently continuous line, it has to be considered more with regard to Carefulness than to Discontinuity.

Artistic training may influence the type of stroke in a sense of greater Continuity or of greater Discontinuity. A certain type of art teaching seems to promote the use of a bold, continuous stroke, while another favors the sketching technique. This training factor, which must be taken into account in evaluating the stroke, can generally be recognized from the ease and suppleness of the subject's movements while drawing and from the quality of the product. The type of occupation of the subject does not seem to have a significant bearing upon the Stroke, for continuous as well as discontinuous lines appear throughout the entire group here examined regardless of differences in the occupational status of the subjects. Continuous lines produced by laborers are, obviously, of a poorer quality than those coming from subjects accustomed to handling pencils. However, this difference is a matter of Form level, not of Stroke.

. . .

Like the Type of line, the Stroke is influenced to a large extent by neuro-muscular factors and may therefore be regarded as a highly reliable criterion.

Continuity of Stroke results from an uninterrupted innervation of the muscles, that is, from an uninhibited discharge of the motor impulse. The significance of this form of motor expression varies greatly, depending upon the combination of criteria in which Continuity occurs; it may go from smoothness and relaxation to reckless impulsivity. In spite of these extreme variations, the continuous stroke seems to present one fairly constant diagnostic trend, pointing to a certain degree of spontaneity, of self-assurance and straightforwardness.

By way of illustration the meaning of a few combinations of Continuity with other important variables are given below.

Continuity + high Form level, when not due to training, which it frequently is, indicates a high degree of psychomotor coordination, easy and effective command of the attention, optimum control, and freedom from restraint. When, in addition to good Form level, the Continuous lines are predominantly *Curved* and feature *Nature* content, a high degree of integration of the conscious and unconscious elements of personality is almost certain to be present. Subjects whose drawings show this combination of characteristics are generally pleasant, tension-free, fairly dynamic and efficient personalities.

Continuity + strong Intensity points to a direct, steady, decisive attitude.

Continuity + poor Form level occurs often with excessively bold, inconsiderate, irresponsible individuals. When this combination is found with *Strong Intensity,* a tendency toward excessive self-assurance, impulsiveness and need for domination may be assumed.

Discontinuity of line may be due either to a more or less conscious, continuous checking of the self and its activity, or to an involuntary, somewhat spasmodic discharge of the motor impulse.

The diagnostic implications of this aspect of the line are widely divergent, depending upon the kind of Discontinuity and, as always, upon the context of variables. The apparently continuous line is produced by the controlled, cautious, sometimes slightly over-circumspect individual, inclined towards lengthy deliberations and self-criticism. The splinter-like line generally appears with subjects characterized by a lack of smoothness in their movements, which may be stiff or jerky, and in their behavior, moods and attitudes. These subjects exhibit a control which is near to inhibition and indecisiveness. They may be spontaneous, but in that case they are generally irritable and restless.

Covering

By Covering is meant the amount of space occupied by the drawings. Some subjects scarcely amplify the stimuli, leaving the squares almost entirely blank; others cover all or almost all the available surface; the majority use an amount of space in between these extremes. The *scant* ways of Covering include the *small* and the *empty* drawings; the varieties of *full Covering* are called *moderate, ample,* and *compact.*

Covering must not be taken literally, for then it would apply only to shaded areas. It must be extended to all drawings suggesting the material consistency of the object represented by some structuring within its outline.   In drawings of the human figure, details of clothing such as a belt, pockets, buttons, suggest concreteness.   The same effect may be achieved in the naked figure by a few lines indicating muscles and anatomical features.   The consistency of man-made objects, likewise, is indicated by some detailing or by some form of elaboration within the outline.

Scant Varieties of Covering

Empty drawings show scarce or no inner structuring or detailing, as d. 59 featuring merely an outline, or make scant use of lines (sets X and Y), or represent objects void of context (dd. 107, 108, 115.)   Whereas empty drawings may be broadly spreading, *small* drawings are those which cover only a limited area of the square, leaving the remaining space practically untouched.   The small drawing thus represents a scanter degree of Covering than the empty one. Extreme examples of smallness appear in set J; milder examples are dd. 73, 74, and 133. Smallness does not necessarily imply Constriction. A drawing may cover but little surface, yet not be constricted, as illustrated by H/5 and H/6 representing embroidered corners of napkins which, although concise and economically executed are unconstrained and adequately proportioned.

.   .   .

Empty drawings are made by rather unemotional, moderately communicative and undemonstrative individuals.   Practically all subjects whose drawings show empty composition (not to be confused with Smallness or Constriction) tend to be orderly and lucid, but lacking in genuine warmth and spontaneity. Emptiness is more favorable with males than with females, and more so with middle-aged individuals than with younger ones.   When appearing with young subjects it tends to reveal an insufficient self-assertiveness and a premature restriction of imagination and ambition.   With adequate completion of the stimuli, Emptiness may reveal a sence of what is essential and relevant, and a strictly matter-of-fact and clear-minded attitude.   With poor completion of the stimuli it is likely to reflect a reduced contact with the environment and an impoverished emotionality.

Small drawings tend to have a negative symptom value. According to the rules of spatial symbolism, one might expect to find these drawings with the modest, unassuming, unassertive type of subject.   The facts, however, do not confirm this supposition, the aforementioned type producing mainly medium sized drawings and also larger ones.   Small drawings seem to be an expression, not of a genuine simplicity and moderation of the ambition but rather of an "imposed" state of restraint, with accompanying feelings of inadequacy or frustration. Depressed subjects also produce fairly small drawings. The possibility of a state of depression is reinforced when Smallness appears in combination with low intensity of pressure, although this combination may also reinforce the first mentioned interpretation and reflect something like a lack of self-confidence or feeling of inferiority. Combined with strong lines, it rather indicates inhibition. When the small drawings feature mainly Nature content the above conclusions are attenuated, pointing rather to an overly modest, somewhat fearful, yet congenial make-up. But when appearing with Abstraction or Objects, Smallness definitely suggests feelings of inadequacy and inhibition.

Full Varieties of Covering

A *moderate* degree of Covering is present when drawing and background are well balanced (set O, most drawings of sets B, some of E, F and I). Such balance is generally achieved when about a third or half of the surface is taken up by the drawing. Moderate Covering presupposes some inner structuring.

When roughly three-quarters or more is taken up by the drawing, the Covering is said to be *ample* (set A, C, K and N). A good deal of structuring is required for this degree of fullness. Drawings of large proportion, void of Shading or Detail are not to be considered as amply covered but as Expanded and Empty.

Where a drawing covers all or almost all of the available space, either because it extends up to the frame (set G, most drawings of S) or because the remaining space is shaded out, the Covering is called *Compact*. Compactness always implies a tight, crowded structure.

•   •   •

Moderate Covering, when supported by other diagnostically related variables, is an indication of adjustment, for it reveals a sense of measure and a healthy balance between dynamism and control. It occurs generally with individuals characterized by a productive assertiveness and a realistic limitation of the ambitions. Moderate Covering is therefore especially favorable with middle-aged subjects. With young subjects its meaning remains positive although it suggests a somewhat premature regulation of the expressive activity.

Ample Covering is a sign of vitality and often of a certain spontaneity. Combined with Strong Lines it may be regarded as a reliable indicator of actually operating driving force, of ardor and aggressiveness. When this combination also includes Animate Nature, it points in addition to a great capacity for enjoying life and productively participating in it. Full Covering is especially desirable with young people for whom, all other things being equal, it suggests emotional resourcefulness and a capacity to express it. Combined with satisfactory Form level, Movement and adequate completion of the stimuli, it indicates a need for achievement which makes for natural efficiency. With poor Form level and strong Lines it reveals a passionate emotionality and a precarious balance due to a predominance of the driving over the regulating forces.

The extreme form of dense Covering indicated as *Compactness* is much less favorable than the preceding form. Its basic diagnostic tendency is toward an excessive vitality and a need to excel and dominate which thwarts social adjustment and maturity. It may also be an expression of compulsiveness and overt aggressiveness. Most of the subjects whose drawings show this characteristic give evidence of emotional immaturity or conflict. However, much depends on the constellation of variables into which Compactness appears. When accompanied by representational content of a varied nature, moderate or soft pressure and high level of Organization, Compactness may be an expression of outstanding potentialities. With young subjects its significance is rather auspicious, but it is very unlikely to be so with older subjects; since excessive need for expression at this age level bears a neurotic connotation.

Expansion

This concept refers to an implicit tendency of certain drawings, especially landscapes (dd. 89 to 96), town views (E/3, G/4, N/4 and 6), interiors (E/6, d. 105) to extend beyond the limits of the squares. Although such drawings represent a unit within the frame, they continue virtually beyond it, aiming in a sense at infinite dimensions. This form of Expansion is indicated here by the name *natural Expansion,* as opposed to another form which, for the purpose of differentiation, can be called *technical Expansion.* The latter is present when only part of a well-defined object is depicted within the frame (D/6, W/5, d. 65, d. 135). Technical Expansion applies thus to a form of fragmentary representation which is, however, not to be confused with Parts (pp. 97–98). This type of Expansion occurs mostly within a context or constitutes the context to another, entirely represented object, as appears in some of the above mentioned examples.

Minor forms of Expansion are found in drawings showing simply a wide *spreading* or scatter of elements over the drawing surface (X/4 tends to be an example of this) or with drawings of relatively large dimensions lacking inner structuring (I/7). Broadly spreading decorative patterns should be scored moderately for Expansion, such spreading often being initiated by the corner position of the stimuli more than by a subjective need to draw in an expanding fashion.

Related, at least in its appearance, to Expansion, is the so-called "bursting
•of the frame." Certain subjects draw with bold broad strokes continuing into
the black margin of the frame and sometimes entering the next square. These
sallies are not always recognizable at first sight; in order to detect them the test
sheet must be slightly tilted until the shining effect of the line is visible on the
dark margin. "Bursting the frame," not seeming to be symptomatic for the
emotionality of the subject, but for his vitality, is scored for Movement, not for
Expansion.

                                        •   •   •

Expansion is one of the indexes for which it is difficult to assign a constant
and specific trend of meaning; indeed, the meaning of Expansion is more fluid,
more dependent upon the context of graphic variables than that of most
other criteria. Furthermore, the high frequency of occurrence of Expansion
makes its meaning very general and therefore less significant in the individual
case. The interpretive cues indicated below must therefore be handled with
due circumspection, keeping in mind that Expansion is largely subordinated to
the characteristics of the Line, Form level, Content and Composition.

All other things being equal, *natural Expansion* appears as a basically
favorable phenomenon. Drawings showing this characteristic are mostly found
among subjects who show a certain ease and relaxation, tending neither toward
forwardness nor toward nonchalance but rather achieving a happy medium.
These subjects also seem to be gifted with a refined, positively attuned sensitivity and a capacity for enthusiasm of a quiet and serene kind, not overflowing
into exuberance. When adequately supported by other indexes, natural
Expansion may reveal a disposition towards magnitude, openness, acceptance.
In brief, it seems to be an expression of an emotionality raised to a higher
level of experience where it acquires social-ethical or esthetic value. In spite
of the basically favorable meaning of natural Expansion, its occurrence throughout the set is not desirable, for it indicates an insufficiently concrete and practical attitude and a deficient ability to concentrate which, considered as a
whole, endangers the subject's efficiency and adjustment to everyday life.
A certain amount of natural Expansion is almost a requisite in drawings of
younger subjects for whom it expresses a need to transcend the various limitations of their status. One or two such drawings in the products of adults
stands for a touch of youthfulness which is likely to enhance the personality.
Beyond this amount, natural Expansion ceases to be favorable and justifies
suspicion concerning the emotional maturity and adjustment of the middle-aged
subject.

The diagnostic trend of *technical Expansion* appears to be significantly
different from that of natural Expansion, referring to the vital component of

the personality more than to the emotional. Technical Expansion must therefore be scored more sparingly since, in the quantitative part of the interpretation, Expansion in general is correlated with Emotion. Only in the qualitative and differentiating phase does the significance of technical Expansion come into its own. When interpreting the fragmentary represented objects which occur in technical Expansion, a distinction must be made between those items which are readily recognizable and those which cannot be identified without comments from the subject. Examples of the first kind are d. 65, the arm holding a bow; W/5, the foot pushing a pedal; d. 135, the arms reaching for a crown. The underlying tendency in these examples reveals a desire to make the picture more meaningful and understandable. When the nature and function of the fragmentary object is not obvious, there seems to be a lack of concern for the onlooker and for communicating with him. Mild examples of such fragmentary representation are: K/5, "Gilded tip of a flag stick, shining in the sun"; C/1 "Point of a pencil directed at dot on sheet of paper"; d. 132, with the arms raising from the lower right hand corner towards the center (this drawing represents a symbolic theme without precise title but with a page of comments). Similar to the former examples, though not so much in regard to Expansion as to deficient representational value is d. 61, "Schematization of the head of a Chinese" (this picture is to be viewed from its left hand corner; the parts of the stimulus represent the mouth and beard of the figure); another example is P/8, "Woman's figure" which, contrary to instructions, is represented upside down. One such drawing within a fully representational set does not seem to call for particular concern unless it is markedly bizarre. But subjects exhibiting several such drawings may have an insufficient desire to deal on an objectively understandable level and to conform socially. This inference is not based upon quantitatively strong data for such cases are rare. However, it encounters support from a few subjects who produced such esoteric compositions and who were characterized by markedly eccentric features.

The meaning of drawings showing a spread composition seems to lie along the line of natural Expansion. *Spreading* appears however to be diagnostically far less significant than actual Expansion. Certain cases of spreading draw the attention because of undue amplification of the object and suggest that drawings presenting such peculiarities are likely to carry a deeper meaning. An example of such amplification—implicit amplification in this case—is drawing 42, the appealing facial features void of any limiting contour letting the face, as it were, expand without limits. This drawing was made by a young girl, very short but with an attractive good-looking face, apparently very conscious of her appealing facial features and extremely concerned about asserting herself through them, possibly by way of compensation for her deficient height.

Another example of this kind is K/4 with the face covering the entire square and even expanding slightly beyond it. In view of the corner position of the stimulus, this example is not particularly illustrative of undue amplification, but it is worth mentioning in this connection. The father of the girl who made this drawing was known to have a beard and moustache and her family was strongly father-centered. The fact that the dark and angular stimulus 4 was as an eye and completed into a face bearing the characteristics of the father is a combination of symptoms which may well deserve further investigation.

Constriction

The constricted drawing is generally a small drawing, though not all small drawings are constricted. Constriction applies to unduly small drawings, in which the whole is not proportioned to the size of the stimulus, that is, when the size of the whole appears shrunken in comparison with the size of the stimulus. In drawing 64, the subject has perceived stimulus 2 as part of a face, but has failed to amplify the whole in accordance with the proportion shown by the part. (The cut-off character of this head, together with the thinness of the lines, accentuates still further the constricted effect of the drawing.) Another, milder, example of Constriction is found in X/2 where the stimulus, repeated several times to represent a flock of birds, grows smaller and smaller; the same characteristic appears in drawing 7 of the same set, where the dotted design placed in the upper left corner is composed of circles smaller than stimulus 7 which, obviously, suggested the idea of the dotted circle pattern. A form of Constriction is found also in Y/1 which is unduly small, not with respect to the size of the stimulus, but in regard to the amount of space available for expansion.

Constriction occurs sometimes in combination with Compactness, for instance, when a small drawing shows a tight, crowded inner structure. Even somewhat larger drawings, when exhibiting over-structured organization as d. 6. imply an element of Constriction.

.   .   .

Constriction has a negative value, indicative of disturbance. This kind of drawing occurs infrequently in the material here collected but its exclusive appearance with uncommunicative, rather tense, withdrawn individuals, gives strong support to the above interpretation. Combined with strong Pressure, Constriction is an almost unmistakable sign of repressed aggressiveness; with low Pressure it points toward anxiety or emotional impoverishment. The tightly structured constricted drawing appears as especially symptomatic for neurotic tendencies, the specific nature of which has to be inferred from other indexes.

Shading

Shading presents three diagnostically significant aspects: intensity, texture and function.

The difference in *intensity* of Shading could be indicated by the same words as used for the various gradations of intensity of the lines. However, for the sake of specificity the terms dark, heavy and black will be used for indicating the strong intensities of Shading; light, transparent and subtle for the soft varieties.

Dark shading appears in A/6 and C/5; *heavy* shading in G/3 and 5; I/1 and 6 are examples of extreme *black* shading produced by excessive, almost compulsive reinforcement of the shading. Set O presents a scale of gradations from the dark, in places almost heavy, to the subtle shades. Drawing 90 is executed in a medium, predominantly *light* shading; d. 99 shows an example of *transparent* shading. *Subtle* shading appears in faintly sketched, almost invisible indications of skies, sun rays, or distant, vague vista effects.

Texture refers to the manner in which Shading is executed. The texture may appear smooth and homogeneous like an even surface (set O), or it may show scrawls and criss-crossings (dd. 93 and 97), straight lines (C/1 and 5) or some mixed and indefinite kind of texture (G/1, 2 and 6).

Another aspect of Shading is its *function*, that is, its greater or lesser appropriateness within the picture. Shading is considered appropriate when it fulfills a representational role, that is, when it contributes to the structuring of the object drawn, bringing out shape and spatial relations in three-dimensional objects, stressing the consistency of certain parts, suggesting movement or fullness (in trees or bushes, for instance). Shading may occur without representational value in Abstract drawings, especially of the decorative kind where it serves the balance and esthetic value of the composition. Finally, Shading may appear in an apparently irrelevant, merely space-filling way.

Scoring for this variable considers only the amount and intensity of the Shading.

. . .

Shading evidences a predominantly emotional personality make-up, tending toward passionateness when it is dark, toward great sensitivity when it is light. Beyond these characteristics—and apparently because of them—it reveals a proneness to emotional conflicts or an actual state of disturbance. Indeed, of the subjects here examined, the majority of those showing a great deal of shading presented emotional difficulties of various kinds and degrees, while practically none of the typically matter-of-fact subjects produced any significant amount of Shading. However, scant Shading is not a sufficient reason to assume emotional balance.

Differences in intensity of the Shading seem to correspond to differences in the strength and especially in the nature of the emotions. The strong intensities reveal strong vital trends which color the emotions with warmth, eagerness and passionateness. When Shading appears with the moderate degree of intensity indicated here as *dark,* these qualities are represented to an extent likely to enhance the personality, endowing it with a capacity for enthusiasm and forceful activity. Stronger intensities do not permit as favorable assumptions, for increased intensity of Shading seems to go with increased emotional vehemence and vulnerability. *Heavy* shading occurs mostly with sensuously inclined subjects whose potentialities for emotional refinement are overpowered by vigorous vital impulses. The same appears to apply to *black* shading which, in several cases, was found to be an expression of hostility, aggressiveness, and neurotic tendencies of an active nature.

The soft degrees of Shading are an almost unmistakable sign of great sensitivity of a sentimental, romantic or idealistic kind. Individuals whose drawings show a great deal of this Shading are generally of a delicate and deep, but vulnerable, emotional makeup. Soft shading is therefore frequently an expression of anxiety, depression or evasion in daydreaming. Specific cues for every degree of softness are difficult to distinguish. The observations made in regard to these varieties pertain, indeed, more to the scale of shades than to the separate steps. In this respect, emotional sensitivity and intensity of shading appear to be inversely proportional; that is, subtle shading points to a greater sensitivity and delicacy of feelings than just light shading, but not to greater vulnerability. On the contrary, emotional discomfort or disturbance is encountered more often in subjects producing light than in those producing subtle shading. This may have to be explained by the fact that transparent and subtle shading, at least when smooth and equal, require a degree of psychomotor control hardly compatible with depression, anxiety, or conflict. Another possibility is that the affectivity manifested by such delicate phenomena is of a kind that is more self-detached, more serene and therefore less prone to conflict.

As to the *function* of Shading, a few appropriate touches of various intensities are a positive sign, suggesting rich emotional potentialities. Inappropriate, irrelevant or excessive use of shading of any intensity has a definitely negative significance. Abstract decorative use of shading can, of course, always be justified by subjective reasons, either on the part of the subject or of the examiner. However, such arbitrary shading, when occurring to a great extent, justifies a certain suspicion and may tentatively be interpreted in the sense of inappropriate use.

Texture offers a cue for clarifying the meaning of the intensity and the function of Shading. Smooth Shading of moderate intensity is an indicator of controlled emotionality; with decreasing intensity it confirms the aforementioned tendency to indulge in daydreaming and sentimental idealism (d. 99). When the texture is neither smooth nor scrawled and appears with medium or light intensity, as in X/2 and dd. 4 and 90, depression or some form of passive neurotic disturbance may be assumed. When the shading is made up of numerous straight and parallel lines, as in C/1 and 5, rigorous control of strong vital-emotional tendencies is almost sure to be present. In general, where the texture shows a rectilinear pattern, as in B/1, E/2, 5 and 6, and d. 105, a rather strict intellectual ruling of the emotions may be assumed. Scrawled texture expresses either overwhelming vitality, or tenseness and conflict. The significance of scrawled texture depends largely upon the scrawls showing a casual and loose structure, or a sharp and angular one. In the first instance, and provided that the intensity is moderate (G/2, Q/2, d. 92), it points to a rich but rather undisciplined emotionality, prone to become vehement. Grossly scrawled or crisscrossed, it indicates an explosive, tense, emotional makeup, or aggressive hostility.

A peculiarity noticed in the products of a few well known subjects is the inclusion of clouds or of smoke in a contour (d. 100). The frequency of this phenomenon is not high enough to justify definite conclusions, but such delineating of amorphous, nebulous elements seems to express strongly repressed tendencies.

Composition

Wholes and Parts

An elementary characteristic of representational drawings is the distinction between a *Whole,* such as a person, a house, a landscape, or a *Part,* an ear, a window, a wheel, etc. The latter, although in a sense wholes also, have no independent existence and are too simple to serve as themes by themselves. An exception to this classification is the "head theme," into which signs 2 and 8 are frequently completed. This object, though fragmentary, must be considered as a Whole because of its complexity and importance in regard to the entity to which it belongs, and because its incomplete character is determined by the technical conditions of the test. Indeed, the given signs suggest certain objects for completion, but while the proportions of these objects are determined by the size of the stimuli, the dimensions of the squares prevent them from being worked out entirely. A condition, however, for heads to be considered as Wholes, is that they show at least a neckline or a tendency toward further development into a bust. Heads lacking this expanding tendency, as in set Z and in dd. 38, 40 and 64 are to be considered as Parts.

.   .   .

The diagnostic value of each of the terms of the concept pair Wholes and Parts is very unequal, because of the unequal frequency with which these variables occur. Practically all drawings represent Wholes; the significance of this aspect of the composition is consequently so general that it can hardly be isolated from the many variables with which it generally appears. Parts, on the contrary, occur fairly rarely, at least in the material underlying this study, and therefore take on increased significance. Examination of context-devoid Parts suggests that such drawings express a defective state of integration of the basic vital-emotional and rational controlling forces. A reservation must, however, be made in regard to the above statement. In the material here examined, Part drawings occurred more often in the products of unskilled, manual laborers, than in any other group. This tends to suggest that educational factors may operate in the production of Parts, although it is not obvious why more education should be necessary for awkwardly drawing a head rather than an ear, for a simple house than for a window. On the other hand, it must be mentioned that none of the laborers who produced Parts appeared to be wholesome, contented individuals—which shifts the balance from the factor occupation-education back to the first mentioned factor: unsatisfactory integration. As for the other, nonmanual subjects who produced Parts, most of them gave evidence of a lesser integrated, somewhat angular or unilateral personality makeup.

The significance of Wholes is derived indirectly from their contrast with Parts rather than directly from comparison with the information concerning the subjects. Thus, it is assumed that Wholes tend to be an expression of satisfactory integration and balance. However, this inference needs the support of other indexes in order to acquire any weight.

Context and Isolation

These aspects of the drawings are closely related to the preceding, Wholes and Parts. Indeed isolated themes, even when they are Wholes, are in relation to objects in a context what parts are to wholes; they represent the same phenomenon, but with broader scope.

Context refers to everything surrounding the object constructed from the given stimuli; it is not to be confused with "elaboration," which refers to inner structure of the picture; for instance, A/5 presents a rather sketchy house in Context whereas B/6 shows a fairly detailed house without Context.

Context may be achieved in two ways; through *integration*, when the object is incorporated into its natural or usual setting, or through *multiplication* when the object is repeated once or several times, or when a few related though independent objects are added, as in X/4, where the stimulus is seen as a geometric form and is surrounded by more of these forms. However, drawings such as 68, with the cord, shoe and spike added to the pick, into which sign 5 is completed, must be considered as examples of Context through integration because a whole sphere of work or leisure is suggested through addition of such meaningful items.

Isolation stands for the absence of "accompaniment" to the theme into which the stimulus is worked. Not only Parts but Wholes are considered to be isolated when they lack the kind of elements which confer a touch of life or reality to the picture. The absence of such touches does not seem to be due to a lack of drawing ability, no particular skill being required for adding a few lines to represent smoke above an ash-tipped cigarette (d. 103), or a path, a hill, bushes or birds around a house. Rather, it seems as if it did not occur to the subject that he could animate or enrich his response in so easy a way; that he does not feel the need for any accompaniment.

．　　．　　．

Context and Isolation reinforce and differentiate the diagnostic trends suggested by Wholes and Parts. When Context is achieved by means of integration, it manifests the presence of synthetic tendencies, not so much of the mind but of the personality in feeling and behavior. It indicates a need to relate, to unify and incorporate things into the total experience where they acquire meaning and emotional value. Context supports, therefore, the assumption of a harmonious functioning of the basic components of personality suggested by the appearance of Wholes. It also points toward a keen interest in reality. This genuine contact with reality, being centered more in the emotional than in the rational sphere, does not always correspond to a sharp "sense" of reality or a capacity for mastering it. However, much depends, in this respect, on the kind of subject matter featured, atmospheric or commonplace.

Context realized through multiplication appears to be much less favorable than Context achieved through integration. Drawings representing unrelated or slightly related independent items are not frequently found among the drawings here examined. They generally appear in sets showing several suspicious indexes. See in this repect set X which, besides the Context through multiplication in drawing 4, shows Emptiness, weak intensity of the lines, incoherent Organization, fairly inappropriate Shading, Constriction and nonrepresentational content. It seems that the individuals exhibiting such an attempt at creating Context feel a diffuse need for relating or participating but are unable to achieve this in a satisfactory way, probably (and this is suggested by other indexes in their products) because of some emotional blocking.

Isolated objects, without anything around to enhance their appearance or meaning, look bare, cold, somewhat disrupted and even unreal, mere representations. These appearances often reflect remarkably well the attitude of the subject whose rapport with the external world is aloof or limited to a narrow range of things. Such a person has no eye for the variety and color of reality and but little receptivity for the warmth and excitement which life may offer. He approaches things and people from a mental point where they seem more general and impersonal; he lacks the kind of binding element which brings unity within and around himself. Such a person is himself isolated and reflects this in his context-disrupted drawings.

Isolated themes may also have a positive meaning, for their negative implications can be counter-balanced by characteristics of execution and especially of content. Isolation may stand for matter-of-factness, capacity to concentrate and to see things in a clear and simple way, whatever the subject's level of intelligence may be. Furthermore, it may point to an aversion for fussiness, for trivia and conventional sentimentality. With adult males such drawings are likely to be an expression of maturity and efficiency, but they are not auspicious with female subjects of any age. However, when occurring throughout the set, Isolation is undesirable, even with male subjects, for it suggests deficient congeniality and outgoingness.

Detail

This concept refers to the representation of organs or parts of objects, living or man-made; it does not apply to Abstract designs. Elaboration within the latter kind of drawing is considered a form of two-dimensional Organization.

Detail must be examined with respect to its *amount* and to its *function*. The function of Detail may be relevant or irrelevant. It may serve the purpose of differentiating the object, or it may encumber the picture with unessential matter, or impair it by far-fetched or bizarre elements.

Scoring for Detail regards only the qualifiable aspect, the amount. The function is, to an extent, indirectly reflected in the scores, low scores generally referring to essential detail, high scores implying abundancy of Detail. The function of Detail, however, receives due attention in the individualizing phase of the interpretation.

.   .   .

The diagnostic clues derived from Detail concern mainly the intellectual aspect of personality, although they also contribute to the understanding of the total structure.

The significance of Detail in the present test is not the same as in the Goodenough test (16), where the number of details constitute an index of the subject's intellectual development. The general design, aim and use of these tests are too different to allow for much similarity in the interpretation. The Drawing-Completion Test shows no direct relation between number of details and degree of intelligence. Indications concerning the level of intelligence can be derived only when both function and amount of Detail are considered in combination with Organization. Some of the tendencies emerging from combinations of these variables follow the discussion of Organization.

Drawings showing a good deal of correctly used Detail prove that the subject possesses clear and differentiated images of things outside of himself; this presupposes keen attention which, in turn, suggests a certain interest in concrete reality and a liking for dealing with it. Detail thus points to a predominantly practical orientation of perception, intelligence and activity. Further interpretation must proceed on the basis of the relation between amount and function of this variable. When Detail is limited to essential features it may be regarded as one indication that the subject is a clear-minded, common-sense person, who disregards minor matters and in whom logic and practicality combine favorably. Thus, Detail may indirectly reflect an intellectual makeup conducive to adjustment and efficiency. When the amount of Detail slightly exceeds the essential its significance is not altered. Even a certain superfluity of Detail is common and quite admissible with younger people and with women, for it reveals their presumed natural affinity for concrete matters. Abundance of Detail, however, is always a negative indication suggesting either a childish need for display, pseudo-achievement and excellency, or a compulsive tendency to be complete and to stress minor matters. At any rate, profuse Detailing of items as small as those commanded by the conditions of the present test is not compatible with the moderation and relative casualness which characterize maturity. Profusion of Detail in drawings of adults must therefore be regarded as suspicious.

Irrelevant Detail also is always suspect. However, one should not conclude too hastily that a detail is irrelevant. After the comments which the examiner must, in such cases, try to gain from the subject, what appeared irrelevant on first sight may become justified to some extent. But even then, such elements have a negative diagnostic connotation because of their subjective character. Irrelevant detail occurs very seldom in drawings of "normal" adults.

Absence of Detail is unfavorable also since this corresponds to a form of Schematism with the negative significance attached to such a manner of drawing. As to absence of certain essential details with profusion of unessential ones, the few examples of this kind here encountered came from intellectually mediocre, often emotionally excitable individuals.

Organization

When applied to representational content, Organization refers to the various ways and degrees to which the actual structure of the object is depicted. With Abstract drawings it refers to the logical planning involved in the arrangement of elements, lines and surfaces making up such drawings. Minor forms of surface elaboration, occurring in representational as well as in abstract drawings, must also be scored for Organization.

Organization appears on two levels of execution: a lower one, the two-dimensional level; and a higher one, the three-dimensional. To the first belong most Abstractions, especially those of the decorative type, and all concrete objects represented in surface. The three-dimensional level includes all representational items depicted in their depth dimension, and such Abstractions which involve perspective, as dd. 9 and 11. Three-dimensional Organization presents also two levels of technical difficulty. One uses varied intensities of Line and Shading to produce effects of depth or vista. The other, higher, level is achieved by linear treatment. Drawing A/4 presents an example of superior linear depth organization not often achieved within the reduced limits of the squares. Three-dimensional, particularly linear forms of Organization must be scored liberally, these forms being largely dependent upon skill and training. Not only the degree of success, but also the choice of three-dimensional objects and the attempt to represent them in their spatial relations should be taken into account while scoring.

The difference, in regard to Organization, between "structure" and "elaboration" is easily recognizable in three-dimensional drawings, but not so well in two-dimensional ones. Yet, proper differentiation of these aspects has some importance in regard to scoring, one aspect scoring higher than the other. An example may clarify this question. Drawings G/1, S/1, d. 6 and d. 7 all show complex patterns. However, the kind of structure found in S/1, with its stimulus centered composition, its organic unity, its strict symmetry, requires a degree of conscious planning not present to a comparable extent in G/1, which is merely elaborate and somewhat mechanically constructed; nor is this degree of conscious planning found in patterns dd. 6 and 7 which seem to have grown out of free fantasy and spontaneous movements (and were actually produced in this way, according to the subjects). The latter patterns, however intricate and original, have a doodle-like character; they are examples of "elaboration" rather than of "structure."

Other, rather subtle, distinctions between graphic variables are those existing between Context, Detail and Organization on the one hand and Carefulness and Organization on the other. A brief comparison of the specific object of each of these variables may therefore be appropriate. Context means that one or more items have been added to the object into which the stimulus is worked; it does not imply that either the main object or the additional items are detailed. Drawing 136 shows Context without Detail; d. 135 shows both. Detail which, as earlier mentioned, applies only to representational content, refers to functional elements of differentiation (parts and organs), not to surface elaboration. Whereas Detail refers solely to the presence of various parts of the object, Organization has to do with their adequate disposal, in conformity with certain logical, natural or practical standards. Organization pertains thus essentially to the structural aspects of the composition, to the correctness of proportions and location. These aspects border, however, on the specific object of Carefulness which, in regard to spatial relationships, is concerned with such matters as equal shaping of identical parts, regularly increasing or decreasing their size or spacing them equally according to the requirements of the particular theme. But while Organization deals with adequate distribution of the elements, Carefulness has to do solely with their formal perfection.

· · ·

Degree and level of Organization are significant in regard to the logical, analytical and synthesizing capacities of the subject, his ability to deal with principles, to understand and visualize complex relationships. This is especially true for drawings showing linear three-dimensional organization. Absence of such forms of organization does not, however, justify reversal of the above conclusion, especially not when the drawings are made with great speed. Organization in two dimensions, such as found in maps and blueprints, is also an indicator of intellectual ability though a less reliable indicator than Organization in three dimensions. Flat forms of Organization, such as mere elaboration, are hardly representative of intellectual capacity.

Following are a few combinations of Organization and Detail found to contain cues as to the subject's level of intelligence. It is presupposed in this that the stimuli are adequately completed and that there are no indexes of marked emotional disturbance capable of upsetting the following "rules."

Superior three-dimensional Organization with scant Detail: high but probably unilaterally speculative intelligence of a synthesizing type.

Superior three-dimensional Organization with a fair amount of Detail: high level of analytical-synthesizing intelligence and satisfactory balance of speculation and practicality.

Superior two-dimensional Organization with scant Detail: presumably good average intelligence; this assumption receives considerable support if the performance is speedy.

Predominance of Organization over Detail at any level of complexity: always a favorable indication of intelligence.

Predominance of Detail over Organization: unfavorable indication in regard to intellectual capacity and emotional maturity.

Medium degree of Organization and of Detail: not conclusive, occurring with subjects of any level of intelligence; with slow performance it tends to show average or below average intelligence.

Poor Organization and scant Detail: not conclusive, dependent on length of drawing time; frequently an indication of low average intelligence; may occur in speedy performances of highly intelligent adults.

Repetition, Duplication and Recurrence

A pattern frequently appearing in Abstract drawings of the symmetrical decorative type consists of mere repetition of the stimulus in a straight line or, owing to the corner position of some stimuli, in a square arrangement (Y/3 and 6, dd. 19 and 21), or in some other, often scattered, way. The poorest of these patterns show a rigidly uniform repetition of the stimulus; some show a slight variation of it (dd. 20 and 23) or an alternating succession of the stimulus and another element (d. 17) attenuating somewhat the flatness and monotony of the repetition. Most symmetrical decorative Abstractions are made up of some such form of repetition. However, when a variety of new elements is added to the stimulus or when the latter is integrated into a complex decorative structure, as in dd. 25 to 32, the elements become absorbed by the whole and a completely new Gestalt emerges. In such cases the repetition is merely material, not functional, and no longer belongs, therefore, with the category under discussion.

Duplication* refers to an arrangement of the repeated elements according to a strictly symmetrical pattern. In set Y, all the drawings except figure 1 show a rigidly regular organization consisting of an exact reversal of the stimulus with or without a connecting element (drawings 3 and 6 of this set).

While *Repetition* refers to a return of the same elements within the single drawing, and *Duplication* to repetition within the pattern, *Recurrence* applies to the reappearance of the same theme—representational or abstract—within the same set of drawings. Recurrence is most frequent with geometric designs, where the basic pattern of the drawings is the same in all or several of the drawings, as shown by set Y, which shows an extreme form of combined Repeti-

---

*This variety of Repetition was first considered as an independent criterion. (Duplication still occupies a separate place on the scoring sheet). The meaning of this aspect of the composition being closely related to the other forms of Repetition, its maintenance as a separate category is actually unnecessary.

tion, Duplication and Recurrence. Representational content, obviously, does not lend itself to continuous use of the same theme throughout the set because of the variety of the stimuli, which resists uniform completion. A maximum of Recurrence is attained in such drawings when the same object appears three or four times in the same set. Recurrence presupposes also a similarity of structure of the recurrent object, as in set Z, with the four almost identical heads. The three human figures in sets C and K do not fall within this category; on the contrary, they represent a form of Variety. When the recurrent object is uncommon—though not necessarily bizarre—as few as two such drawings may be significant.

.   .   ○

The various forms of uniformity here discussed belong to the unfavorable group of diagnostic indexes. In regard to intellectual functioning they reveal a scarcity of associations, defective mental mobility and suppleness, a lack of originality and a marked tendency towards perseverance. With respect to behavior and activity, they point to a lack of autonomy and creative initiative, sometimes to submissiveness and docility. When occurring with Abstract content Recurrence indicates either emotional poverty or repression. With representational content its significance may be quite different, not related to a lack of emotional capacity or expression but to a tendency toward fixation and obsession.

The above interpretations presuppose that Repetition and Recurrence are rather largely represented, either throughout the set or in a majority of drawings; within an unfavorable constellation of indexes, fewer than half of the drawings may be sufficient to cause suspicion. One drawing, or even two, showing repetition of the stimulus is common in the present test and does not justify any concern. It may simply be regarded as an attempt at fulfilling a task without aiming at excellence. Notice must be taken, however, of the kind of stimulus for which the subject shows such reduced receptiviy, this being more significant than the mere fact of Repetition. As for Recurrence, when appearing with representational content, it always calls for attention, unless it occurs with very common themes as human figures, houses, flowers. Yet, even in these cases, it may take on particular significance.

Repetition and Recurrence may be due to a temporary state of emotional or general disturbance such as anxiety or depression, in which the subject is unable to think of adequate and varied ways of completing the stimuli. In such cases, the above mentioned deficiency of the intellectual and volitional functions are, of course, not to be regarded as basic characteristics of the subject's personality.

The negative significance attached to Repetition and Recurrence finds confirmation in the literature on drawings by psychiatric patients, which reports Repetition in its various forms as one of the most frequently encountered characteristics of these drawings.

Variety

Variety refers to a modal aspect of the Content, rather than to Execution. Real Variety is present when the set of drawings shows different classes of drawings, Pictures and Designs, Nature and Objects, Decoration and Technical designs. A variety of items belonging to the same category such as Inanimate Nature, Fantasy or Utility is not real variety, but rather uniformity. Within Animate Nature, however, such a series remains to be considered as Variety because of the great specificity of the manifestations of human and animal life.

.   .   .

Variety results almost necessarily from adequate completion of the stimuli, which themselves are varied. Variety is then a favorable symptom, suggesting diversity of interests, facility of expression, pleasure at creating, intellectual flexibility and, to a certain extent, also emotional flexibility and capacity for adaptation. When supported by other tendencies of related diagnostic value, Variety may be an expression of an excessively vivid imagination or a need for excellency. All other things equal, Variety is a positive indicator, although it does not have the degree of validity which its opponent, Repetition, has in regard to negative trends.

Closure

Certain subjects show a tendency to surround the stimulus by an encompassing line or to integrate it into enclosed structures as if they wanted to catch it and prevent it from expanding freely. In some cases this tendency appears as a real urge. Without hesitation, the subject encloses every stimulus which lends itself to this practice (1, 2 and 4), works stimuli 6, 7 and 8 in some closed pattern also, and sometimes finds a way to confine the remaining stimuli 3 and 5 in a similar fashion.

Sometimes the contour is double or multiple and may develop into a fairly complex geometric-abstract pattern which is occasionally "afternamed." Such afternaming occurs especially with stimuli 1 and 4 which are then called targets, or with 8 completed into a circle and 6 into a square, which in turn receive an appropriate name. Whether such drawings are determined by an unconscious tendency to enclose or by a conscious aim to represent objects or abstractions cannot be made out with certitude but must be inferred from the predominant trends manifested in the complete set. It is, therefore, safe to divide the scores for such drawings over Closure and either Utility or Technical Abstraction.

·   ·   ·

Closure seems to express a need to restrain, to concentrate, to protect or to isolate. Its specific trend of meaning is, however, not clear. The majority of Closures are found in drawings of controlled, fairly uncommunicative, somewhat "static" personalities. But it seems that the meaning of this rather peculiar reaction goes beyond this interpretation.

Information concerning a few well-known subjects tends to show that Closure may refer to the existence of a depth problem of which the subject is confusedly aware and about which he is particularly cautious and seclusive. Another explanation which appeared plausible in several cases presents Closure as expressing a lack of inner security, and more specifically a fear of losing the inner self through contact with the surrounding world. People whose drawings exhibit this characteristic often seem to hold tightly to something in life: habits, possessions, principles or convictions. Therefore, they generally appear conservative, circumspect and somewhat rigid. However, in order to acquire significance, Closure must occur with a certain frequency or else be supported by other indexes. When largely represented, Closure is almost necessarily combined with Recurrence and hence justifies serious suspicion.

Orientation

By Orientation is understood something fairly simple, namely, a particular composition of the drawing on a slanted line producing an effect of "pointing upward." Orientation can be achieved within both representational and non-representational content.

Faint manifestations of this variable appear in geometric-decorative Abstractions like Y/4 and 5 or d. 20. Such drawings deserve only a low score for Orientation (½ to maximum 1 point), their upgoing movement being counterbalanced too strongly by the static effect of their symmetry. Within representational content, equally faint manifestations are found in A/4 and C/4, where the upward direction of the main lines is determined chiefly by the location of the stimulus, which serves as a focus and termination point of lines of various, not ascending, directions.

Certain elements of the composition may also be given a slight or moderate score for Orientation. Among these are: smoke effects, when represented in a decidedly upward direction as in C/3 (not in A/3); steeply rising histograms or stairways, such as occur often as completions of stimulus 3 (B/3); upward footprints, as appear not uncommonly with stimulus 7; upward flights of birds, as in d. 94.

Outstanding examples of Orientation are found in C/5 where the beam of light projected by the flashlight and breaking through the darkness brings out sharply the dynamic impulse contained in the stimulus. The same intense effect is achieved by D/5, less dramatic in its composition than C/5 but executed in a sketchy, casual way that heightens its vividness. Arrow themes also contain a strongly oriented movement. See in this respect E/1, whose intensely aiming effect cannot be surpassed on this level of simplicity of composition. A similar, though much weaker, example ·of Orientation appears in D/1 and V/5.

Orientation, not being a frequently encountered characteristic, must be scored generously.

·   ·   ·

The general trend of meaning of Orientation is favorable, provided that it is present to a marked degree; otherwise it carries little specific meaning. Orientation seems to be an expression of a particularly strong dynamism, of audacity, and decisiveness. Most subjects whose drawings show this characteristic prove to have a positive attitude toward life and problems, and a healthy ambition. These assumptions receive considerable support when Orientation appears in combination with good or satisfactory Form level, superior Organization and a few Originals. Within such a constellation of variables, Orientation is likely to stand for efficiency and creativeness. When combined with a high degree of Carefulness, it is almost certain to be an expression of immoderate striving toward excellence. With low Form level, mediocre Organization and Fullness, an unjustified high level of aspiration and an overeagerness for apparent achievement is likely to be present. An element of Orientation is particularly desirable in the drawings of male subjects.

Carefulness

This concept covers a number of characteristics, such as quality of the line, either perfectly straight or fluently curved; completeness of contours; exactness of angles and symmetrical parts; regularity in the sequence of certain elements; smoothness of shading and similar characteristics, giving the drawings a neat and orderly aspect.

Carefulness is not to be confused with Form level, as indicated earlier. It is more technical, more "material," and implies obvious efforts, whereas Form level is achieved in a more or less spontaneous, natural way.

·   ·   ·

Carefulness results from adequate psychomotor coordination and sustained attention; it is, therefore, a direct expression of control, order, and perhaps of foresight. When exhibited in products as small as those under discussion, the significance of Carefulness is still increased.

Depending upon the degree to which it appears and, as always, upon the general context of indexes, Carefulness may stand for highly commendable traits: zeal, accuracy, reliability, prudence; or for seriously impairing tendencies: meticulousness, compulsiveness, perfectionism and intolerance. Combined with indicators of emotionality—that is, with regard to content, Nature and its various expressions; with regard to execution, Expansion, Fullness, Curved lines—a fair degree of Carefulness strikes a most favorable note (see analysis of set A, p. 138), indicating a wholesome balance and a constructive interaction of the conscious and unconscious forces. But when appearing to a high degree with a constellation of variables made up predominantly of indexes of intellectuality and control, as in set B, the enhancing value of Carefulness is considerably reduced. Set B is not seriously affected, however, by the weight of this variable, because of the adequate and realistic completion of stimuli and the moderation of Pressure and Covering whose meaning counterbalances that of over-Carefulness. However, in view of the content of this set and its narrow range of Variation, Carefulness reveals a certain emotional aridity and a leaning toward obstinacy and unilaterality.

A moderate degree of Carefulness seems auspicious with adults, for whom it indicates a compromise between a desire to keep up with satisfactory standards of performance and a sensible, relaxed way of viewing things. It is remarkable, however, that practically none of the superiorly endowed, efficient and mature individuals examined here display a high measure of Carefulness in their products. With younger subjects, late adolescents especially, a fair amount of Carefulness is desirable and almost a requisite. For these subjects it is an expression of a high level of aspiration, an appreciation for quality, a healthy sense of competition and a favorable development of the control functions.

Casualness

Casualness refers to a loose, informal, sometimes stylish, sometimes slightly negligent way of drawing, which may enhance or impair a picture depending upon many factors. Among these, the appropriateness of a casual treatment of the subject matter is important. Casualness is likely to confer a vivid, supple and light touch to a drawing and is therefore particularly suited for Nature content, to which it lends expressiveness and life, or for Movement, which it enhances with vividness. (Compare, with respect to their dynamic quality, C/5, stereotyped in its careful execution, and D/5, flashy and lively in its casual treatment.) For Objects, which must look solid and consistent and require, therefore, a firm and precise execution, such a casual way of drawing is inappropriate.

When composition and treatment are too loose, the drawing acquires a scribbling-like appearance, as in set N and especially in set R, which appear frankly incoherent. In such cases, the scores must be divided in various proportions between Casualness and Scribblings.

.   .   .

As for most expressive phenomena, the meaning of Casualness is fluid, and may be indicative of rather divergent traits and attitudes. However, when moderately represented, the general diagnostic trend of Casualness is one of adaptability, relaxation, spontaneity and tolerance. The more specific meaning of this variable depends, first, on the age level of the subject. For the middle-aged individual a fair degree of Casualness, as appearing in set D, points to a well-adjusted, undramatic and mature attitude. For younger subjects, such as late adolescents, only a slight degree of Casualness is permissible. Any marked looseness — unless it is an art technique — indicates a deficient discipline, excessive independency, and a lack of readiness for expending effort and living up to reasonable standards.

The significance of Casualness depends further upon the appropriateness of its use. When occurring with organic subject matter or with objects in motion, it expresses a life-centered attitude and an ability to adjust to changes. When used for representing Objects it points toward a certain instability or a state of conflict.

When Casualness becomes mere negligence and incoherence, its meaning changes considerably. It becomes then an almost unmistakable sign of serious impairment of the controlling and directing functions or of acute emotional disturbance of an active type.

Movement

Movement may be encountered in various forms: (1) nonobjective, (2) cosmic, (3) mechanical action, (4) human activity.

Nonobjective movement is contained in the earlier described motor Scribblings. A dynamic element is found also in asymmetrical Abstractions, especially in those exhibiting curly, undulating structures and flamelike contours, as the drawings of set O. Symbolic Abstractions also frequently suggest the idea of movement, either through a concentration of the lines to a particular point or through a convergence of ascending lines (a faint illustration of the latter kind is found in d. 132).

Cosmic movement appears in agitated clouds and skies (dd. 97, 99), lightning (L/8, R/6), seas (dd. 93, 95), rain and sunrays (d. 98, D/8), or fire and smoke, when the latter are not part of differentiated, representational drawings, in which case they become indicative of mechanical or human action. In more representational drawings, cosmic movement is manifested through volcanic eruptions (G/5), windbeaten trees (d. 87), blowing flower petals, floating flags or garments, etc.

Mechanical action shows the greatest variety and may be implicit or explicit. Implicit action is suggested by the vivid, sharply oriented position of objects associated with activity, tools (M/7), instruments (B/5), arms, or by the particular disposition of a number of objects (d. 71) or other meaningful relations between them (C/1 and 5). Explicit forms are those where the actual functioning of the object is indicated. It is found in drawings which depict the movement itself, for instance by showing the path of an object such as a bullet or an arrow by means of a few light strokes (E/1); or indicating a flying airplane by concentric lines in the area of the propeller, a speeding vehicle by clouds of dust or puffs of steam (A/3), a working factory by smoking chimneys, etc. Other, quite intense manifestations of Movement—neither exactly implicit nor explicit and perhaps more human than mechanical, since there is no rigid delimitation between these categories—are found in those drawings representing an object together with the operating hand (d. 66), arm (d. 65), foot (W/5), or leg.

Human activity is the most significant form of Movement. Like mechanical action it may be explicit, as in dd. 45 and 46, or implicit, as in F/4, where the idea of social activity predominates over the materially represented Objects. Aspects worthy of attention in such drawings are: the kind of activity performed, recreative (dd. 67, 69, 70, 91), social (S/6, "Pledging"; Q/7, "Bear Meeting"), work or labor (d. 45); in cases of group activity, the nature of the relations between the figures, whether of authority (S/6, T/7), equality (d. 134), aggression, cooperation, etc.; the fulfiller of the central role, his age level and sex. When animals are featured, notice should be taken of whether their activity is properly that of animals, or whether it is human.

•   •   •

The urge to represent objects in motion or in action seems, in this kind of projective material, to be an indication of a vividly imaginative and vitally strong, often creative personality. The more specific significance of Movement depends mainly on the particular form in which it is expressed.

Nonobjective movement, such as Scribblings, points to strong impulses of brief duration, to an audacious but unpredictable makeup and to proneness to aggressive action. In symbolic content matter, Movement appears as a positive sign, counterbalancing the utopian-contemplative tendencies often found with the kind of subjects producing symbolic drawings. The specific meaning of Movement in asymmetrical Abstractions such as set O, is hard to determine because of the strong weight, in these drawings, of the variables Curved Lines, Abstractions and abundant Shading, which prevent the weaker variables from revealing their diagnostic contribution.

Cosmic movement, expressed in undifferentiated or scarcely differentiated content, does not seem to be auspicious, especially when depicting violent phenomena (stormy seas and skies, lightnings). It is found in the products of subjects characterized by strong and excitable emotions, rather obscure thinking and reduced efficiency and who, at the moment of taking the test, may be very tense. Within differentiated representational content, cosmic movement is able to convey highly significant but highly specific meaning. Some of the themes, volcanic eruptions, geysers, comets, are unique; that is, they occur only once within a great number of results and can not, therefore, be adequately interpreted on the limited basis of comparison data underlying the present study. Other themes, though original, occur several times and allow some testing of hypotheses borrowed from deeper forms of exploration. An example showing the diagnostic specificity of the drawings, in their content and content-determined modal aspects, such as Movement, is the following. A tree, shaken and stripped by wind, occurred four times as a completion of stimulus 2. Each of the subjects who produced this kind of drawing was known to have objectively grounded feelings of frustration and, therefore, to be more or less despondent. Another theme, similar in its appearance, is the 'flower with blowing petals," made three times from stimulus 7. The frustration hypothesis which seems to apply satisfactorily to the "stripped tree" theme did not, however, appear to be appropriate in any of the cases of the "stripped flower" theme, none of the authors of these drawings showing any evidence of emotional tension, depression or frustration. A tentative explanation for the discrepancy in the meaning of apparently similar themes might be found in the fact that the flower petals, parting from low-placed stimulus 7, are blown upward or in various directions, whereas the falling leaves, appearing as completions of the high-placed stimulus 2, necessarily show a downward direction. In free drawings, these characteristics of the drawings could be interpreted as a function of "spatial symbolism." However, where the location of the object is determined to a large extent by the location of the stimuli, this interpretation seems less justified. On the other hand, considering the fact that the stimuli permit a broad range of completions, the use of cues, provided by the spatial distribution and direction of certain elements, seems legitimate. This example of similar phenomena with divergent meaning, since it refers to a limited number of cases, is, of course, of no conclusive significance. However, the finer symptomatic aspects of the drawings are, statistically, never numerous, and their diagnostic value seems bound to remain tentative. The sole possibility for using them lies in the search for more such subtle indexes in the set in order to find mutual confirmation of their diagnostic hints.

Mechanical action appears to be diagnostically very favorable, perhaps because it implies the operation of conscious factors of selection and direction, whereas the uncontrollable cosmic forms of movement suggest passivity and lack of power in the operating object. Since the subject generally identifies himself in some way with the object depicted, this assumption appears plausible. Frequently the content of these drawings is directly revealing of the interests, preoccupations or aspirations of the subject—at least, no instance has been encountered where human or mechanical action was completely opposed to the interests and attitudes of the subject. For instance, professional subjects tend to draw pencils (C/1), scientific instruments (B/5, W/2), etc.; artists draw painting tools (M/7) or musical instruments (G/3, 7). The same is true for human action. None of the seclusively inclined, controlled and socially somewhat withdrawn kind of subjects produced drawings featuring several interacting human figures. In fact, drawings of the latter kind are infrequent, even among outgoing subjects; the extremely reduced drawing space obviously accounts for the relative infrequency of such drawings. Therefore, absence of interacting human figures, suspicious as it may be in other techniques of investigation, is not disquieting here. Moreover, such drawings do not appear to have a particularly favorable meaning in the present test, for they occur mostly with socially overactive, excitable, playful and emotionally somewhat immature individuals. Offering slight support for this assumption are children's drawings (collected here for the sole purpose of comparing their more obvious characteristics with the drawings of adults), which exhibit to a relatively high degree human figures in some primitive form of interaction. Children's drawings also show more explicit than implicit movement. In accordance with this observation is the fact that implicit movement, among adults, was found predominantly with subjects of above-average intelligence, endowed with constructive, efficiently used potentialities. Explicit Movement appears generally with male subjects of an enterprising, uninhibited, often somewhat excited type, who display an almost childish pleasure at performing the test. Implicit action appears, therefore, on the whole, as the more mature and auspicious form of Movement. However, any form of Movement, when abundantly represented, as in set C, may well correspond to overactivity and overeagerness for achievement, especially when combined with great carefulness and high Originality. The Movement variable in set C reaches an unusually high degree: intense implicit movement in 1 and 5 and, to a lesser extent, in 2 ("Threatening Bomb"); explicit movement in 3 and 7 (a slight element in the smoking pipe of d. 8); even drawings 4 and 6, though static in their representation, feature vehicles (4 represents a coal wagon in the distance, losing coal). So marked a dynamic trend is an almost certain sign of a strong desire to dominate which, depending upon other characteristics of the total product, may correspond to a mere need for self-affirmation or be an expression of genuine leadership qualities.

As to "bursting the frame," when duly supported by other indexes it evidences a defective balance between vital drive and psychomotor or general control and suggests a lack of consideration for boundaries and restrictions—an interpretation which encountered frequent verification in the material studied.

Originality

The original drawing is one whose content occurs rarely. Like every other variable, originality presents several degrees scored on a three point scale and going from the practically unique theme to the more or less unusual, that is, one whose frequency does not exceed about 10 per cent. However, not every rare theme is to be scored for originality. Two further conditions must be fulfilled: first, the drawing must be representational or have a specific meaning such as most technical abstractions have (decorative abstractions are not scored for originality unless they present a remarkably personal style such as set O); second, the stimulus-drawing relation must be excellent.

Acquaintance with a fair amount of material is required for correct scoring of the original drawing. Often the beginner will consider as unique a content which is actually not unusual and may even be rather common. Examination of the selection of drawings reproduced herein and of their scoring is particularly recommended for adequate evaluation of this variable.

· · ·

The capacity to integrate the given stimuli into original wholes seems to indicate an intellectual resourcefulness tinged by emotion. High scores for originality occur mostly with intellectually lively, creative and versatile individuals, while subjects with below average intelligence show practically no originality in their products. Originality is, however, not a reliable indicator of intellectual capacity, for it is often lacking in the drawings of superiorly intelligent people, especially older adults. However, since the performance of these subjects is often very brief, the absence of originality is, to an extent, compensated by the promptness of their response which — provided that the stimulus-drawing relation is satisfactory — allows for conclusions similar to those derived from originality. The diagnostic difference between original content and briefness of performance seems to lie in the emotional makeup of the subjects which, in the latter case, is generally less rich, less warm but also less complicated than in the former.

Popularity

The popular drawing forming the counterpart of the original one is defined by the frequency of its occurrence. Like the latter, it must also be representational and adapted to the particular qualities of the stimulus. Symmetrical decorative or geometric designs, such as dd. 17 to 24, are not considered as populars though they are frequently produced. Being mere repetitions of the stimuli, their pattern is necessarily frequent; however, these drawings are lacking the reality content required as a sign of common conscious experience adopted here as a criterion for popularity.

· · ·

The identity of associations of different people with stimuli as faintly structured as those used here suggests a similarity of perception and experience conducive to thinking and acting as others do. In fact, it was found that less than 10 per cent of the group examined failed to feature popular themes, while the remainder featured at least one, often more. In regard to the popular drawing, the general rule according to which the absence of a given variable is less significant than its presence is not applicable, for the absence of this kind of drawing appears to be as symptomatic as, or more symptomatic than, its presence. A complete lack of popular themes is generally indicative of a markedly idiosyncratic makeup and even of disturbance, unless the drawings represent simple decorative or geometric designs. On the other hand, predominance of populars together with absence of originals generally corresponds either to a flat, primitive and mediocre personality or to a genuinely simple, unsophisticated and adaptive nature (set H).

Clearness — Vagueness

These variables pertain to the over-all aspect of the drawings. Clearness results from a combination of characteristics such as firmness and continuity of the lines, complete outlines, careful execution, sober treatment. Vagueness, on the other hand, is due to weak and sketchy lines, compact coverage, inappropriate use of shading, negligent execution, incoherent composition. With atmospheric content or fantasy content, a certain vagueness may enhance the drawings as well as their meaning; it is inappropriate, however, with utility objects or with technical abstraction, where clearness is desirable for both the picture and the diagnosis.

· · ·

The frequency of occurrence of clearness and vagueness in the material under discussion is very unequal. Clearness is found in the majority of the drawings — apparently due to the fact that most people lacking artistic training tend to represent things in a simple manner. This means that the specific meaning of clearness cannot easily be isolated from the variety of configurations into which it occurs. From a logical point of view, clear drawings presuppose clear images, sharp perception and attention; clear compositions give evidence of a certain organizational capacity, a moderate need to structure and a desire to be comprehensible, which are qualities conducive to adjustment and maturity. However, because of the range of concomitant variables, strict confirmation of these inferences is hard to obtain.

The significance of vagueness, on the other hand, especially the chaotic or incoherent kind of vagueness which is rather rare, is easier to ascertain. When it occurs with inappropriate subject matter, such as objects or technical content, it is almost certain to have negative value. None of the subjects examined who produced obscure, overcrowded, overshaded or otherwise complex drawings where wholesome and balanced; rather, they were somehow peculiar in the sense of highly self-involved, extremistic, problem-prone and socially uncomfortable. These conclusions, though not derived from quantitatively strong data, are nevertheless likely to possess appreciable validity, for they were confirmed to variable degrees in every case.

Consistency — Inconsistency

These concepts apply to the drawings as a set. They pertain to the execution of the drawings compared with one another in the same way as Variety pertains to their content. The consistency or inconsistency of the execution comes out most clearly in the characteristics of the lines, their intensity, type and continuity, and in the coverage, full or empty, expanded or constricted; other characteristics, such as the amount of detail or the degree of organizaton and carefulness, may also be so considered.

In one important respect the single drawing is also to be examined in regard to the consistency of its execution, namely, in regard to the intensity of the lines. Differences of intensity may be appropriate in drawings in the third dimension where perspective calls for intensity gradations in the lines, but are inappropriate in two-dimensional drawings unless these differences aim at decorative effects. Actual inconsistency in the single drawing as well as in the set corresponds, therefore, to marked inequalities in the execution not justified by the nature of the content or forming a sharp contrast with the predominant characteristics of the complete set.

•   •   •

Consistent treatment of a set of drawings is found most often with subjects manifesting a relative equality of mood and behavior. Such equanimity may be of a different nature and have different value depending upon whether it stems from a quality of the temperament, from emotional dullness or from consciously acquired control. Which of these possibilities underlies the particular case must be recognized on the basis of the given set of indexes.

Inconsistency, in the sense of unmotivated shifts in the predominant characteristics of the execution, is always negative, pointing to a moody, unpredictable, often unreliable makeup. When inconsistency occurs as a single instance, that is, when only one drawing in a set shows a degree of intensity, coverage, carefulness or elaboration conspicuously different from the others, such deviation may be related to the particular object depicted. Questioning the subject about this object may then lead to interpretations very different from the aforementioned. The single case of inconsistency may also have to be explained by its rank in the order of execution of the set. Sometimes the first and often the last drawing is different from the others in that it shows less content or elaboration. In these cases the inconsistency may be due to factors such as the newness of the situation, or fatigue or pressure for time and must be interpreted accordingly.

In view of the variety of the stimuli, complete consistency in the execution is not to be expected in the present test. Moreover, such consistency is not always positive and desirable. In given constellations of indexes, a strictly consistent execution may correspond to flatness and rigid conformism, while certain shifts in the execution may express a colorful and versatile makeup.

III. The Diagnostic Operations

A. Scoring

QUANTITATIVE evaluation, although not essential in projective techniques, plays an important role in the present test because it not only determines the structure of the "Personality Profile" but affects the qualitative differentiation or individualization of the diagnosis.

Strictly objective scoring presupposes the existence of precise standards of reference or norms. Free drawings, like all products of creative activity, do not permit establishment of rigorous norms. The objectivity achieved in matters so greatly and subtly varied is only approximate, but may, in given conditions, attain a valuable degree. Conducive to such a degree of objective treatment is the availability, first, of differentiated definitions of the things to be scored, and second, of a means for methodical and easy analysis of the material and for recording the scores. Chapter II, with its description of the phenomena in their chief modalities, aimed at providing the first of these conditons. The second is found in the scoring blank (page 119) which is an indispensable tool for thorough examination of the drawings.

The scoring blank presents two halves facing each other. Along the sides appears a list of the criteria or variables entering into the quantitative part of the diagnosis (the other criteria are considered only in the qualitative part). The numbers across the top of the blank correspond to the eight drawings of a full set. Scoring may proceed in either a horizontal or a vertical order. In the first case the drawings are considered one by one in regard to the complete set of criteria from "Animate Nature" on top of the left hand column to "Schematism" at the bottom of the right hand column. Thus the scores are recorded in a vertical order. In the second case the criteria are taken one by one and each drawing is examined for the same criterion before passing on to another drawing. This results in horizontal recording of the scores. The latter procedure has proved to be the more expeditious and the more consistent because it allows for greater continuity in the evaluation of a given variable within various drawings.

118

Scoring Blank

CRITERIA		Total Score	Drawings 1	2	3	4	5	6	7	8	CRITERIA		Total Score	Drawings 1	2	3	4	5	6	7	8
NATURE	Animate										FANTASY	Fancy									
	Physiognomy											Phantasm									
	Inanimate											Symbolism									
	Atmosphere											Original									
OBJECTS	Utility										ABSTRACT	Symmetric									
	Ornaments											Asymetric									
Style												Technical									
Movement											Careful										
COVERAGE	Full										Casual										
	Empty										SHADING	Light									
	Expanded											Dark									
	Constricted										Orientation										
Organization											Closure										
Detail											Parts										
LINES	Curved										Scribbles										
	Straight										Duplication										
	Strong										Repetition										
	Soft										Schematism										

Interpretation Blank

Anim. Phys.	Ina. Atm. Sof.	Phys. Orna.	Expa. FAN.	OBJECTS	Organized	Anim. Mov.	Emp.Con.Strai.
Expan. Curv.	Sy. As. SHA. Po	Styl. Organ.	Orig. Asy.	Detail	Technical	Ful. Strong	Stro.Clo. Rep.
Casual	Scri. Sche.	Symmetr.	Dark			Dark, Orie.	Duplic. Car
Open	Seclusive	Combinative	Creative	Practical	Speculative	Dynamic	Controlled
EMOTION	IMAGINATION		INTELLECT			ACTIVITY	

When scoring is terminated, the scores obtained by each of the eight drawings in regard to every criterion (that is, all the scores appearing on the same line of one half of the blank) are added, up and their sum is noted besides the name of the corresponding criterion in the "Total Score" column. In case the total score is a half point (see following paragraphs), the half point is dropped, such a degree of accuracy being out of proportion with the probability character of the conclusions.

Scoring proceeded originally on the basis of a three step scale. One point was awarded for weak representation of a given variable, two for marked and three for extraordinarily strong representation. This approach to the intensity aspect of the material did not, however, prove to be satisfactory. Drawings are material objects only in a limited and secondary sense. They are essentially forms of human expression with all the diversity inherent to such phenomena; hence, their evaluation cannot even be approximated when too reduced a measuring stick is used. Too great differences of intensity lie between the point where a characteristic is merely present and that where it is marked, or between the point where it is marked and that where it becomes excessively so. When the rating includes only one point between two extremes, the intermediary degrees of intensity have to be forced rather arbitrarily into one of two categories, with the result that the scoring may become greatly inconsistent and the diagnosis may be flattened or distorted. For instance, if the variables indicative of Outgoing Emotionality (see interpretation blank, page 119) happen to be overrated and those for Seclusiveness underrated, the outcome may show as emotionally balanced an individual who is predominantly seclusive and in certain cases may even present a reversed picture of his emotional structure.

Extension of the scale in view of a more accurate and more objective evaluation thus proved necessary. To this end each of the steps of the three-point scale was split up — a procedure which corresponds actually to a doubling of the steps but which is more suitably called a splitting-up because of the type of symbols used and because of the idea behind it. These symbols are the cross (X) representing a point, and the slant line (/) representing a half point. The half point, besides its function of representing the intermediary intensities between the basic divisions (weak, marked and unusual) serves a specific purpose. First, it is used for recording faint manifestations of characteristics which are not sufficiently pronounced to receive a full point and are easily overlooked in the interpretation when no provision is made for their scoring. Examples of phenomena deserving a minimum score are the following. For Animate Nature a half point can be given to a tiny human figure in a town view or to a schematic bird within a landscape (A/3); for Inanimate Nature, to nature-related objects, such as a flower pot or a framed landscape decorating the picture of an interior (E/6); for Atmosphere, this score is appropriate for a cloud in the sky of an otherwise matter-of-fact picture (B/1), or to smoke coming out of a chimney (D/3). The half point serves further as a guiding mark in cases where the scores have to be revised for one reason or another (lack of differentiation within the profile or disagreement with the results of other techniques and the like). Since the half point often represents a hesitancy on the part of the examiner to award a higher or lower score, re-evaluation of such items often straightens out the difficulty.

The use of symbols instead of figures for recording the scores serves to reflect as directly as possible on the scoring sheet the constellation of variables contained in the drawings. The effect of the distribution of the symbols over the scoring blank, and the fact that the intensity of the variables is reflected in the number and type of the symbols, creates a pattern representing an immediate diagnostic communication to the trained examiner. This abstract pattern is not intended as a substitute for the original product, it is only an aid for bringing out more clearly that which in the drawings appears in intimate fusion, some of its elements dominating, others functionally absorbed, some appealing or perhaps repelling to the onlooker and therefore magnified at the expense of other elements. Representational content in particular and quality of the execution influence the examiner almost irresistibly when he interprets the material in a global, somewhat appreciative way. As a counterweight to the diagnostically "syncretic" character of the drawings, the scoring blank provides for a methodic, clear and complete inventory of the variables (complete in terms of the study here presented). Another advantage of the use of the blank is the fact that, through the effect of the spaces left open after termination of scoring, attention is drawn to the variables *not* represented within the drawings. The absence of certain variables, though generally not as significant as their presence, is nevertheless a worthwhile aspect of the material, capable of clarifying and emphasizing the diagnostic trends contained in the variables actually represented. When the examiner interprets directly from the drawings, the absent characteristics are often not taken into account and a real contribution is lost.

The meaning of scores in the present test is not the same as in most other tests where it is relative to external, statistical data. Here the meaning of the score obtained by a given variable is dependent predominantly upon the configuration of scores of the group of variables to which it belongs. For instance, in regard to the group of variables correlated with the *outgoing* aspect of Emotion, the meaning of a 9 point score for the variable Expansion will vary considerably depending upon the weight of the scores for Animate Nature, for Casualness and for the other variables of the group in question. Likewise the total scores obtained by the various components of the profile must be interpreted as functions of each other. Thus the significance of the total score for *Outgoingness* can only be determined as a function of the scores obtained first by its counterpart *Seclusiveness* and further by each of the other components of the schema. If the total scores for Emotion show a proportion of 10:15, the significance of these figures may be in certain cases — dependent especially upon the amount of time put into the performance — approximately the same as in the proportion 20:30. The absolute values thus not being essential in the present case, the effect of individual differences in the ratings of various judges or of the same judge at different times is of no primary importance, provided of course that a given level of rating be maintained with approximate consistency. However, while the general level of the scoring is not essential, the standards for differential evaluation of the variables must be at least similar to those used originally in the construction of the test, if the conclusions are to be valid. Full description of those standards not being feasible, a series of samples have been selected (see Part III) to cover a broad variety of phenomena and to bring out the finer differences in the evaluation of similar phenomena. It is hoped that examination and intercomparison of these samples will provide a workable start in the adoption of standards of evaluation approximating those which underly the conclusions here reported.

B. Interpretation

1. The Personality Profile

This part of the interpretation provides a basis for the process of individualization leading up to the final conclusions. The value of the profile is essentially typological; therefore, largely similar profiles may be obtained from subjects with considerable differences of individual makeup.

The blank used for this first operation appears on page 119. On top are the abbreviated names of the criteria grouped according to the relations found to exist between them and the various functions of the personality schema represented along the bottom of the blank. In order to facilitate identification of these abbreviations a transcription in full of the criteria as grouped on the interpretation blank is given in table 4.

TABLE 4. *Reproduction in full of the abbreviated content of the interpretation blank showing the composition of the groups of variables as correlated with the components of the personality schema.*

EMOTION	*Outgoing*	Animate Nature; Physiognomy; Expansion; Curves; Casualness.
	Seclusive	Inanimate Nature, Atmosphere; Soft Lines; Symmetric Abstraction; Asymmetric Abstraction; Shading (both light and dark); Parts; Scribbles; Schematism.
IMAGINATION	*Combinative*	Physiognomy; Ornaments; Style; Organization; Symmetric Abstraction.
	Creative	Expansion; Fantasy (including Fancy, Phantasm and Symbolism); Originality; Asymmetric Abstraction; Dark Shading.
INTELLECT	*Practical*	Objects (both Utility and Ornaments); Detail.
	Speculative	Organization; Technical Abstraction.
ACTIVITY	*Dynamic*	Animate Nature; Movement; Fullness; Strong Pressure; Carefulness; Closure; Duplication; Repetition.
	Controlled	Emptiness; Constriction; Straight Lines; Strong Pressure; Carefulness; Closure; Duplication; Repetition.

The order of succession of the variables as grouped on the interpretation blank corresponds to the order in which they appear on the scoring blank, to facilitate use of both.

The small box in the lower right hand corner of each of the compartments carrying the criteria (see blank) serves for recording the sum of the scores obtained by each criterion of a given group. Notation of each of these scores beside the corresponding criteria, as shown by the scoring blanks in part III, is of appreciable help in the subsequent analysis of the profile.

The scale in the center of the blank allows for registration of 60 points, a level which is seldom surpassed. Each line of the scale represents two points, the even numbers are marked *on* the lines, the odd numbers *in between* the lines. The points thus marked on the scale are finally connected by a line. The relative evenness or the peaks and depressions of this line provides a first, general picture of the subject's personality structure.

2. Individualization of the Diagnosis

The introductory part of the interpretation examined the drawings solely in regard to the weight of clusters of variables; the main part, to be discussed now, considers the weight and particular characteristics of the variables. Through comparison, mutual modificaton, combination and cross-checking of the indexes thus brought out, meaningful relations are established and a unique diagnostic picture gradually emerges. Unlike the construction of the profile, which is a simple and mechanical procedure, its individualization is complex and delicate, requiring ready knowledge of the meaning of all the criteria in their main modalities and variability.

The various aspects of the material to be considered, including both the product and the performance, are the following:

The drawing time.

The receptivity versus insensitivity of the subject to the stimuli as evidenced by: (1) the stimulus-drawing relation and (2) the order of execution of the drawings.

The nature and structure of the criteria making up the profile.

The absent variables.

The nonscored variables.

The particularities which drawings occasionally show.

For the examination of the above aspects to lead up to a properly individual diagnosis certain basic personal data must be taken into account. These data are the subject's sex, age, level of education or type of occupation. Blind diagnosis is, of course, feasible, and may be of interest for theoretical purposes, but is of little use for clinical practice. Projective material being essentially polyvalent, it can be constructed into a number of personality pictures among which a proper choice can be made only through focusing the diagnostic process in regard to the above-mentioned personal data. A few words about these fundamental data will, therefore, precede the indication of the manner in which the test results — drawings and drawing time — are examined.

The Personal Data

Sex

The sex of the subject is always an important factor in the interpretation of creative products. It is, however, of particular significance in the D.-C. T. because of the symbolic value of the stimuli in regard to sex. As indicated on page 37 these stimuli can be classified into masculine and feminine. The first group includes stimuli 3, 4, 5 and 6, whose straight geometric character calls for completion into material-technical objects and involves primarily the rational and organizational functions of the mind. Because of the predominance of these func-tions in the typically masculine makeup, this group of stimuli is considered repre-sentative for the male sex. The remaining stimuli 1, 2, 7 and 8 have the round and supple character of the organic world which generally appeals more to the predominantly emotional-imaginative character of the feminine mind.

Most individuals are more or less responsive to both categories of stimuli with a variable degree of preference for the signs representative for their own sex. Others show a unilateral or strongly predominant sensitivity to the stimuli of either their own or the opposite sex. For instance, subject O, a man, reveals a sensi-tivity which, in terms of the stimuli used here, appears exactly reversed; not only does he prove remarkably responsive to the curved stimuli but also completely insensitive to the straight ones which he works into baroque curlicue designs. Almost the same degree of insensitivity for the signs representative of the sex of the subject appears in drawings 17 to 24 made by a female. Contrarily, W, a man, and especially H, a woman, give examples of unilateral affinity for the symbols of their own sex.

Predominance of a given type of line, straight or curved, entails almost necessarily the predominance of a given type of content, either material-con-structive or organic. While a spontaneous preference for a given type of line and content is in itself significant but may be due to accidental factors, preference for one type or another gains increased significance when it occurs in situations eliciting contrary types of reaction, such as in four of the eight situations pre-sented by the test blank. In such cases the preference is likely to express some-thing about the subject's attitudes rather than about his momentary interests and feelings. According to the implications of the stimuli in question, preference for one category of stimuli expresses either a positive or a negative attitude towards the role and attributes of the subject's own sex, while complete unilat-erality of responsiveness points to a limitation of his capacity for experiencing or — when such unilateral affinity exists in regard to the symbols of the opposite sex—to possible disturbance of fundamental aspects of his personality. Thus it appears that the conclusions derived from the stimulus-drawing relation may present fundamental differences depending upon the sex of the subject. Infor-mation about this data is therefore indispensable for the results of this test to acquire their proper diagnostic value.

Another aspect of the drawings, less important than the former and not exclusively pertaining to the present test but well worth considering is the content as such, regardless of its relation to the stimuli. Among the broad range of items grouped under the various categories of content, especially Nature and Objects, some occur so frequently with one sex and so seldom with the other that they almost become sex indicators. As mentioned earlier, children

appear often in the drawings of women but rarely in those of men and therefore take on greater significance when occurring with the latter. The same is
true for flowers. While they may appear in several drawings by a woman without
pointing to any particular degree of affectivity, flowers in a man's drawings,
however few or sketchy, are a practically certain sign of emotional delicacy or
tenderness (unless several indexes within the set point to immaturity or effeminacy). Atmosphere, especially the somewhat romantic-idealistic variety, is
another indicator of emotionality taking on far greater significance when occurring with men than with women. On the other hand, the drily humorous kind
of atmosphere found in T/4, "Bachelor's Bliss" (with cigar, cup of coffee, cat and
newspaper), is seldom encountered in women's drawings. Sex discriminative
aspects are found also under Physiognomy. For instance, the particular flavor
of drawings 53 and 123 did not appear in the drawings of the women examined,
while the snug and tender touch in drawing 122 is most unusual with men. As
for Objects, while appearing with almost equal frequency in the drawings of
either sex, most objects featured by women tend to show a note of refinement
or adornment; those by males often have a bare, merely utilitarian or technical
character. The specific aspects of the respective sphere of interest of the sexes
also tend to be reflected in the drawings. In the material collected here, engines,
machines, apparatus and industrial scenes or buildings occurred only with men,
whereas kitchen utensils, scissors, thimbles, ornaments and clothes were largely
predominant with women. Certain criteria of *execution* other than those mentioned earlier also tend to present sex-related aspects, though not as distinctly as
the criteria of content. Thus, Strong Lines, Organization in three dimensions, and
Movement are found more frequently in the drawings of men than in those of
women, whereas Soft pressure, Carefulness and Natural Expansion are slightly
predominant in the drawings of females. These tendencies in the distribution of
the items of content and in the characteristics of execution are, of course, not
clearly delineated and show a certain overlapping. However, they are distinc-
tive enough to be significant and to take on particular meaning when the
relation between the sex-conditioned characteristics of the drawings and the sex
of the subject is reversed.

Age

Both content and execution vary somewhat with the age of the individual.
For instance, the symbolic-idealistic content of set S, the esthetic-romantic scenes
of M, or the playfully imaginative themes of T are found almost exclusively
with young subjects. While such content may be expressive of unusual resources
when featured at this age level, it generally reveals an immature or unrealistic
streak when occurring on a higher level — though in rare cases it may reveal an
unusually fresh and creative turn of mind. The kind of subject matter com-

monly found in the drawings of older adults is somewhat more matter-of-fact, less rich and inclusive and less original. The latter characteristics are, however, not exclusively representative of this age range, for they occur frequently in the drawings of young subjects. In the latter case, however, they lack the favorable implications which they have in the former, where they indicate a healthy reduction of the need for emotional expression. With younger subjects, a large predominance of commonplace objects, while it may occasionally reflect a genuinely simple and humble make-up, is generally indicative of a certain mediocrity. either emotional or intellectual.

The execution of the drawings shows similar age-related differences. Careful and elaborate treatment, while dependent far more upon personal characteristics than upon age, appears nevertheless more frequently with the younger population than with the older and appears also to have more favorable implications in youth than in age. For instance, the extraordinarily precise and careful treatment of set B is likely to stand for high standards of performance and readiness for effort when occurring with young subjects but may be interpreted as compulsive meticulousness when appearing in the products of older subjects. Similarly, while the gross treatment shown by set I has no unfavorable implications in the case of a 50 year old laborer, the execution of set P by a sophisticated man of 24 is immediately suspect for it suggests a weakly integrated, probably disturbed, individual.

The subject's age is to be taken into account also when the drawings are interpreted as a function of the time put into the performance. With comparable quality of execution and amount of content and elaboration, the drawing time has a tendency to decrease as age increases. This, obviously, is not due to a parallel increase of speed and age, but results apparently from the fact that the individual's attitude toward tasks such as this tends to become more casual, less concerned with excellence, details and originality. Briefness of the drawing time tends to enhance the diagnosis whereas length seldom does. In regard to the older adult a long drawing time is never indicative of maturity, whatever the quality of the product. For the younger person a long performance, when justified by the quality of the product, may enhance the diagnosis, for it bespeaks important qualities of the will and high standards of achievement. As to the very brief and very poor performance, it is generally due to uncooperativeness, contempt, or hostility unless it occurs with subjects of below average general endowment.

Occupation and Education

Knowledge of the subject's occupation is more important to our purpose than knowledge of his education, since the occupation reflects education to an extent sufficient for this purpose. The only specifically educational element to be taken into account for adequate interpretation is art training. It is required especially for correct evaluaton of Form level, an over-all quality of the drawings which serves as a basis for the interpretation of a number of variables. Art training obviously tends to heighten the form level of drawings and necessitates modification of the meaning implied in this characteristic. When high form level is achieved by artistically untrained subjects its significance is, of course, very different from that with formally trained persons; the same holds true for poor form level.

Art training influences not only the execution of the drawings but also certain aspects of their content. Complex subject matter involving three-dimensional organization, as in sets A, C, M, and S, can hardly be expected from people lacking any kind of previous exercise or unaccustomed to handling pencil and paper. The latter distinction introduces occupation as a modifying factor of the interpretation. This factor is of particular importance for valid individualization of the diagnosis, as will appear from some examples. Take for instance, the plain utilitarian content and crude treatment of set I; it clearly evidences toughness and intellectual-emotional primitivity, yet in this particular case it allows for a largely favorable diagnosis, for it shows the subject, an older mine worker, as a forceful, commonsense, stable, probably reliable individual who is able to cope with the hard realism of his particular type of life. The same drawings produced by someone of a higher cultural level would convey a basically different meaning, for their heavy awkward, lines, lack of curves and complete disregard for the delicate stimuli 1 and 7 reveal an almost brutal vitality, rigid self-assertiveness, exclusive interest in earthly things and completely obtuse emotionality. Conversely, the diagnostically unfavorable implications of set X would be far worse if these drawings came from a laborer instead of from the student in philosophy who actually made them. In the first case, the faint execution of these drawings, their lack of concreteness and meaning, and their scattered unintegrated character would suggest grave inadequacy and even psychotic tendencies. In the second case the conclusions are less harsh, for the remoteness of the scholar's concerns from tangible reality, the nature of this activity, marked by cautious deliberation rather than by vigor and impetus, all attenuate the implications of the life-estranged character of his drawings.

Examining the content of the drawings in relation to the subject's occupation is of interest not only in regard to the broad categories (Nature, animate or inanimate; Objects, commonplace or more refined; Abstraction, decorative or technical) but also in regard to the specific items. It is worthwhile to find out whether, for instance, these items are related or unrelated to the subject's field of occupation, and, if related, what kind of interests they reveal, whether these interests are directed toward a "higher" or "lower" occupational level than the subject's own, etc. Does a shopkeeper, for instance, draw scientific instruments or charts? Does the scholar feature such content or does he represent commonplace things? Does the woman reveal the interests of the homemaker or those of the technician? Inspection of the drawings in relation to the educational and occupational status of the subject thus contributes appreciably to the differentiation and individualization of the conclusions.

The Material

Time

A statistically average length of time for the group under discussion was 20 minutes. However, this average has but little significance since it pertains to very different performances and very different subjects. Time is therefore a purely relative element and must be considered in relation to the product, its form level, complexity, the stimulus-drawing relation and personal data on the subject.

There is, however, a range of time which, all other things equal, appears to be diagnostically more favorable — perhaps because of the general character of moderation in the amount of content, level of execution and search for originality of the drawings made within such a span of time. This range is from about 15 to 40 minutes, depending upon the amount and quality of the products and their adequacy in regard to the given stimuli. Examples of such drawings are sets D and H, which are slightly above the lower limit of this range, and set K which is representative for the higher limit. However, when a product is poor in every respect even 15 minutes will, obviously, be too long and diagnostically unfavorable. As to the speedy but good performance, which may be as brief as three or five minutes, it is generally indicative of superior intellectual endowment, energetic makeup and often of satisfactory adjustment. For such brief performances to be qualified as good the only requisite is adequate completion of the signs since further qualities are hardly achievable within so short a span of time.

Analysis of the Profile

First the profile has to be considered in its over all structure: that is, the weight of every component has to be examined in regard to the weight of all and every other one. As mentioned earlier, the specific meaning of a given component, for example, the outgoing pole of Emotion, is dependent upon the importance of the opposed, seclusive pole. It is also affected by the structure of Imagination, since the outgoingness of a person with strong creative imagination differs from that of a person giving no evidence of creativity. The same is true of the relative weight of the scores for Intellect. A profile showing a good deal of practical intellect allows diagnosis of a sounder kind of outgoingness than a profile showing a deep dip at this point. Likewise the combination of outgoingness with a strongly controlled Activity will be significantly different from one where dynamism is predominant.

After this intercomparison of the components in their over-all value comes the main part of the process of individualization. It consists of an analysis of the total score obtained by each component of the profile in terms of the nature and intensity of the criteria involved, followed by their translation into diagnostic terms and ending with a particular synthesis representing the closest approach to personality made possible by this test.

A total score may be made up in very different ways. It may be the sum of the scores of all the criteria correlated with a given component, and the contribution of each of these scores may be about equal or may differ considerably, or the total score may be made up by only one or two criteria with no or only a negligible contribution from the other criteria. Such marked differences in the composition of the total scores are significant even from a merely structural angle. Their chief importance lies, however, in the kind of criteria involved, for this aspect of the data forms the very basis from which the specific meaning of *outgoingness, seclusiveness, dynamism,* etc., is derived in the particular case. This quantitative-qualitative operation is carried out mainly on the basis of the scoring sheet, yet must be done with continuous reference to the drawings so that their particular modalites be duly taken into account.

Stimulus-Drawing Relation and Order of Execution

The main elements for interpreting the stimulus-drawing relation have been indicated in an earlier section (pages 35–41). In spite of the importance of this part of the diagnostic mechanism, it will not be given further attention here, since the rather elaborate illustration of this point appearing in Part II (pages 146–148) may be considered a sufficient complement.

As for the diagnostic indexes derived from the order of execution of the drawings, they represent only a secondary source of data, often showing a striking coincidence with the main trends contained in the total product but on the whole not as valid or reliable as the stimulus-drawing relation.

The following characteristics of the order of execution have been proved to be particularly worthy of attention.

a. Marked preference for either the masculine or the feminine stimuli as expressed through the subject starting the series by these stimuli and completing three or all of them in immediate succession.

b. Contradiction between the order of execution and the stimulus-drawing relation, the former showing a preference for one group of stimuli, the latter for the opposed group.

c. Objective order of execution, that is, according to the order of succession of the squares. Such a way of dealing with the opportunity for choosing may represent a systematic, matter-of-fact, self-certain and mature approach, or it may point to a lack of affectivity, depending upon the constellation of diagnostic indexes and the sex of the subject.

d. Scattered order of execution, showing alternate completion of masculine and feminine stimuli. This order points to either versatility or inconsistency, dependent upon the context of data.

e. Starting the series with stimulus 5, the conflicting structure of which is commonly regarded as difficult to deal with. This characteristic of the performance is generally unfavorable, suggesing a somewhat negatively oriented make-up or an affinity for problem situations. Noteworthy is the fact that no woman in the group examined started the series with this stimulus. Even early completion of it, that is, within the first three drawings, occurred seldom among either men or women.

f. Starting the series with sign 7, also a most unusual procedure, especially with men, who generally consider this stimulus as the least appealing and the most difficult to complete. Women, on the other hand, show no particular difficulty with it; yet, only 1 per cent chose it as a starting point.

Absent Criteria

Examination of these criteria may be part of the analysis of the profile or a separate operation. In the first case, the absent criteria are considered in the order of their succession within the groups of criteria appearing on the *interpretation* blank, and the significance of these absences is directly integrated in the conclusions derived from the analysis of the profile. In the second case the *scoring* blank is used and inspected for spaces left open, especially at the level of important criteria such as Animate Nature or Objects, whose absence immediately commands watchfulness in further examination of the material. Other criteria on whose absence it is important to be informed from the outset are Emptiness, Constriction, Phantasm, Parts, Scribbles, Duplication, Repetition and Schematism. Open spaces at the level of these criteria remove provisionally all grounds for serious concern. Thus by a glance at certain points of the scoring sheet a foundation is provided upon which the more subtle elements of individualization can be brought out more significantly.

Nonscored Criteria

These criteria are: Form level, Reinforcement, texture and function of the Shading, Wholes, Context-Isolation, Clarity-Vagueness and Popularity. Several of these criteria have usually received consideration before the present phase is reached either because they are closely related to other criteria or because they must be taken into account in regard to earlier phases of the interpretation. Among these criteria are Form level, which is examined at the outset in regard to the subject's occupation or in regard to the length of the performance; Reinforcement, which is almost inseparable from the other aspects of the lines; Popularity, which is implicitly considered in its counterpart Originality, etc. However, the interpretation of test material being one of studying gradually broadening constellations of indexes repeated examination of certain elements is integral part of the process.

Particularities

These personal, often inconspicuous, touches are to be regarded as a secondary source of information, no objective basis for their interpretation being available. Yet, their contribution may be particularly valuable because of their highly individual character, capable sometimes of underscoring certain diagnostic trends, differentiating complex points or removing ambiguity.

Effective integration of these details in the total diagnostic picture is a function of the examiner's general knowledge of expression phenomena, of his experience with the particular text, and of his intuitive skill in the handling of symbols.

Bibliography

1. Abel, T. M.: Free design of limited scope as a personality index. Character & Personal. *7:* 50, 1938.

2. Anastasi, A., and Foley, J. P.: A survey of the literature on artistic behavior in the abnormal.
   I. Historical and theoretical background. J. Genet. Psychol. *25:* 111, 1941.
   II. Approaches and interrelationships. Ann. N. Y. Acad. Sc. *42:* 1, 1941.
   III. Spontaneous productions. Psychol. Monogr. *52:* No. 6, 1940.
   IV. Experimental investigations. J. Genet Psychol. *25:* 187, 1941.

3. —: An experimental study of the drawing behavior of adult psychotics in comparison with that of a normal control group. J. Exp. Psychol. *34:* 169, 1944.

4. Arundel, R. M.: Everybody's Pixillated: A Book on Doodles. Boston, Little, Brown and Co., 1937.

5. Bender, L.: A visual motor gestalt test and its clinical use. Res. Monogr. Am. Orthopsychiat. A. No. 3, 1938.

6. —: Gestalt principles in the side-walk drawings and games of children. J. Genet. Psychol. *41:* 192, 1932.

7. Berger, E.: Der Sandersche Phantasietest im Rahmen der psychologischen Eignungsuntersuchung. Arch. ges. Psychol. *103:* 499, 1939.

8. Birzele, K.: Das Reproduzieren von Bildgestalten als Hilfsmittel zur Charakterbestimmung. Indust. Psychotech. *15:* 65, 1938.

9. Bonisch, R.: Uber den Zusammenhang seelischer Teilstrukturen. Neue psychol. Stud. *15:* No. 1, 1939.

10. Buck, J. N.: The H-T-P Test. J. Clin. Psychol. *4:* 151, 1948.

11. —: The H.T.P. Technique; a qualitative and quantitative scoring manual. J. Clin. Psychol. *4:* 317, 1948; *5:* 37, 1949.

12. Cameron N.: Functional immaturity in the symbolisation of trained adults. J. Psychol. *6:* 161, 1938.

13. De Vletter, W.: Het Medaillon. Assen, Van Gorcum en Comp. N. V., 1942.

14. Elkisch, P.: Children's drawings in a projective technique. Psychol. Monogr. *58:* No. 1, 1945.

15. Fischer, G. H.: Ausdruck und Persönlichkeit. Leipzig, J. A. Barth, 1934.

16. Goodenough, F. L.: Measurement of Intelligence by Drawings. Yonkers, World Book, 1926.

133

17. Harms, E.: Kinderkunst als diagnostisches Hilfsmittel bei infantilen Neurosen. Z. Kinder-psychiat. 6: 129, 1940.

18. —: The psychology of formal creativeness. I. Six fundamental types of formal expression. J. Genet. Psychol. 69: 97, 1946.

19. Hellersberg, E. F.: The Horn-Hellersberg test and adjustment to reality. Am. J. Orthopsychiat. 15: 690, 1945.

20. Hippius, M. T.: Graphischer Ausdruck von Gefühlen. Ztschr. ang. Psychol. 51: 257, 1936.

21. Hutter, A.: Het wereldbeeld der Schizophrenen en hun Kunst. Nederl. Tijdschr. v. Geneesk. 78: 1306, 1934.

22. Ihms, M.: Charakterologische Untersuchungen an strafgefangenen Frauen. Ztschr. ang. Psychol. 56: 129, 1939.

23. Kerr, M.: Children's drawings of houses. Brit. J. M. Psychol. 16: 206, 1937.

24. Kienzle, R.: Das bildhafte Gestalten als Ausdruck der Persönlichkeit. Esslingen, Burgbücherei, 1932.

25. Klages, L.: Ausdrucksbewegung und Gestaltungskraft. Leipzig, J. A. Barth, 1923.

26. Kohlmann, Th.: Psychologische Untersuchungen mit Rorschach und Wartegg Versuch an Psychosen in der Electroschockbehandlung. Wiener Ztschr. f. Nervenheilkunde. 1: 382, 1948.

27. Krauss, R.: Ueber graphischen Ausdruck. Ztschr. Psychol. Beiheft 48, 1930.

28. Krout, J.: Symbol elaboration test (S.E.T.): the reliability and validity of a new projective technique. Psychol. Monogr. 64: No. 4, 1950.

29. Krueger, F.: Ueber psychische Ganzheit. Neue psychol. Stud., 1: 1, 1926.

30. —: Das Wesen der Gefühle. Leipzig, J. A. Barth, 1930.

31. —: Der strukturelle Grund des Fühlens und des Wollens. Ber. 15. Kongr. dtsch. Ges. Psychol. pp. 181-189, 1937.

32. Kurbitz, W.: Die Zeichnungen geisteskranker Personen. Ztschr. ges. Neur. u. Psy. 13: 153, 1912.

33. Lamparter, H.: Typische Formen bildhafter Gestalten. Ztschr. Psy. und Physiol. der Sinnesorgane Ergänzbuch 22: 217, 1932.

34. Lewis, N. D. C.: Graphic art productions in schizophrenia. A Proc. Res. Nerv. & Ment. Dis., 1925. 5: 344, 1928.

35. Lembke, W.: Ueber Zeichnungen von "frechen" und "schüchternen" Schulkindern. Ztschr. päd. Psychol. 31: 459, 1930.

36. Machover, K.: Personality Projection in the Drawing of the Human Figure. Springfield, Charles C Thomas, 1949.

37. Muller-Freienfells, R.: Charakter und Erlebnis. Jahrb. Char. 2-3: 21, 1926.

38. Naumburg, M.: Studies of the "free" art expression of behavior problem children and adolescents as a means of diagnosis and therapy. Nerv. Ment. Dis. Monogr. No. 71, 1947.

39. Pickford, R. W.: Some interpretations of a painting called "abstraction." Brit. J. M. Psychol. 18: 219, 1939.

40. Prinzhorn, H.: Bildnerei der Geisteskranken. Berlin, Springer, 1922.

41. Prudhommeau, M.: Le dessin chez l'enfant. Paris, Presses Universitaires, 1947.

42. Rupp, H.: Raumliche Klarheit und Intelligenz. Ber. uber d. 11. Kongr. exper. Psychol. pp. 132-134, 1930.

43. Sander, F.: Experimentelle Ergebnisse der Gestaltpsychologie. Ber. uber d. 10. Kongr. exper. Psychol. pp. 23-88, 1928.

44. —: Funktionale Struktur, Erlebnisganzheit und Gestalt. Arch. ges. Psychol. *85:* 237, 1932.

45. —: Gestaltpsychologie und Kunsttheorie. Neue psychol. Studien. *4:* 319, 1932.

46. —: Zur neuen Gefühlslehre. Ber. über d. 15. Kongr. dtsch. Ges. Psychol. pp. 23-52, 1937.

47. Schadeberg, W.: Ueber den Einstellungscharakter komplexer Erlebnisse. Neue psychol. Studien. *10:* No. 4, 1934.

48. Vetter, A.: Diagnostische Erfolgungen mit dem Warteggtest. Grenzgebiete der Medizin. *1:* 241, 1948.

49. Volkelt, H.: Ganzheit und Struktur: Grundbegriffe. Neue psychol. Studien *12:* 1, 1934.

50. Waehner, T. S.: Formal criteria in children's drawings and paintings. Am. J. Orthopsychiat. *12:* 95, 1942.

51. —: Interpretation of spontaneous drawings and paintings. Genet. Psychol. Monogr. *33:* 3, 1946.

52. Wachter, P.: Ueber den Zusammenhang der typischen Formen des Gestalterlebens mit den temperamentskreisen Kretschmers. Arch. ges. Psychol. *104:* 1, 1939.

53. Wartegg, E.: Gefühl. Neue psychol. Studien *12:* 99, 1934.

54. —: Gefühl und Phantasiebield. Industr. Psychotechn. *13:* 251, 1936.

55. —: Gefühl und Phantasiebield. Ber. über d.15. Kongr. dtsch. Ges. Psychol. *15:* 70, 1937.

56. —: Gestaltung und Charakter. Ztschr. ang. Psychol. Beiheft 84, 1939.

57. Wellek, A.: Typus und Struktur. Arch. ges. Psychol. *100:* 465, 1938.

58. Zierer, E.: Dynamics and diagnostic value of creative therapy; the body-space test. Acta. med. orient. *9:* 35, 1950.

Part Three: Discussion of Cases

SUBJECT A, male, 21 years, student in chemistry, excellent academic achievements. No training in art.

Significance of the Drawings

1. Flower.
2. Seagull over ocean.
3. Speedy train.
4. Cloister hall.
5. House in the mountains.
6. Old book.
7. Caterpillar on a branch.
8. Fish.

Order of Execution: Regular (in the sequence of the stimuli). Drawing Time: 65 minutes.

Discussion

Profile

The over-all appearance of the profile is favorable. All functions are represented and cover a broad area of the scale, suggesting rich potentialities, versatility and a relatively even, gap-free development. There is no sharp opposition of peaks and dips, and no disquieting predominance of any one component over the others. (As explained earlier, a certain predominance of Activity is usual within this test; the degree of predominance shown here is positive for a young male, especially when Dynamism outweighs Control to about the extent appearing here.) However, in view of the heavy weight of Dynamism, of Emotion and of Imagination, a Control as strongly developed as revealed by this profile seems to require considerable effort, and allows the assumption that A experiences a good deal of tension.

The degree of Emotion and Imagination exhibited here is exceptional for a male, though admissible at the age level of A. In itself such strong development of these functions arouses suspicion regarding A's contact with reality and his capacity for adjustment. However, in the total configuration of his profile it is not immediately indicative of deficiency or disturbance. In view of (1) the approximate balance between the two poles of Emotion; (2) the slight predominance of Combinative Imagination over Creative; (3) the well-balanced and strongly developed Intellect; and (4) the weight of Control, a well-integrated personality may tentatively be assumed.

The very broad covering of the scale is not a sign of maturity. However, in view of A's youth, this characteristic is favorable and bespeaks a rich general

139

endowment. Its occurrence with a male subject reveals a need for expression generally found in individuals still in the process of maturation, though sometimes also in the neurotically inclined.

Analysis of the Profile

Emotion. The composition of the total scores for this function is satisfactory. The Outgoing pole encompasses the full range of variables. Examination of the drawings reveals, however, that the score for Animate Nature refers exclusively to animals. Absence of human figures is always significant; when it occurs within an entirely representational set, proving the subject's ability to express himself by means of drawings, such absence justifies suspicion concerning the state of the subject's relationships with people.

Further examination of the variables making up the score for the Outgoing pole shows a very weak score for Casualness. In itself this is no negative indication; it suggests that A is not the easy-going lighthearted type but that he takes things seriously, although he is nowise inclined towards rigidity. The latter assumption is based on the rather large amount of Curves, for a man, and rather small amount of Straight lines, which suggest flexibility and capacity for emotional identification.

Another variable worth considering is Expansion, which shows a rather strong weight for a male. This variable gains more significance when interpreted with regard to certain characteristics of the Seclusive group of variables. Immediately reassuring in this group is the absence of Parts, Scribblings and Schematism, suggesting that A is free from serious disturbance. The Seclusive aspect of A's emotionality is made up exclusively of *primary* indicators of emotionality, that is, Inanimate Nature, Atmosphere, Softness and Shading (the secondary indicators being Symmetrical, and Asymmetrical Abstraction). When occurring in the drawings of a male, the high scores for Inanimate Nature and Atmosphere call for special attention. These variables, together with Expansion, reveal markedly sentimental-idealistic leanings. Whether these leanings have a positive, enhancing value, or correspond to romanticism, daydreaming or reality-estranged idealism must be made out on the basis of (1) the indexes of realism and rational-volitional functioning (especially Objects, Details, Organization, Straightness, Carefulness); (2) the qualitative aspects of Atmosphere. Examination of (1) allows favorable presumptions, every one of these variables being satisfactorily represented. As for (2), the quality of the Atmosphere here depicted, it is on the whole sound, broad, restful, harmonious, not too emotion-loaded, not somber or depressing, though not cheerful, not abandoned, yet lonely (in d. 4 "Cloister" there is a slightly spiritualistic and austere connotation.) From these indications it appears that the aforementioned combination of emotion indexes (Inanimate Nature, Atmosphere, Expansion) may be considered as expressing a desire for expansion, for contemplation and a deep feeling of participation with the universe at large (see in this respect the large variety of Nature: animals, trees, flowers, foliage, mountains, water, skies, clouds, sunrays). In view of this diversity of nature-phenomena, the absence of human figures becomes even more conspicuous and takes on increased significance. The absence of Abstraction, both Symmetrical and Asymmetrical, accentuates the life-relatedness of A's emotions; these variables are, indeed, representative of affectivity diluted by either intellectual or spiritual tendencies, and sometimes indicative of a neurotically inclined emotionality.

In regard to the Seclusive pole, only Shading remains to be examined, in itself and in relation to the other variables. The variety of Shading used here covers the full scale of intensities with the exception of the diagnostically unfavorable Black Shading. Such a variety reveals a particularly rich, deep and versatile emotional sensibility, ranging from ardor and enthusiasm to the most delicate sensitivity. In the present context of indexes, the absence of Black Shading shows that A's emotionality, though strong, is neither vehement nor primitively heavy. The occurrence of Dark Shading in these drawings bespeaks a passionate nature, not one of sensuous drive and aggressiveness, but, in view of the given context of indexes, rather an eager and colorful one. The rich intensity-variation of the shading, together with its abundance and the kind of Nature items featured (small, smoothly moving animals, flowers, skies, water) reveal a great capacity for love, tenderness and understanding—which makes the absence of human figures appear even more striking.

The texture of the Shading is neither smooth and indicative of dreaminess as with subject O, nor strictly rectilinear, revealing compulsiveness and rigidity as with C, nor scrawled, expressive of overt aggressiveness and disturbance as in set R. In most of A's drawings, the texture of shading is slightly casual as in d. 2, tending to show a rectilinear pattern as in d. 7, and actually becoming rectilinear in d. 6. Such a texture has a rational-volitional value which counterbalances favorably the strength and all-pervading character of A's emotionality, without, however, overflowing into compulsive control.

The function of A's Shading is, on the whole, appropriate although it is predominantly esthetic, that is, not required by the necessity to bring out the material consistency or the three-dimensional character of the objects featured. Remarkable, in regard to the function of the shading in A's drawings, is the fact that in d. 6 it is used, not to represent the concreteness and tangibility of the book, but to enhance the book, to illuminate it, as it were, by means of a sharply-contrasting background. Likewise, in d. 3, it is used, not for accentuating the heavy smoke puffing from the engine, as it is usually, but for picturing

a cloud, sunrays and a delicately sketched sky. Such use, though quite acceptable from an esthetic point of view, bears a very personal accent and supports
the assumption concerning the somewhat earth-detached character of A's
emotionality.

In spite of the favorable conclusions suggested by the various aspects of
A's Shading, it remains a fact that abundant shading is a sign either of emotional
problems or of a proneness to such problems. In A's case, the hypothesis concerning an actual state of problems with accompanying consciously experienced
disturbance, is not likely to be confirmed. His drawings show no signs of
hostility or overt aggressiveness. Acute anxiety or conflict must also be discarded
it seems, considering the combination of Inanimate Nature, Atmosphere, Expansion, Curves, Consistency in the Execution, and general harmony of the content.
However, some support is found for the hypothesis concerning the existence of
an unconscious or faintly conscious problem, not actually felt as disturbing but
determining certain aspects of A's emotional state. In relation to this hypothesis,
the absence of human figures immediately comes to mind. Moreover, the occurrence of Expansion and Atmosphere suggests that the abundancy of shading
expresses a deep melancholic trend which may be tied up with some negative
experience in the sphere of human relations.

Another element, unimpressive in itself but likely to acquire some meaning
in the present context, is A's particular way of distributing the shading. This
distribution shows a constant need to produce contrasts of light and dark, to
divide every petal of the flower in d. 1 and every leaf in d. 7 into a clear and
a dark half, etc. This way of handling Shading, a prominent indicator of emotionality, may have some directly expressive value, pointing to a deep state of
conflict. More support for this hypothesis will emerge as the discussion proceeds.
However, further examination of the material is necessary to permit a choice
between these hypotheses.

Imagination. The total score for the Combinative aspect of this function
is made up almost entirely by Organization. This variable represents the intellectual component of the group; therefore, its strong predominance is particularly favorable in view of A's markedly emotional makeup. The presence of
Style within this group also strikes a favorable note, since Style expresses a blend
of intellect and emotion. The absence of Ornaments is auspicious too, for, when
occurring with males, this variable suggests a certain mediocrity or inadequacy
of interests and aspirations. Likewise, the absence of Symmetrical Abstraction must be appreciated since its presence generally reflects a flat, uninspired
form of imagination.

The Creative aspect of A's imagination also has a largely intellectual composition, as appears from the significant weight of the score for Originality. The

latter, together with the earlier discussed Expansion, form a combination which suggests that A's creative thinking is oriented toward vast projects, extending far beyond his immediate needs and interests. The absence of Fancy and Phantasm underscores the realistic and sound character of A's imagination; about the same can be said of the absence of Asymmetrical Abstraction, since this variable suggests that the personality is governed chiefly by unconscious impulses. Moreover, the absence of both Symmetrical and Asymmetrical Abstractions shows that A is neither conventional nor unconventional but, considering the total picture of indexes, that he is healthily personal.

The earlier examined weight of Dark Shading suggests that A's creative imagination is fostered by a strong vital impulse. This allows the assumption that the creative ability exhibited in his drawings is not due to an inspiration of the moment or to a passing effort, but is inherent in his basic makeup and offers, therefore, a promise for consistent lasting productivity. Support for this assumption is found in the marked predominance of the intellectual indexes in A's imagination. Such a composition presents greater chances for consistency than a predominantly emotional set of variables, such as Physiognomy, Ornaments, Fantasy and Asymmetry.

To summarize, examination of A's imagination shows that, far from representing a threat to his reality functioning, as occurs frequently when imagination (especially its creative aspect) is strongly developed, its significance is thoroughly positive, enhancing his sensibility and fostering his activity.

Intellect. The composition of the scores for this function indicate a superior level of analytic synthesizing intelligence (see proportions of Organization and Detail), of a predominantly speculative kind (strong weight of superior three-dimensional Organization), yet satisfactorily realistic (comparatively large amount of Detail), but not oriented towards material reality (low score for Objects). The latter indication reinforces the earlier inference concerning A's earth-detached attitude and so does the kind of Objects featured. Indeed d. 4, the "Cloister," and d. 6, the old book, do not evidence specifically material interest; as for the telephone poles and engine of d. 3, their commonplace character is considerably weakened by their atmospheric context. The quality of three-dimensional Organization is unusually high and evidences a superior logical capacity, but suggests also a tendency toward top achievements. The Detail variable speaks thoroughly in favor of A's intellectual makeup and functioning, indicating that, despite his predominantly speculative orientation, he is not indifferent to concrete reality or unable to deal with it. The amount of Detail featured gives evidence of sharp perception, keen attention and a capacity to visualize which are valuable assets for organizational-constructive functioning of the mind. The thoroughly adequate use of Detail suggests common sense;

its amount reveals that A, though perfectly able to recognize what is essential, is unable to stick to cold, strict essentials but feels a need to express himself with nuances.

Slightly unusual for a male is the fact that Technical Abstraction is not represented among the indexes of Intellect. This, however, does not detract from A's intellectual value, for Technical designs are primarily expressions of a rationalistic orientation of the personality, not of intellectual capacity. The absence of Technicals contains a hint of the qualitative nature of A's intellect. In the present configuration of functions, with the predominance of emotion, imagination and speculativeness, absence of Technicals suggests that A's intellect is not of a mechanical but rather of an intuitive nature. Furthermore, considering the relatively low score for Objects, for a male, it may be inferred that this intuitive kind of intelligence has a somewhat metaphysical orientation. This does not imply that A's contact with reality is suffering from such an orientation. Such supposition is contradicted by the exclusively representational character of his drawings, the variety of the content, the amount of Detail, the number of Populars, which all point to keen observation and genuine identification with the surrounding world.

Activity. Analysis of the scores for Dynamism reveals the existence of a strong vitality (Fullness, Strong Pressure, Darkness) of an ardent and even impetuous kind. These variables combined with Animate Nature and Curves suggest that A has a positive attitude toward life and a genuine capacity to enjoy it. The combination of Strong Lines and Dark Shading with Originality and Movement indicates an enterprising, enthusiastic, productive personality, moved by a spontaneous urge for self-development and expansion. The high score for Movement suggests that A's drive is of a lively, articulate, mobile kind. Various kinds of Movement are represented: cosmic, mechanical and animate. The slight manifestations of cosmic Movement (d. 2, rolling waves, d. 3, sun-rays) have a mild accent. Mechanical action is scant for a male, appearing only in drawing 1, which supports the aforementioned assumption that A's intellect, despite its superior capacities, is not typically masculine. Animate activity is predominant, both in amount and in intensity (d. 2, 7 and 8).

It is expressed through the medium of animals, but this does not necessarily diminish the projective, "self-portrait" value of these drawings. The kind of Movement featured, is, by the very nature of these animals, smooth and flexible, although in d. 2 it is also vigorous. The particularly skillfully conceived picture of the fish in 8 is noteworthy for its interesting, rather elegant, but somewhat contorted posture. *If* the symbolism of such aspects of drawings is valid, it may be assumed that A, though succeeding in what he proposes to achieve, is not without experiencing discomfort in doing so. Something like effort and achievement but also like tension seems to be expressed too by the somewhat fierce expression and the strong, sharply marked features of the bird in d. 2. These elements of free interpretation, while insignificant in themselves, fit with the total picture of a forceful individual, eager for achievement and quality and consequently obliged to make strenuous efforts. The other variables, making up the dynamic pole of Activity, reinforce the conclusions drawn earlier from the general aspect of the profile.

The Control pole presents a constellation of variables entirely void of disquieting signs (such as Constriction, Emptiness, Repetition, Duplication) which suggests that A's control corresponds to purposeful firmness and endurance rather than to inhibition or perseveration. The combination of Strong Lines with high Form level (a nonscored variable) points to efficiency, decisiveness and self-assurance. However, when the Form level is particularly high (and it may, in this case, be considered as such in view of the fact that no eraser was used), and when the total product shows great Carefulness, a tendency toward overcontrol may be suspected. This supposition ties in with the earlier expressed assumption concerning a somewhat high-strung control. However, considering the moderate score for Straight Lines, the fluency of the Curves, the delicacy of certain lines and the touches of Subtle Shading, the control exerted by A appears to be neither rigid nor compulsive but rather to represent a strong lead for a strong impetus. The effectiveness of A's control appears also from the perfect quality of the long straight lines in d. 4 which suggests firmness, consistency and tenacity. The particularly strong weight of Carefulness shows that A sets himself high standards of achievement; considering A's youth, this Carefulness is entirely commendable.

A slightly puzzling element in the variable composition of the Control pole is the occurrence of Closure. This variable appears here only in d. 1, which presents firm encircling of the group of dots added to the stimulus. Closure seldom occurs with great frequency and as little as one instance therefore calls for attention, especially when it is fairly pronounced (the intensity of pressure with which the circle is drawn is, indeed, almost excessive). The hypothesis concerning inner insecurity and lack of inner freedom, sometimes confirmed in cases of Closure, is not plausible in this case considering the indexes already discussed and those still following. Another explanation, pointing toward the existence of a depth problem about which the individual is not fully aware or consciously concerned, is more likely to be adequate, for it meets with one of the hypotheses formulated about the lack of human figures. However, this coincidence does not permit a final conclusion, the specific meaning of Closure not being sufficiently well known and the amount of Closure here exhibited not offering a strong enough basis.

Nonscored Criteria

Basically in favor of inner integration, of sound contact with reality and adjustment, is the fact that A produces exclusively representational content, all of which pertains to the Reality category and includes both Nature and Objects. The Variety of topics also points in the same direction and bespeaks, moreover, great mental mobility, versatility of interests and emotional outgoingness. The appearance of several Populars (d. 1, 2, 3) emphasizes A's basic adjustment and common sense. The fact that none of these Populars are of the banal flat kind, together with the number and the quality of the Originals, suggests that A, while capable of feeling and acting on an everyday level, strives and belongs, nevertheless, to a higher plane.

The fact that all the drawings are Wholes and that all feature Context underscores A's need for harmony, unity and association. These variables support the hypothesis that the absence of human figures does not signify a break between A and humanity at large, but is due either to a conflict with one or a few persons of great emotional significance to A, or to a strong sublimation of vital tendencies.

The remarkable Continuity of the Lines suggests that A's strong control has a physiological component, namely a state of neuromuscular relaxation and steadiness, and an excellent psychomotor coordination. These assets are likely to lower the tension involved in the control of as lively and dynamic a nature as A's and to allow him to be fairly spontaneous and straightforward while remaining smooth and pleasant.

The perfect Consistency of Line and Covering emphasizes the earlier encountered indexes of stability, equality of mood and consistency of behavior. These indexes, together with the strongly emphasized Carefulness, allow the conclusion that A is a thoroughly reliable and (considering the aforementioned variables, plus Expansiveness, Fullness and Inanimate Nature) a sincere person.

The specific, qualitative aspect of Atmosphere has been given due consideration in the preceding discussion. A's drawings do not contain many Physiognomic indexes. The bird in d. 2 is the only item carrying some physiognomic expression. With its broadly spread, uplifted wings, particularly strong and large beak, and sharp eye, this bird expresses something like effort, strength, wilfulness, fierceness and almost aggressiveness, which fits in perfectly with the total picture—save for the aggressiveness. The latter trait is, however, not quite without support and is to be retained for examination with the earlier mentioned negative indexes. From their mutual comparison and combination, more insight in the dynamics of A's personality is likely to be gained.

Particularities

An inconspicuous, but very unusual, detail in A's drawings is the tiny V-shaped bird, all alone in the broad sky of drawing 3. Such birds form an almost inseparable element of the conventional landscape or seascape, but they almost always appear in groups of two, three, or a flock. Considering the vastness of the seaview, with the faraway ship, depicted in d. 2, the solitude of the "Cloister" and especially the total absence of humans, it may be inferred that the tiny, lonely bird in d. 3 possesses self-projective value and is an expression of deep loneliness (A happens to be known as homeless and somewhat drifting by himself). In relation to this assumption, the abundant Shading may express a melancholy feeling deep underneath A's adjustment.

Another unusual detail is the cloud in the upper left corner of d. 3 veiling the sun, and the sunrays coming out from behind it. Such elements can only be interpreted in the light of a broad, intuitively handled symbolism. However, it can hardly be called far-fetched in the present context of indexes (especially absence of humans) to consider the possibility that such a detail may reveal a glimpse of A's problem: deprivation of a direct outlet for the source of affection which he carries in him.

Stimulus-Drawing Relation

Stimulus 1 is recognized in its round, small, organic and central qualities, which bespeaks the versatile character of A's sensibility. Affinity for the organic character of the stimulus prevails. Its centrality, although perfectly acknowledged, is not emphasized (as it is, for instance in sets D or E). This might suggest that A, because of his versatility, tends not to concentrate sufficiently on what he recognizes as central or essential. This hypothesis, while justifiable in other cases, does not encounter support from any side in the present context of indexes. On the contrary, most indexes point to purposeful activity, decisiveness and consistency. Rather, the lack of emphasis on the central quality of the stimulus—which is its geometric logical quality—is linked to the repeatedly mentioned remark about A's intelligence which, despite its superior logical-practical capacity, seems to be of a predominantly intuitive nature.

The free-floating character of the stimulus—which is, indeed, far less pronounced than its other qualities—is not recognized. On the contrary, the stimulus is integrated into a firm structure of similar elements where it loses its individuality. Such incorporation tends to indicate a capacity to associate closely and on a level of equality, at least within limited groups. A touch of free interpretation concerning this particular use of the stimulus may be appropriate here. According to the symbolism generally applied in interpreting projective material, it seems as if S, rather than wanting to stand out, prefers to be identified with a group of firmly united (see strongly drawn circle around dots), equal and related (stamina of the same flower) individuals. (This interpretation fits, apparently, in the present case since A comes from a broken home.) The affinity for the smallness of the stimulus, denotes, furthermore, great sensitivity and a sense of detail.

The kind of object into into which this stimulus is worked, the broadly spread, regularly and decoratively shaped flower, points to expansiveness, gentleness and charm of an almost feminine nature. However, the particularly strong pressure denies effeminacy.

Stimulus 2. The organic and dynamic qualities of this stimulus receive perfect treatment, which indicates a life-related sensibility, flexibility, alertness and activity. The position of the stimulus within the square is remarkably well used also, evidencing organizational capacity. The dimensions, the activity and the forceful execution of the big sea gull express unusual strength and willfulness. However, the background of a vast sea view and faraway ship with waving line of smoke lends a markedly emotional, somewhat dreamy connotation to the total picture and weakens the vigor of the chief element.

Stimulus 3. The mechanical-constructive qualities of straightness, firmness, and progressive increase are well recognized, pointing to technical-constructive abilities. The upward-directed quality of the stimulus is, however, not acknowledged, which suggests a somewhat reduced ambition and aggressiveness. The masculine character of the drawing (especially the engine; not so much the telephone poles, which are a common response of females as well) is considerably weakened by the context of a broad, deep sky with extremely delicate sunrays. This element adds to the already mentioned supposition about A's metaphysically oriented aspirations.

Stimulus 4. The square form and the localization of the stimulus are most adequately utilized in this perspective of a long hall. Its constructive and static qualities are perfectly acknowledged which, together with the remarkable organization in three dimensions, bespeaks again logical-technical capacity, consistency and stability. The dark quality is also recognized and is used in a logical way, not in an emotional manner as, for instance, in K/4 or L/4—which weakens the earlier formulated hypothesis about anxiety.

Affinity for stimulus 4 often reveals interest in material reality and a matter-of-fact outlook. Indexes of the latter quality are rather scant in this record, but they do exist. The hypothesis concerning interest in material reality does, however, not encounter any support within the record. Moreover, the object into which stimulus 4 is worked ("Cloister"), while being entirely material, has an esthetic-religious accent that weakens the aforementioned hypothesis.

Stimulus 5. This stimulus is recognized in its mechanical-constructive quality but not in its dynamic implications which shows, once more, that A has great logical-constructive ability but is somewhat lacking in aggressiveness and ambition. Remarkable, again, is the fact that he has worked the conflicting structure of stimulus 5 into a harmonious, restful, somewhat romantic picture suggesting a gentle, conciliating, somewhat feminine makeup and, perhaps, a tendency to dilute the purposefulness of his activity by his emotional-esthetic leanings.

Stimulus 6. The straight and mechanical character of this stimulus, which calls for construction into a consistent object, receives excellent treatment in this three-dimensional, sober, well balanced drawing providing one more indication of A's organizational-constructive abilities. However, the unemotional, commonplace, strictly mechanical character of stimulus 6 disappears in the highly esthetic composition which again reveals A's fundamental emotional-esthetic tendencies.

Stimulus 7. Both the finely structured and the organic quality of the stimulus are brought out with outstanding skill in this original drawing. This emphasizes once more the intimate blend of A's intellectual and emotional functions, composed of differentiated perception, sharp attention, analytic-synthesizing capacities on the one hand, and affinity for living nature, smoothness and flexibility on the other.

Such remarkably successful dealing with small and complex material as stimulus 7 reveals, however, a degree of sensitivity and a concern for details which borders upon meticulousness. The stamp of A's constant need for harmony and beauty appears this time in the context of gracefully bent, decoratively shaded leaves.

Stimulus 8. The simple, broad and regular shape of this stimulus, inviting an easy and simple solution, receives a surprising treatment in the unusual theme of this drawing. Such a drawing emphasizes A's dislike for easy solutions. He feels, rightfully, able to cope with difficulties, has probably developed a tendency to challenge himself, and thus easily aims at top achievements. The rich evidence of logical-constructive abilities already obtained is once more confirmed by the particularly skillful three-dimensional drawing which, at the same time, underscores A's affinity for the organic, smooth and fluent qualities of the stimulus. The appealing, tastefully chosen elements of context again bear witness to A's deep concern for beauty and his nature-relatedness.

Order of Execution

The methodic sequence in the execution of the drawings introduces a most welcome element in the total picture of A's personality. In the present context of indexes, such conforming to the objective order of succession of the stimuli points to an objective, simple, mature, self-assured manner of approach presenting a favorable counterbalance to the predominantly emotional makeup which emerges from numerous indexes. On the other hand, this order of treatment of the stimuli gives a certain support to the somewhat strict self-discipline and slightly compulsve tendencies transpiring here and there. It is certain that, in view of the remarkable quality of the total product, this regular order of execution shows a capacity for easy and successful dealing with whatever situation comes along.

Drawing Time

In view of the careful, accurate and fairly elaborate execution of the drawings, and especially in view of the fact that no use of the eraser was permitted—which, obviously, required longer planning—the long time of 65 minutes is permissible. With a young person, such as A, this length of time reveals a readiness to make the necessary efforts for the high standards of achievement at which he aims. However, the combined effect of long drawing time, careful execution, high quality of the Originals and extraordinary affinity for stimulus 7, suggests a need for top achievements and perhaps a slight tendency towards perfectionism.

SUBJECT B, male, 24 years of age, single, B.A. in Philosophy. Politically active.

Significance of the Drawings

1. Industrial scene.
2. Microscope plate.
3. Industrial production curve.
4. Design for table cloth.
5. Syringe.
6. Modern building.
7. Footsteps.
8. Mushroom.

Order of Execution: 5, 8, 6, 7, 3, 4, 1, 8.   Drawing Time: 40 minutes.

Discussion

Profile

The covering and configuration of this profile is typical of the adult male personality in which the rational-volitional functions dominate the emotional-imaginative. If Dynamism and Control showed better balance or, preferably, if Dynamism predominated slightly, this subject's profile could be considered, provisionally, representative of the well integrated, adult male.

Analysis of the Profile

Emotion. The quasiabsence of Nature, Animate as well as Inanimate (the mushroom in d. 8 is, indeed, a poor indicator of life-relatedness) accentuates the poverty of B's emotional life and points to a reduced capacity for identification with living objects—or to strong emotional repression, which is more likely to be the case in view of the considerable development of Control appearing in B's profile. Total absence of Casualness is generally indicative of a high-strung, overserious and perfectionistic makeup. The scantness of Curves in B's drawings adds weight to this assumption. There are signs of great sensitivity (touches of extremely weak Pressure); however, considering the configuration of emotion indexes, this points more in the direction of susceptibility than of delicacy of feelings. B's great affinity for the finely structured stimulus 7 and the finical execution of most of his drawings give strong support to the latter assumption.

Imagination. The weight of Organization, which makes up almost the entire score for the Combinative pole, emphasizes B's markedly intellectual orientation. Style and Abstraction are faintly represented. These generally indicate a certain affectivity; however, the angular, rigid and geometric character of both the Style (d. 6) and the Abstraction (d. 4) displayed here can hardly be considered as expressions of emotion, but only of a certain esthetic sensibility.

Intellect. The composition of this function shows a well balanced, practical-theoretical intelligence. Examination of the drawings reveals, however, that the score for Organization refers almost exclusively to two-dimensional Organization, which is not a sign of superior intellectual endowment. The presence of Technical Abstraction of a very simple kind (3) points to the same conclusion (at least when the drawing time is relatively long). The enhancement of this simple drawing by written indications suggests a tendency within B to cover up by apparent achievements for his lack of superior intellectual capacities.

Activity. B appears to have a good deal of vitality (fairly Strong Lines of most of the drawings, Black Shading in d. 4). However, the combination of moderate Covering, predominance of Straight Lines, and especially the overcareful execution of the drawings evidences rigid control. Factors that account for the predominance of control are the subject's markedly intellectual attitude and his tendency to meticulousness, which, together, lead him to analyze his moves and to "label" his inner motives as he labels his drawings (see dd. 2, 3 and 5). Thus he fails to utilize fully the natural drive which he possesses. There are no direct signs of inhibition. The score for Orientation points to ambition but the score for Movement is rather low, suggesting that B's achievements may remain beneath his aspirations. The score for Closure suggests circumspection and perhaps overcautiousness.

Nonscored Criteria

The exclusive Reality content of the drawings (even d. 4 is titled a table cloth) points to sound contact with reality and interest in objective matters. The general sphere of interest expressed in the set is that of work, production, and study, which suggests an investigating and industrious attitude. The quality of the drawings is high, but this appears to be due to good planning and careful execution rather than to natural ease.   The forms are extraordinarily sharp and the composition is clear, which again stresses the intellectual component in B's personality.   The Continuity of the lines appears remarkable on first sight; yet, upon closer examination, it appears to be the result of very skillful Reinforcement.   In the present configuration of symptoms this suggests great capacity to deliberate carefully and to proceed cautiously.   Signs of concern about balance in the drawings are also preceptible; this suggests a certain esthetic sensibility and perhaps a subdued latent affectivity.   The latter inference receives some support from the touch of light Shading in d. 1 and the fineness of execution of d. 7, and from the fact that all the drawings are Wholes and that most of them show a touch of Context.

Particularities

B's drawings exhibit several particularities, which all point in the same direction.   These are, first, the written specifications appearing in dd. 2, 3 and 5, which generally point to a somewhat compulsive need for accuracy; further, the over-detailed, over-carefully represented elements in dd. 2, 7 and 8.   The mushroom in d. 8 is a Popular but is never depicted with the finely featured fringe which it shows here.   Such over-detailing points to a degree of meticulousness and a need to structure that bears a negative connotation.   Another characteristic of B's drawings is their static character, suggesting great rigidity.   The complete lack of casualness, revealing a definite lack of spontaneity, together with the score for Closure complete the picture of a cautious slightly paranoid individual.

Stimulus-Drawing Relation

Except for stimulus 1, which is felt neither in its organic roundness nor in its central quality, the stimuli are all well integrated into matter-of-fact, masculine solutions. However, the dynamic quality of stimulus 5 is not brought out properly, the drawings are on the whole static and the score for Originality is weak. Outstanding Originals are not necessarily indicative of great intellectual capacity. However, when a subject displays great Carefulness and elaborate Detailing, the weakness of his Originals reveals almost certainly that he is not superiorly endowed but is trying to compensate by effort.

Order of Execution

The stimuli are not treated in their objective order of succession.   In the present constellation of indexes, the subjectivity revealed by this irregular order of execution can be explained not by emotional factors, but rather by a certain concern about trivia.   B, quite typically, starts with the conflicting stimulus 5 and ends with the supple stimulus 2.   Special affinity for the difficult stimulus 5 is generally indicative of a like for tackling difficulties, a trait which fits with the implications of the strong weight of Straight Lines.   B's enclosing the moving, lively stimulus 2 is also in agreement with the total picture of a rigid, overcontrolled, unemotional personality. Noteworthy also is the rather early treatment of stimulus 7, which males often dislike because of its extreme fineness. This, again, fits in with the tendency toward complication evidenced by several other indexes.

Drawing-Time

The length of time, 33 minutes, is not excessive considering the particularly careful execution. It is however not representative for a fully mature and adjusted personality for whom a more casual and more rapid manner is regular.

S UBJECT C, male, 25 years old, graduate student of social and political sciences. Excellent academic achievements.

Significance of the Drawings

1. Pencil aimed at a starting point on a sheet of paper.
2. Hitler head, angry and afraid because of the sight of a bomb.
3. Large factory.
4. Wagon of coal in the distance losing coal along the way. Bridge and canal.
5. Flashlight throwing light on revolver and cartridge.
6. Streetcar.
7. Reclining woman with glass of champagne.
8. Man's head.

Order of Execution: 4, 8, 2, 3, 7, 5, 6, 1. Drawing Time: 115 minutes.

Discussion

Profile

The Profile of C and that of A show remarkable similarity. In order to avoid repetition, C will be considered only in regard to the characteristics which differentiate him from A.

The general appearance of C's drawings allows for an even more favorable—tentative—diagnosis than that of A. (1) It is more masculine, owing to the lesser weight of Emotion, plus the stronger weight of Intellect. (2) Because of this structure it suggests less tension in the achievement of Control. (3) The more externally oriented perceptive-reactive functions (Outgoingness, Combinative Imagination, Practical Intellect and Dynamism) show a constant predominance over the more internally oriented speculative-inhibitory functions (Seclusiveness, Creative Imagination, Speculative Intellect and Control), which permits easier and more complete adjustment to life for C than for A.

Analysis of the Profile

Emotion. The most striking feature emerging from the comparison of the indexes of Emotion is the difference in the kind of Animate Nature presented by each subject. Where A has completed signs 2, 7 and 8, into animals, C has worked them into humans. From this it should not be concluded offhand that C has a greater capacity to establish and entertain relationships with people. Such a conclusion must be verified by examination of many other indexes. Several divergent explanations may underlie the absence or presence of human figures.

This difference in Animate Nature entails considerable difference in the kind of Physiognomy. The physiognomic elements contained in C's drawings are the kind that is generally highly self-projective. The military uniform and the expression of anger and tension in drawing 2 indicate tendencies towards self-assertion, domination and irritability. The head in d. 8, slightly bent and wearing glasses as if the person were reading or studying, conveys an impression of concentration. This indication, unimposing in itself and perhaps even ambiguous, acquires significance, however, when combined with the remarkable planning involved in C's drawings, which reveals great capacity for concentration and stresses the intellectual character of his personality. A detail which accentuates the self-portraiting value of d. 8 is the fact that C himself wears glasses and smokes a pipe. The mustache which adorns his human figures is, however, not portraiting C's actual appearance; this facial ornament being most unusual in his group and country. Some cue-value for the understanding of the most unusual occurrence of two mustached heads within the same set of drawings may perhaps be found in the fact that C's stature is rather frail, which, possibly, thwarts his tendency to dominate. When confronted with a projective task he feels unconsciously prompted to make a self-portrait which, by way of wish fulfilment, he idealizes with these symbols of masculinity. The Physiognomic content of d. 7 shows a markedly erotic character. The extraordinary successful representation of this theme may be considered highly symptomatic for C's interest in the opposite sex. Remarkable in this drawing is the fact that the woman is a glamor girl in formal array, not just a sexually appealing type as in set D or some kind and unassuming type of woman. She is the "expensive" sort, likely to appeal to the self-assertive, self-enhancing individual who emerges from the total picture of indexes contained in these drawings.

The fundamental differences between the emotional makeup of C and A is further emphasized by the contrast between the combined scores for Expansion, Inanimate Nature, and Atmosphere obtained by each subject. The total absence of Inanimate Nature in C's drawings, though not necessarily unfavorable or suspect when occurring with a male subject, is surprising in drawings as richly representative and varied as these.   It shows with almost unmistakable certitude that his emotionality is not the same gentle, good natured and romantic kind as A's.

A lesser, though not unimportant, difference appears in the texture of the Shading. In C's drawings 1 and 5 the texture is unique in its strictly parallel straight lines and points to a complete lack of casualness and flexibility. Combined with the extreme intensity of the Shading appearing in d. 3, indicative of excessive vital drive, the rigidity suggested by the texture may be assumed to have a compulsive flavor.

From the indexes examined thus far it appears that, while A's emotionality is of a sensitive, kindhearted, serene and sublimated nature, C's is more passionate, irritable and aggressive.

Imagination. The main difference in this function consists of the presence in C's drawing of more Physiognomy and in A's of more Expansion. These indexes suggest that C's imagination is oriented toward more vital and personally important goals, A's toward more impersonal and broader objectives. The presence of Style in A's drawings agrees with the above-mentioned inference and shows A to be intellectually and emotionally more refined.

Intellect. The differences in this respect appear more clearly from the drawings than from the scores.   They lie mainly in the kind of objects appearing in each set of drawings.   The objects featured by C have a markedly commonplace, technical-industrial character, whereas A's have a somewhat poetic-contemplative connotation (save for d. 3). The fact that the Black Shading appearing in C's drawing is used for representing the factory in d. 3 offers a slight support to the inference concerning C's interest in material reality denoted by several other indexes.

Another sign opposing the more clear, conscious rationalism of C to the esthetic, intuitive leanings of A appears in C's need to number clearly his street-car in d. 6, while A simply suggests the inscription of a title on his book, leaving the onlooker—and perhaps himself—free to imagine the rest.

Activity. In regard to this function the differences are to be found mainly (1) in the relatively heavy weight of Orientation in C's drawings; and (2) in the kind of Movement featured by each subject.

Orientation seldom attains a high score; its occurrence therefore has particular significance. The amount of Orientation found in C's drawings suggests dynamism, audacity and ambition, and gives strong support to the indications of this kind already encountered. Together with the weight of Organization and Originality in C's drawings, Orientation points to great efficiency. However, the combination of high scores for Orientation, Carefulness, Movement and

Strong Lines indicates an almost excessive need for achievement, for excellency and for recognition.

The kind of Movement appearing in each of the sets highlights once more the differences existing between the subjects under comparison. Mechanical Movement is strongly predominant in the drawings of C, while it is almost lacking in those of A. Moreover, two of C's drawings containing Movement imply violence and aggressiveness (2 and 5). The others refer to production and transportation or have an intellectual-technical character (d. 1). This, together with the earlier mentioned characteristics, show that on the whole C has the masculine, aggressive makeup of a business man while A appears more as a humanist.

Nonscored Criteria

The perfect Balance, the presence of Context and the successful decorative use of Shading in most of the drawings of each set reveal great esthetic sensibility. C, however, is not likely to possess real artistic capacities since he is too predominantly rational-practical and too rigid to allow for genuinely artistic inspiration and expression. In the given configuration of indexes C's high score for Originality points to intellectual creativity rather than artistic potentialities.

The remarkable Continuity characterizing A's lines is not found in C's, which suggests that he is more tense and lacks the naturally smooth and pleasant makeup of A. Compared with the other drawings, d. 4 also shows a certain inconsistency in the Covering and in the quality of the Form level. The Inconsistency is slight but its significance ties in with the earlier encountered signs of lesser equanimity on the part of C.

Stimulus-Drawing Relation

A striking difference appears in the treatment given by each subject to stimuli 4 and 5. While C recognizes and emphasizes the dynamic quality of stimulus 5, but makes a rather poor picture out of stimulus 4, A shows the reverse, proving insensitive to the dynamic-conflicting quality of stimulus 5 but remarkably receptive for the stability of stimulus 4. This supports the inference about C's greater drive and ambition and suggests also that he has a preference for complex matters. Indeed, his drawings show, on the whole, better treatment of the complex than of the simple stimuli. Both subjects have great affinity for the finely structured stimulus 7. Viewed in the total context of indexes emerging from C's drawings, this points more to irritability and meticulousness than to delicacy of feelings.

Order of Execution

Whereas males often execute the drawings in the order of succession of the stimuli, thus manifesting a casual and uncomplicated objective attitude, C considers each of the stimuli attentively and deliberates long before acting. This is one more indication of C's need for excellence and of his tendency to take things over-seriously. Very unusual is the fact that a subject starts the series with the stimulus for which he shows least sensitivity (stimulus 4). This may perhaps be related to C's promptness to react to opposition. The early treatment of stimuii 8 and 2 is surprising in the present context, but may be due to the fitness of these stimuli for self-portraiture.

Drawing Time

115 minutes is definitely too long for an adult male and suggests that C's need for top achievement, accuracy and recognition has an almost neurotic character.

SUBJECT E, female, 21 years old, college education; fulfils a supervisory clerical and organizational function in an industrial plant. Very good intelligence.

Significance of the Drawings

1. Straight to the goal.
2. Pagoda.
3. Entrance of the Exposition of Liége, 1939.
4. ". . . he was standing at the second left hand window of the twenty-second floor when suddenly . . ."
5. The tractor my cousin dreams to have.
6. Interior.
7. Border.
8. First flight of Professor Piccard into the stratosphere.

Order of Execution: 8, 6, 4, 5, 2, 1, 3, 7. Drawing Time: 65 minutes.

The earlier discussion of A presented a young man with superior intellectual and general endowment; well integrated, showing no signs of maladjustment or serious impairment (although there were signs of problems), but with a somewhat feminine, yet perfectly sound personality structure. The following discussion refers to a young woman of approximately equal intelligence, general endowment and education as A, equally well integrated and adjusted, but with a predominantly masculine makeup (the latter being understood in the sense of a marked predominance of the rational-volitional functions over the emotional-imaginative).

Again, only the differences between these two personalities will be briefly sketched.

Very unusual in the drawings of a young woman are: (1) absence of Inanimate Nature—only drawings 2 and 6 (the flowers in the vase) show slight touches of Nature; (2) quasi-absence of Animate Nature (only a few tiny figures in the background of d. 8); (3) quasi-exclusive occurrence of Objects and Technical

Abstractions; (4) the matter-of-fact nature of these Objects; (5) quasi-absence of Atmosphere; (6) occurrence of writing in two drawings—7 and 8; (7) intense Orientation appearing in d. 1; (8) Strong Lines; (9) scant Curves; (10) absence of easy or slightly playful, casual solutions such as decorative Abstractions; (11) high quality and amount of Organization; (12) ample use of Straight Lines.

The combination of these indexes forms a reliable basis for concluding that E has a clear, conscious, unemotional, rational-volitional makeup, sharpness of mind, concentrated attention, endurance, initiative, accuracy, consistency, purposeful activity and efficiency which are the characteristics of the typically masculine structure.

Examination of the stimulus-drawing relation confirms the aforementioned conclusions and evidences in particular E's overstrong control.

Stimulus 1 is seen in its centrality, as evidenced with emphasis by the title "Straight to the goal." The dot, which is frequently felt as free-floating, is seen by E as a stable point.

Stimulus 2 is acknowledged in its curved but not in its typically organic and supple quality. On the contrary, its mobility is firmly curbed in this static and material object.

Stimuli 3 and 5 are recognized in their constructive but not in their dynamic quality.

Stimulus 4 is recognized in its stability, its materiality, its constructive qualities and, to an extent, in its darkness. Remarkable in regard to E's rationalistic and almost compulsive need for logic is the fact that she works out a motivation for the darkness of the stimulus (which is inappropriately used for a window): "The building is seen from the street-level, the windows appear darker and darker as they get farther and farther away from the onlooker." Consider, in this drawing, the progressive darkening of the windows.

Stimulus 6, likewise, is seen in its constructive qualities and receives excellent treatment.

Stimulus 7 is completely denied in its organic, feminine, soft, appealingly decorative qualities and is used in a purely abstract-intellectual manner.

Stimulus 8 is felt in its geometric character, not in its organic quality.

Summarizing the characteristics of the stimulus drawing relation we see that E, though working each of the stimuli in a logically perfectly acceptable picture, fails to respond to any of the specifically feminine qualities but works them all into firmly constructed objects or abstractions.

SUBJECT H, female, 18 years, student in home economics. Satisfactory academic achievement.

Significance of the Drawings

1. Little Bird.
2. Duck.
3. Trees.
4 and 6. Decorative motifs for napkins.
5. Initials (the subject's own) on corner of handkerchief.
7. Rabbit.
8. Cat.
Order of Execution: 8, 2, 3, 1, 4, 6, 5, 7. Drawing Time: 35 minutes.

The personality emerging from this set is one who, like F, is outspokenly feminine, though of a completely different type. This set of drawings represents the prototype of the products obtained from the type of young woman who is: *typically feminine* (affinity for the organic stimuli; complete insensibility for the mechanical-constructive "masculine" stimuli; quasi-absence of Straight Lines); *mild and kindhearted* (small, tame animals; strong predominance of Curves); *unromantic* (absence of Atmosphere and of Fantasy, plus total context of indexes); *warm but not passionate* (life-relatedness of the content; fairly Strong Lines but absence of Fullness and of Dark Shading); *unassuming* (simple, domestic animals and simple symmetrical Abstraction; very moderate Covering); *unsophisticated* (absence of Expansion; commonplace character of the content); *not inclined toward great refinement, meticulousness or trivia* (insensibility to the finely structured sign 7; scant Detail); *realistic and well adjusted* (representational character of the drawings; abstract drawings titled as objects; all items refer to H's occupation and direct sphere of interest; absence of Fantasy); *commonsense* (all the drawings are Populars); *quiet and docile* (total absence of Movement; static character of the set; domestic kind of animals; absence of Orientation); *conservative and reserved* (absence of Movement; carefully closed contours; slight Recurrence in drawings 4, 5 and 6); *conventional* (absence of Originality; Symmetrical Abstraction); *slightly fearful* (Reinforced lines; Emptiness, plus total context); *unambitious* (no Orientation, no Originality).

SUBJECT L, female, 23 years old, student in social work. Satisfactory academic achievements.

Significance of the Drawings

1. The house stands on earth. The dot is the sun. The figures around the sun are new planets except the long one which is a cloud.

2. A man floating on a cloud around his own private dream castle.   The earth is down below him.
3. Whirlpool.
4. Prison for people who are supposed to be crazy.   It's out by the sea.
5. Snake pit.   Snakes can bend their bodies all kinds of ways but humans can't.
6. The circle at the top is a peaceful person.   One thing after another piles up to anger him until he sees X which could be something he greatly loves or hates.   If he hates X he curses and swears and forgets it, withdrawing back to peace again.   If he loves X he forgets about his anger, throws it out of his mind as insignificant and finds peace again.
7. Confusion.
8. Paratrooper forced to jump on a stormy night.   Everything is black and ugly but the one shining star.

Order of Execution: 3, 4, 8, 1, 5, 6, 7, 2.   Drawing Time: 35 minutes.

SUBJECT O, male, 18 years old, college student, average school grades.

Significance of the Drawings

1. Yearning and Expectation.
2. Winter.

Order of Execution: 8, 5, 6, 7, 1, 2, 3, 4.   Drawing Time: 65 minutes.

Discussion

Profile

The over-all appearance is unfavorable mainly because of the combined effect of lack of Practical Intellect and strong weight of Creative Imagination.   In view of this basic pattern, the strongly developed Emotion, though not unfavorable in itself, and the sharp peak at the level of Control take on a negative significance.   Whatever correction analysis of the profile may bring, O's personality must be considered precariously balanced, showing overwhelming emotionality, unrealistic imagination and intellect, and probably also inhibition.

Analysis of the Profile

Emotion.   The variables correlated with each aspect of this function are very irregularly represented.   The scores are practically concentrated on Curved lines, for the Outgoing pole, and on Asymmetrical Abstraction and Shading, for the Seclusive pole.   Whereas a fair amount of Curves is indicative of adaptability, flexibility, relaxation, generosity and life-relatedness, its excessive occurrence is a much less favorable augury, especially with a male subject.   As a rule, considerable use of Curved lines with almost complete absence of Straight lines points to manic tendencies or, for a male, to a unilaterally feminine personality makeup. The first of these interpretations must be rejected because of the strong Control which characterizes the Profile and also because of the abundancy of smooth Shading, which points to neurotic tendencies tinged by depression. The hypothesis concerning an outspoken feminine personality structure is therefore more likely to be confirmed. In the case of a male, such a structure is obviously conducive to serious inadequacy and even disturbance, which may affect the entire personality in its intellectual and volitional aspects as well as in its emotionality. Whether O is feminine only in a diffuse, general way, or whether a specific sexual problem is involved as well must be deduced from further examination of the material.

The drawings contain also indexes of marked sexual concern, as appears from the erotic implications in both theme and title of d. 1 and in the sexual character of certain elements of the other drawings, especially d. 8. The almost obsessive repetition of such elements and others like the flame element and other edge elements, together with the abundance of Shading, points to disturbance within the deeper areas of personality. The uniform occurrence of Asymmetrical Abstractions fits in with the latter assumption, for when this variable occurs to such an extent, it is generally symptomatic of disturbance of a sexual, hostile or aggressive nature. Since the latter two hypotheses must be discarded in the present constellation of indexes, it may be assumed that O presents both a state of general inadequacy and a specific sexual problem.

Imagination and Intellect. Both these functions present the same structure and evidence weakness of the reality component. Examination of the drawings shows that the Organization score refers solely to elaboration in plane, not to linear perspective. This suggests that O's Speculativeness consists more of daydreaming than of productive logical thinking. Complete absence of Objects, Technical Abstraction and consequently of Populars indicates a lack of common sense, practicality and masculine interests.

Activity. The irregular representation of variables found throughout the Profile characterizes also both poles of this function revealing the precariousness and one-sidedness of O's personality. The Dynamic pole of the Activity shows marked deficiency of the indexes of masculinity, vigor, initiative and wilfulness. The particularly high score for Carefulness must be interpreted in the sense of inhibition since the other alternative for this variable, compulsiveness, fits less well in the present configuration.

Stimulus-Drawing Relation

Striking with regard to a male subject is the fact that all the mechanical-constructive stimuli are rejected without exception. The attitudes underlying such complete lack of affinity prevent O from utilizing the capacities, revealed by his high Form level, for constructive effort, objective and logical thinking, and purposeful activity of a practical kind. His affinity for the feminine-organic stimuli accentuates his lack of virility and the unilaterality of his structure.

Order of Execution

In conformity with the over-all picture of indexes O starts with the feminine stimulus 8 and works it into a design with marked sexual accent, parts of which appear in most of the other drawings. Significant also is the conclusion of the series with two typically masculine stimuli, 3 and 4, to whose straightness and angularity O proves completely insensitive.

Summary

As revealed by his drawings, O appears as a one-sidedly emotional individual. Feminine qualities, sensibility, refinement, affection, flexibility, smoothness, reserve, are over-emphasized, while masculine traits, constructive abilities, self-assertiveness, decisiveness, dynamism, realism, logical thinking and purposeful activity are completely lacking. Sexual concern is apparent and the possibility of sexual inversion may be considered. O does not, however, appear to be consciously hindered by his inadequacy and seems to maintain a surface balance and integration. His lack of contact with concrete reality and the weakness of his rational-volitional functions do not, at the present state, permit much perspective for efficient activity except in the social or esthetic sphere, toward which his delicate sensitivity and creative tendencies are conducive.

SUBJECT P, male, 29 years old, fiction writer.

Significance of the Drawings

1. Just curlicues repeating itself; the possibility of an infinite regression.
2. A face like that given to the mother in children's books and also the lips repeated and enlarged; the face is dissolving.
3. The least imaginative of the designs (as design).
4. Nothing.
5. Neptune and his triton, also an albatross and the ocean; the triton is a cross-bow firing at the bird.
6. Nothing.
7. Streptococci and gonococci; the latter are also eyes.
8. Woman's Figure.

Order of Execution: 2, 1, 8, 6, 5, 3, 7, 4. Drawing Time: 12 minutes.

SUBJECT S, male, 17½ years old, college student, majoring in psychology. Superior academic success; extraordinary general endowment. Strong artistic leanings and a certain amount of art training.

Significance of the Drawings

1. Decorative flower-fountain combination.
2. Boy's head.
3. Flowers; kind of lilies; they are being besprinkled by a divinity (figure in left-hand corner). Another figure, which is a kind of force, reaches for the flowers but his hand does not dare take them; it becomes rigid when it approaches them. (Subject says that he cannot explain very well what he has drawn.)
4. Subject does not know himself. The line structure into which the stimulus is worked is a combination of an arrow and a compass figure. The line structure starting from the left-hand side represents a kind of focus, sending out long rays. An insect is caught between two of these rays.
5. A scene in ancient Greece, gardens, terraces, colonnades. In the foreground a figure in garments of that time, carrying a bird. The watering pot into which the stimulus was originally completed has no connection with the whole of the drawing. (Subject would have removed it had erasing been permitted.)
6. Pledging young people. They pledge to various emblems. Above them is a divinity. Subject cannot explain the curling lines in the middle of the picture nor the element appearing between the two lines forming the sharp, right-hand upper corner.
7. Primeval forest scene. A reptile coming out of the water; a butterfly leaving the branch of the tree, a big mushroom and other vegetation; in the right-hand lower corner a gnome (in S's language called "Spirit of the Earth"); the whole scene overshadowed by a strong tree.
8. A vase with flowers. Subject finds the latter uninteresting, conventional and banal, as also d. 2.

Order of Execution: 2, 4, 1, 3, 8, 7, 5, 6. Drawing Time: 65 minutes.

Discussion

This subject shows a great deal in common with Subject A. Both have a markedly emotional, esthetic, idealistic makeup, superior logical capacities, versatility of interests, a refined and deep sensibility, a healthy need for expansion, a dislike for banality and a humanistic orientation.

However, S does not have A's strong—perhaps slightly heavy—vitality, nor the degree of passion which characterizes A's emotionality; neither does he seem to have to the same extent as A a capacity for warmth and affection. Especially, he does not share in A's sense of reality, his practical qualities, his commonsense, his quietness and equanimity and his ability to deal with commonplace situations. In regard to the latter statement, see the scantness of Objects, of Strong Lines and of Populars in S's drawings.

S is not lacking vitality as proved by the Fullness—in several cases Compactness—and the degree of Movement contained in his drawings. But his vitality is channelled, as it were, through extremely differentiated esthetic-intellectual mechanisms. This results, apparently, in a lesser vigor of S's reactivity but not in a lesser endurance or tenacity, as appears from the extraordinary Continuity of his lines, Consistency of pressure, incomparable quality of the Straight Lines (see d. 4), and his remarkable capacity to execute complex symmetrical patterns with almost mechanical precision (d. 1). Also, this more differentiated and less vigorous vitality seems to permit S to govern his energy with more suppleness and easiness than the person with a more primitive vital-emotional makeup. On the other hand, the particularly refined nature of S's emotions makes him prone to over-sensitivity.

The individual character of S's personality resides in his unusually pronounced esthetic-idealistic orientation, which is not so much the effect of sublimation, as is the case with A, but more like genuine affinity for these values. The latter inference reposes on the combination of the content of his drawings (especially dd. 3, 6 and 7) with the extraordinary high Form level, the subtle Movement thrilling through his drawings and the remarkable fluency of his Curves. Quite personal also is the strongly metaphysical leaning revealed by the Symbolism and its specific content (divinities in dd. 3 and 6; gnome in d. 7, called "Spirit of the Earth"). In the present configuration of indexes a marked ethical-social trend is revealed also by the political, religious and ethical symbols to which the youth represented in d. 5 is pledging himself. These indications of Content are supported by the delicate, almost dematerialized, aspects of the Execution. Noteworthy, in regard to d. 5, is the different intensity of Lines in which it is executed, compared with the other drawings. This particularity is likely to express the greater meaning which this theme (youth pledging to ideals) has for S.

The entire set of drawings produced by S is, apparently, rich in psychoanalytical implications. Since the material presented here has not been studied from that point of view an interpretation of this kind cannot be given, but a few hints may be pointed out. Drawings 3, 6 and 7 seem to be partifularly full of deeper meaning, considering the divinities which they feature and also the localization of these divinities, either high and facing the direction of progress (that is, in terms of spatial symbolism, from left to right) or seated low (d. 7) and backwardly oriented. In all likelihood these drawings express something like a conflict between "higher" and "lower" forces, between idealistic aspirations and earthly urges. The confusion accompanying this state of conflict seems to be expressed, with extraordinary directness, in the variety and contradictory character of the symbols featured in d. 6.

SUBJECT T, male, 20 years old, student in education. Average academic achievements.

Significance of the Drawings

1. Decorative motif on flower or leaf theme.
2. Butterflies. One of them is attracted by a flower.
3. Fence, with view of park behind.
4. Bachelor's bliss.
5. Decorative motif.
6. "Life on a clothesline" (birds as clothespins).
7. Singing lesson.
8. "This is for people with childish thoughts: a funny character blowing as spirit out of his little pipe."

Order of Execution: 1, 8, 1, 2, 6, 5, 3, 4. Drawing Time: 45 minutes.

SUBJECT U, male; 46 years old; storekeeper in a factory; grammar school education, and SUBJECT V, male; 59 years old; dealer in grain; high school education.

Significance of the Drawings

Subject U. 1. A cross; a decoration in cross form.
2. A Victory-V.
3. A cross, maybe on a churchyard.
4. A Victory-V.
5. Nothing. Could also be a Victory-V.
6. A cross.
7. Hammer and sickle.
8. Allied soldier (the picture carries the liberation date of the subject's town).

Subject V. 1. Eagle's eye.
2. The human being.
3. Stars and Stripes.
4. Chesboard.
5. Arrow aimed at heart but intercepted by the shield of "the other."
6. A large and a small cross.
7. A medieval weapon.
8. Hammer and sickle.

Under the title "Explanation," Subject V writes in addition:

"America (d. 3) and Russia (d. 8) are playing a game on the chessboard of the world (d. 4). Each of them attempts to strike at the heart of the other with an arrow (d. 5) or with another weapon (d. 7). Humanity (d. 2) observes this with a sharp eye (d. 1) and takes up the small cross (d. 6) in order to be able to carry later the large one.

Order of Execution: Subject U: 3, 8, 4, 5, 7, 2, 1, 6. Subject V: 8, 3, 7, 2, 4, 1, 5, 6.

Similarities

The profiles of these subjects are almost identical and are not auspicious. This conclusion is based primarily on the combined effect of the extremely meager Practical Intellect and the relatively strongly developed Creative Imagination both of which are very unusual with subjects of the age, sex and education of U and V. The disproportioned weight of Control is, in itself, not necessarily a problem indicator; neither is the scantness of Emotion, which is not uncommon with this kind of subject. ·However, in the presence of the aforementioned negative indicators, this state of the subject's Emotion and Control is aggravating rather than attenuating.

The chief characteristics of the variable-composition are: (1) the poor representational character of the drawings, pointing to a lack of closeness in the subjects' contact with visible reality; (2) the scantness of Nature, indicating that they are not life-related, warm and sensitive; (3) the absence of Objects of a commonplace kind and scantness of Objects altogether, emphasizing the meagerness of their interest in concrete matters; (4) the profusion of Symbols suggesting a tendency to substitute meanings for facts and objects, with the complications and distortions likely to arise from such an attitude. Attenuating the negative implications of such marked Symbolism is the fact that the ideas expressed relate to actual events, war and war problems (these drawings were made in 1946 and 1947); furthermore, the symbols used have no esoteric character but are of a conventional, readily understandable sort which allows the assumption that the subjects, although lacking nearness and directness in their dealings with their surroundings, are not out of contact with reality at large.

In sum, U and V are not the outgoing, congenial, simple kind of persons who delight in human relationships and concrete hobbies, but rather complicated, somewhat withdrawn people who like to speculate on broad, impersonal matters and to form opinions in which they (especially U) tend to believe stubbornly.

Differences

The main specific characteristics of U's drawings are, first, his perseverative, almost compulsive repetition of the stimuli and their construction into two monotonously alternating themes, the cross and the Victory V. This reveals not only the narrow range of his associations but suggests also a tendency toward fixation and obsession.

U's need to depict subject matter that relates exclusively to one sphere of experience, war, is even more significant since he is known not to have been personally harmed in any particular way by the war. The uniformity of his drawings is thus, apparently, not due to deep emotional experiences but rather to a kind of mental impoverishment or fixation. Another characteristic of U's drawings is his excessively Strong Lines, Black Shading and marked Reinforcement. In the present configuration of indexes (especially with the marked Repetition, the Symmetry, the absence of Casualness and scantness of Curves) the combination of excessive Pressure, Black Shading and Reinforcement is likely to have serious implications. Not only does it support the aforementioned tendencies toward obsession and perseveration but it reveals a primitive impulsive vitality, violently curbed and, therefore, liable to dangerous outbursts. The acute tension thus created between strong impulsiveness and equally strong repression predisposes U to hostility and, because of his tendency to persevere, to resentment.

As for V, the most characteristic feature of his product is his need to systematize, that is, to interrelate everything, as appears from the explanation of his drawings. As is well known, such tendencies to systematize are often encountered in paranoid individuals. The assumption concerning a paranoid streak in V's personality is also supported by the many aggressive elements contained in his drawings: d. 5, Arrow aimed at a heart; d. 7, Medieval weapon; d. 8, Hammer and sickle; d. 1, Eagle's head with sharp beak. Linking up with these indications of paranoid-aggressive tendencies is the insecurity, suggested by the Discontinuity, the Reinforcement and slight Inconsistency in the Pressure of V's lines. Remarkable also, with this over-ideationally inclined individual, is the schematic cut-off head (d. 2) showing only the upper "intellectual" part without any tendency to continue toward the bodily parts of the figure. The head appearing in U's drawing shows not only part of the trunk, duly shaded to bring out its consistency, but also an excessively marked tie, symbol of masculinity. The difference in the vitality of U and V appears with even more strength from the difference in the Intensity of their lines. The more casual execution of V's drawings and the slightly greater amount of Curves suggest however that he is free from the tension expressed by the combined rigidity and heaviness of U's lines.   V is also free from the mental rigidity manifested in U; there is a certain Variety in the content of his drawings and the titles reveal a certain refinement, or perhaps, a certain need to display erudition.

From this comparison of the main features contained in each of the sets it appears once again that, despite quasi-identity of their profiles, subjects may differ considerably in their individual makeup.

Part Four:
Illustrations and Commentary

Subject A

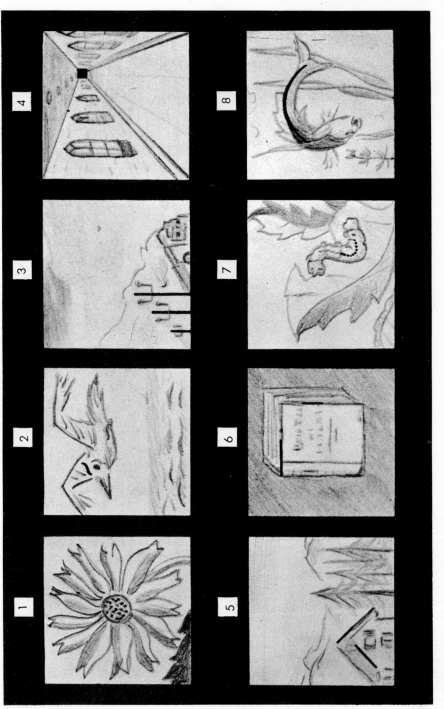

CRITERIA		Total Score	Drawings 1	2	3	4	5	6	7	8
NATURE	Animate	6		XY	/				X/	XX
	Physiognomy	3		XX					/	/
	Inanimate	8	X/	X	X		X/	X	XX	X
	Atmosphere	7		XX		XX	XX	X	XX	X
OB-JECTS	Utility / Ornaments	6			XX	XX	X	X/	/	/
	Style	3				X/	X	X		
	Movement	8		XXY	XX	YY	YY	YY	X/	X/
COVERAGE	Full	16	XX	XY	XY	YY	YY	YY	YY	XX
	Empty									
	Expanded	5		X/	X/		X/		X	
	Constricted				/		/	/	/	/
	Organization	19	X/	XX/	XX/	XXY	XX/	XX/	XY/	XY/
	Detail	10	X/	X/	X	XX	/	/	X/	X/
LINES	Curved	9	X/	X	X		/		XX/	XX/
	Straight	9		/	X	XYY	X/	XYY	X/	/
	Strong	14	XX	XX	X/	X/	Y/	YX	XX	XX
	Soft	4	/	X	X/	X				

CRITERIA		Total Score	Drawings 1	2	3	4	5	6	7	8
NATURE	Fancy / FANTASY									
	Phantasm									
	Symbolism	1							/	
	Original	8				YY		X	XXX	XX
	Symmetric / ABSTRACT									
	Asymmetric							X/		
	Technical									
	Careful	15	XY	X	X/	XXX	X/	YY	XY	X/
	Casual	3	X	X	/	X/		/	/	XX
	Light / SHADING	5	/	X	Y	/	/		X	
	Dark	5	/		/	X/		XX		X
	Orientation	1				X				
	Closure	1	X					/		
	Parts									
	Scribbles									
	Duplication									
	Repetition									
	Schematism									

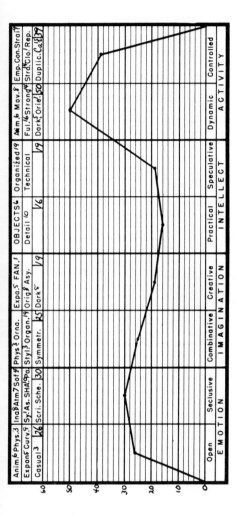

Subject B

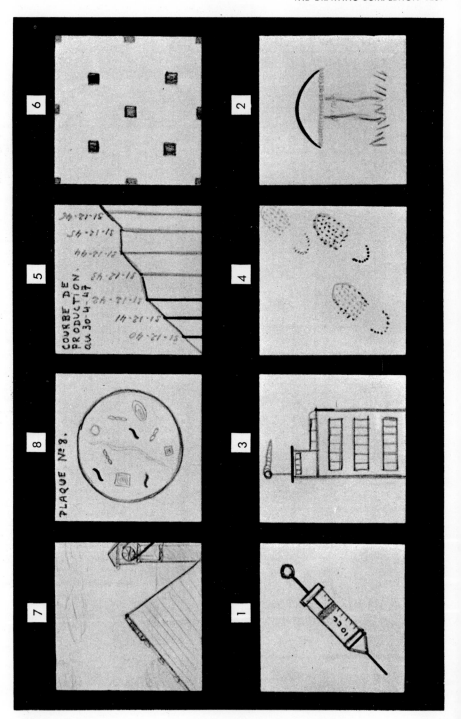

CRITERIA		Total Score	Drawings 1	2	3	4	5	6	7	8
NATURE	Animate									
	Physiognomy									
	Inanimate	1								X
	Atmosphere	6								/
OBJECTS	Utility	8	XY/	X		X	XX	XX		
	Ornaments									
Style		1		/	X			X	/	
Movement		3	X	/			/	X		/
COVERAGE	Full	2	/		X		/	/	/	
	Empty	1	/							
	Expanded	1						/	/	
	Constricted									
Organization		8	X/	X	X/	X	X	X/	X	/
Detail		10	X	XX	X		XX	X/	XX	X
LINES	Curved	4		X/		/	XX	XXX	XX	Y
	Straight	11	X/		XX	XX	XX	X/	XX	X/
	Strong	8	X/	X	X					
	Soft	6	X/	XX	X		/	X	XX	/

CRITERIA		Total Score	Drawings 1	2	3	4	5	6	7	8
FANTASY	Fancy									
	Phantasm									
	Symbolism									
ABSTRACT	Original	2		/		/	/		/	
	Symmetric	1				X				
	Asymetric									
	Technical	6	XX	XXX	XXX		/			X/
Careful		19	XX/	XXX	XY	XXX	XXX	XX	XX	X/
Casual			XX	/				/		/
SHADING	Light	2	XX				X			
	Dark	3			X	XX	X	/	X	
Orientation		3		X	X		X		X	
Closure		1		X						
Parts										
Scribbles										
Duplication										
Repetition										
Schematism										

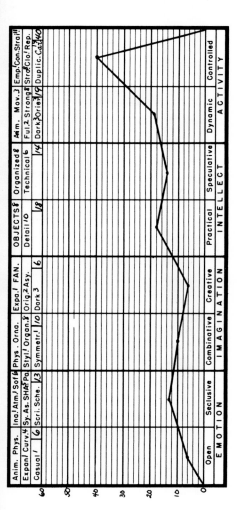

	Anim. Phys.	Ina. Atm. Sof.	Phys. Orna.	Expo. FAN.	OBJECTS 8	Organized 8	Anim. Mov. 3	Emp. Con. Strai.
	Expan. Curv. 1	Sy. As. SHA.	Styl. Organ. 8	Orig. 2 Asy.	Detail 10	Technical 6	Ful. 2 Strong 8	Strd. Clo. Rep.
	Casual 1	Scri. Sche. 13	Symmetr. 1 10	Dark 3	18	14	Dark Orie. 3 6	Duplic. Cat. 40
	6		6					
EMOTION	Open	Seclusive	Combinative	Creative	Practical	Speculative	Dynamic	Controlled
			IMAGINATION			INTELLECT		ACTIVITY

Subject C

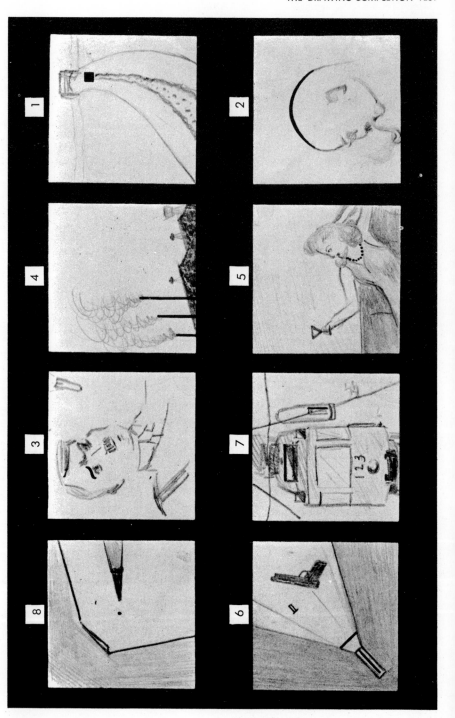

CRITERIA		Total Score	1	2	3	4	5	6	7	8
NATURE	Animate	7		XX					XXX	XX
	Physiognomy	7		XXX					XXX	X/
	Inanimate									
	Atmosphere	4	X		/	X	XX	XXX	XX	
OB-JECTS	Utility	11	X		XXX	X	XX	XXX	X	/
	Ornaments	1							X	
	Style			/	/				X	
COVERAGE	Movement	9	XX	X	X	/	XXX	XX	X	/
	Full	13	XX	XX	X	X	XX	XX	XX	X
	Empty									
	Expanded	2	/			X	/			
	Constricted									
	Organization	16	X	XX	XX	X	XX	XXX	XXX	XX
	Detail	10		X/	/	/	X/	XXX	X/	X
LINES		6							X	
	Curved	11	XXX X	/	X/	/	XXX XX	XX	XXX	X
	Straight	12	XX	XX	XX	X/	/	XX	X	X
	Strong	3		X		X				X
	Soft									

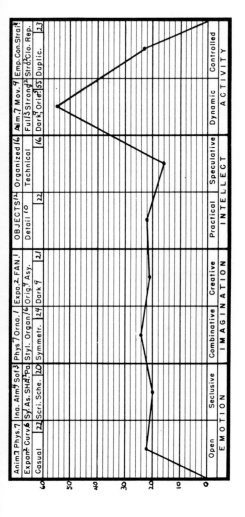

CRITERIA		Total Score	1	2	3	4	5	6	7	8
FAN-TASY	Fancy									
	Phantasm									
	Symbolism	1		X						
	Original	9	XX	X			XX	X	XXX	
	Symmetric									
AB-STRACT	Asymetric									
	Technical									
	Careful	14	XX	X	X/	/	XXX XX	XX	XXX	X
	Casual									
SHADING	Light	3	X					/	X/	/
	Dark	9	XX	X	XX		XX	/	X/	/
	Orientation	5	X		X	X	XX	/	/	
	Closure									
	Parts									
	Scribbles									
	Duplication									
	Repetition									
	Schematism									

Subject D

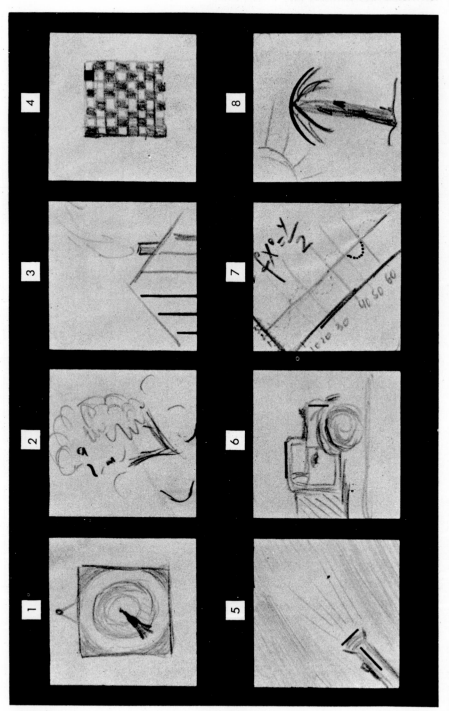

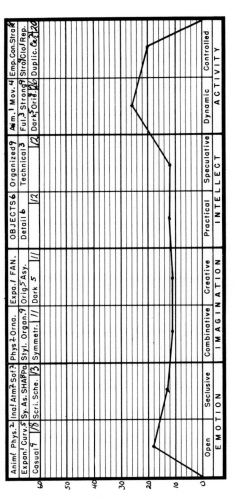

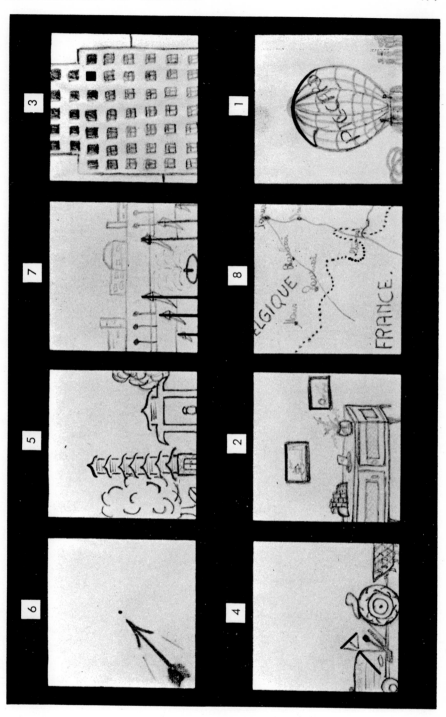

Subject F

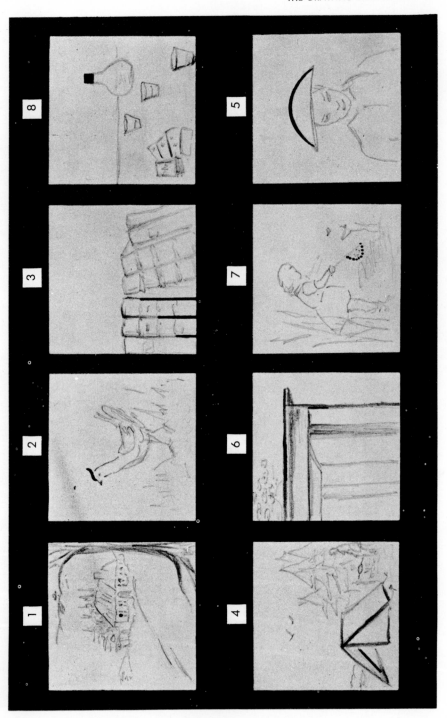

CRITERIA		Total Score	Drawings 1	2	3	4	5	6	7	8
FAN-TASY	Fancy									
	Phantasm									
	Symbolism									
AB-STRACT	Original	7		X		XX		X	XXX	
	Symmetric									
	Asymetric									
	Technical									
SHADING	Careful	9	XX	X	XX	X		X	X	X
	Casual	5	X	X	/		X		X	/
	Light	1			/			/		/
	Dark									
	Orientation									
	Closure									
	Parts									
	Scribbles									
	Duplication									
	Repetition									
	Schematism									

CRITERIA		Total Score	Drawings 1	2	3	4	5	6	7	8
NATURE	Animate	5	X/	X		X	X		XX	XX
	Physiognomy	3	XX	/		X/	X	/	X/	X/
	Inanimate	5		X		/	X	/	X	
	Atmosphere	5	X		x/	X/	X	X	X	
OB-JECTS	Utility	6								
	Ornaments									
	Style	3	X	/	/	/	X	X/	XX	
	Movement	3	/	/				/	/	
	Full	1						/	/	
	Empty									
COVERAGE	Expanded	3	X				X	/	/	
	Constricted									
	Organization	13	XX	X/	X/	XX	XX	XX	X/	X.
	Detail	8	XX	X/	X/	X/			X	/
	Curved	6	X	X	/	X	X	XX	XX	X
LINES	Straight	5			X/	X		X	X	X
	Strong	3		X/	X			/		/
	Soft	9	X/	X/	X	X	X	/	X/	X/

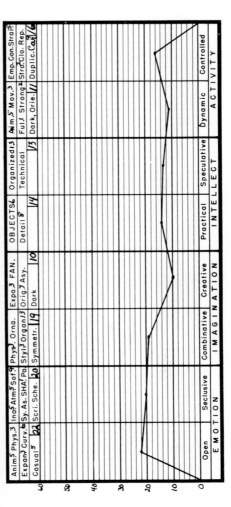

	Emotion				Imagination				Intellect				Activity	
	Open	Seclusive	Combinative	Creative					Practical	Speculative			Dynamic	Controlled

Subject G

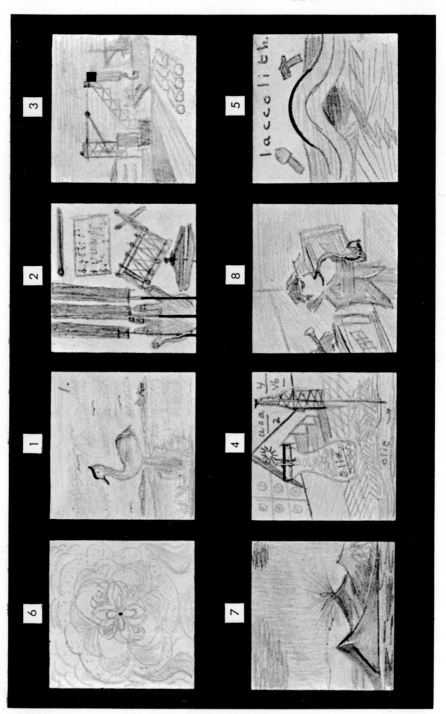

Subject H

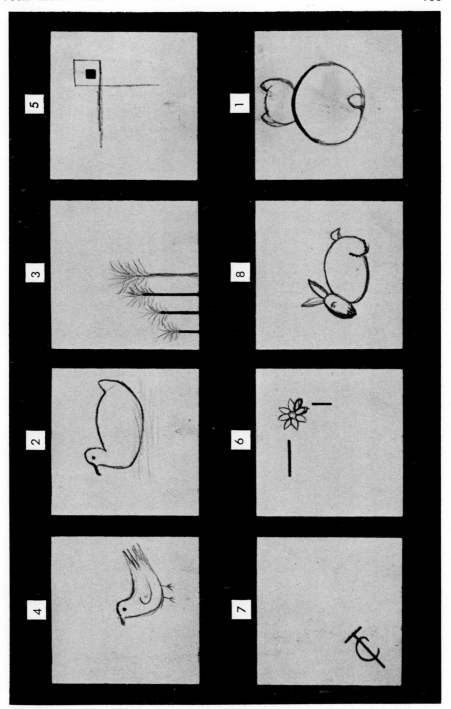

Subject I

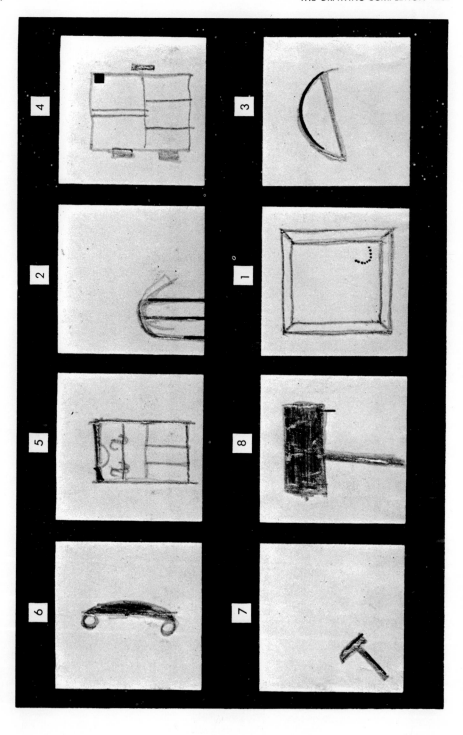

Subject J

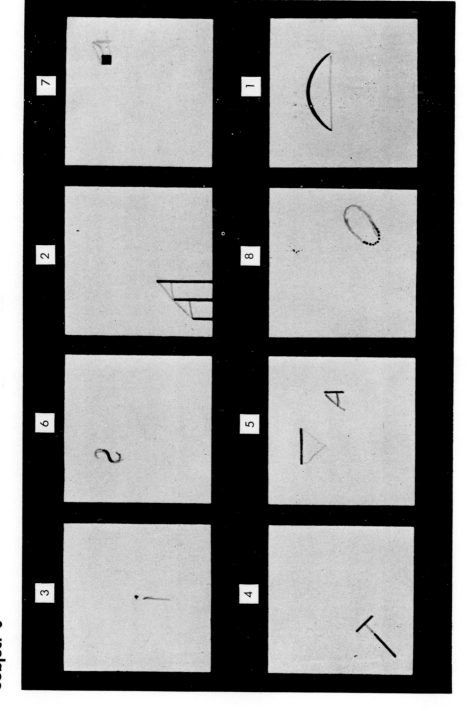

Subject K

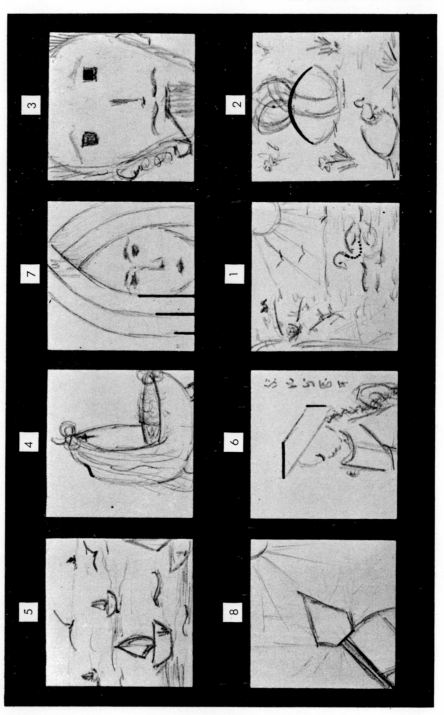

	CRITERIA	Total Score		1	2	3	4	5	6	7	8
NATURE	Animate	7		/		X/	X/		X/	X/	X
NATURE	Physiognomy	6			XX	XX			X/	/	/
NATURE	Inanimate	4		X			/			XX	X
NATURE	Atmosphere	7		X	/			/		XXX	XX
OB-JECTS	Utility	5		X	XX			X			/
OB-JECTS	Ornaments										
	Style	1				X					
	Movement	6		X			/	XX		XX	X
COVERAGE	Full	8		X	/	X	X/			XX	X/
COVERAGE	Empty										
COVERAGE	Expanded	4		X			X			X	X
COVERAGE	Constricted										
	Organization	13		XX	XX	XX	XX	X	X	XX	X/
	Detail	6			X/	/	X		/	X	XX
LINES	Curved	8		X	X	X	/	/	X	X/	XX
LINES	Straight	5		/		/	X	XX	X	/	
LINES	Strong	11		X/	X/	X	X/	XX	X/	/	X/
LINES	Soft	7		/	X	X		XX/	/	X/	

	1	2	3	4	5	6	7	8	Total Score		CRITERIA
						X		X	2		Fancy
										FAN-TASY	Phantasm
	X	X							2		Symbolism
	X	X				X	X	4		Original
											Symmetric
						X			1	AB-STRACT	Asymetric
											Technical
/	X	XX	XX	X/				X	8		Careful
X	X				X	X	X	5		Casual
		/	(				/		2		Light
			/		X				SHADING	Dark
		X		X				2		Orientation
						/		XX	1		Closure
											Parts
											Scribbles
											Duplication
											Repetition
											Schematism

Anim. 7	Phys. 6	Ina. 4	Atm. 7	Sof. 7	Phys. 6	Orna.	Expa. 4	FAN. 2	OBJECTS 5	Organized 13	Anim. 7	Mov. 6	Emp. Con. Strai. 9
Expan. 4	Curv. 8	Sy. 3	As. 1	SHA. 2	Pa.	Styl. 1	Organ. 13	Orig. 4	Asy.	Detail 6	Technical 1	Ful. 8	Strong 11	Stro. 1	Clo. 1	Rep.
Casual 5	30	Scri. Sche.	22		Symmetr.	20	Dark	10		11	14	Dark, Orie. 2	34	Duplic. Ca. 8	25

	EMOTION		IMAGINATION		INTELLECT		ACTIVITY	
	Open	Seclusive	Combinative	Creative	Practical	Speculative	Dynamic	Controlled

Subject L

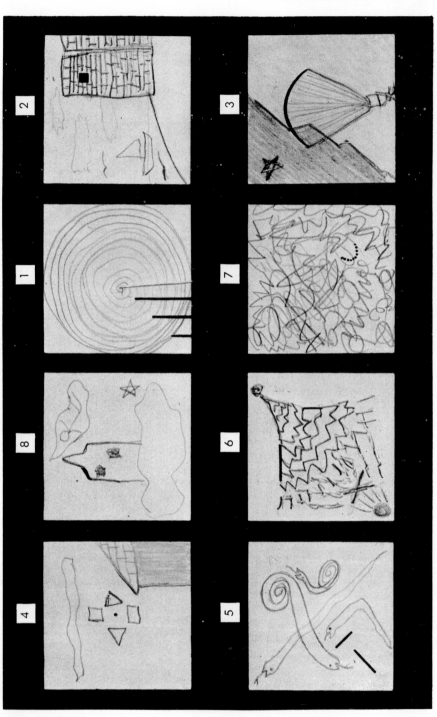

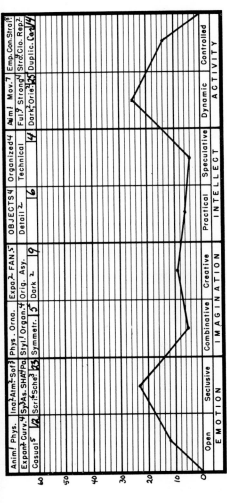

Subject M

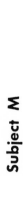
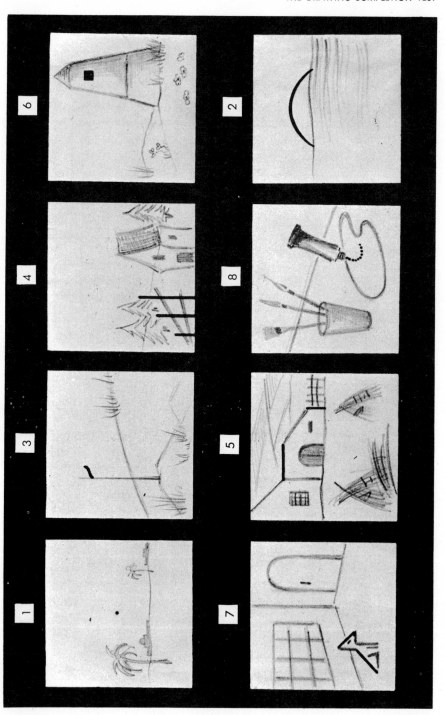

CRITERIA	Total Score	Drawings 1	2	3	4	5	6	7	8
Fancy / FANTASY	1	X/							
Phantasm									
Symbolism									
Original	4		X					XXX	
Symmetric / ABSTRACT									
Asymetric									
Technical									
Careful	17	XXX	XX	XX	XX	XXX	X/	XXX	X
Casual									
Light / SHADING	3	/		/	/	/	/	/	
Dark	3			/	/			X	/
Orientation									
Closure	1				X				
Parts									
Scribbles									
Duplication									
Repetition									
Schematism	2					XX			

	CRITERIA	Total Score	Drawings 1	2	3	4	5	6	7	8
NATURE	Animate	1					X			
	Physiognomy	7		X/	X	X		X		
	Inanimate	9	XX	X	XX	X		X		
	Atmosphere	9	X	X	X	X/	X	X/	XX	X/
OB-JECTS	Utility / Ornaments									XX
	Style	5	X/		X	X	/	X		X
	Movement	2		X					/	
COVERAGE	Full	1	/					X		X
	Empty	2	/	/						XX
	Expanded	6	X	X	X		X	X		
	Constricted					X			XX	/
	Organization	12	XX	X	X/	X/	XX	X/	XX	
	Detail	5	/	/	X	/	X	X	X	X
LINES	Curved	5	XX	/			XX	/	X	
	Straight								X	
	Strong	7		/	X/	X/	XX	X	X	
	Soft	3	X	X	X/					X

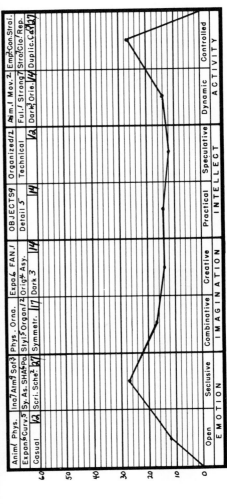

Anim/ Phys.	Ina7 Atm9 Sof3	Phys. Orna.	Expo6 FAN./	Organized/2	Anim./ Mov.2	Emp?Con.Strai.
Expan6Curv.5	Sy.As.SHA?Pa	Styl.5 Organ/2 Orig# Asy.		Technical	Ful./ Strong7	Stro7 Clo.Rep.
Casual	/2 Scri.Sche2	Symmetr. /7	Dark 3	Detail 5 /4	Dark?Orie./4	Duplic.Cc?/2?

Open | Seclusive | Combinative | Creative | Practical | Speculative | Dynamic | Controlled

EMOTION | IMAGINATION | INTELLECT | ACTIVITY

Subject N

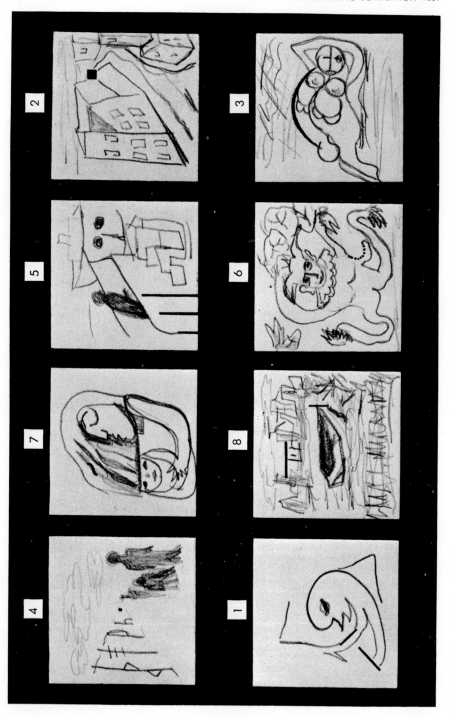

CRITERIA		Total Score	Drawings							
			1	2	3	4	5	6	7	8
NATURE	Animate	7	X/	X/	X	X	/		X	X/
	Physiognomy	4	/	/	/	X	/	/	XX	X
	Inanimate	4	/		/			/		
	Atmosphere	4	X		X	X	X/	X/		
OB-JECTS	Utility / Ornaments	4			X	X/	X/	X/		X
	Style				/					
COVERAGE	Movement	7	X	XX	X	XX		XX	XX	XXX
	Full	10	/	X	X		X	XX	XX	X/
	Empty	1					X			
	Expanded	2			/			X		/
	Constricted									
LINES	Organization	6	X	/	X	X/	/	/	X	X
	Detail	5			/	/		X	X/	X
	Curved	6	/	X	/		X	/	X/	X/
	Straight	4	X	X	X/	X	/	/	X	X/
	Strong	7	/	XX	/	/	/	X	X	X
	Soft	3	X		/	/	/	/		X

CRITERIA		Total Score	Drawings							
			1	2	3	4	5	6	7	8
FAN-TASY	Fancy									
	Phantasm	5		X	/		X		XX	/
	Symbolism								XX	X
AB-STRACT	Original									
	Symmetric									
	Asymetric									
	Technical									
	Careful									
	Casual	2	X	X						
SHADING	Light									
	Dark	5						X		
	Orientation	1			/	/				
	Closure									
	Parts									
	Scribbles	6			/	X		XX	X	/
	Duplication									
	Repetition									
	Schematism									

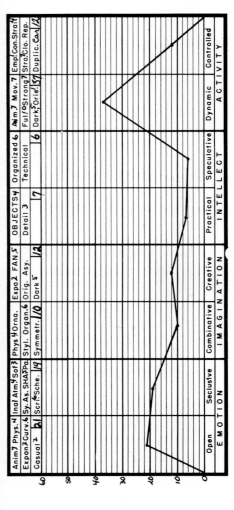

Anim.7 Phys.4	Inal.Atm.4 Sof.3	Phys.4 Orna.	Expa.2 FAN.5	OBJECTS4	Organized 6	Aim.7 Mov.7	Emp.Con.Strai.4
Expan.2 Curv.6	Sy.As. SHASPa.	Styl. Organ.6	Orig. Asy.	Detail 3	Technical	Ful.OStrong7	Stro.Clo. Rep.
Casual 2	21	Scri.Sche. 19	Symmetr. 10	Dark 5	12	17	6	Dark;Orie. 37	Duplic. Cov. 12
Open	Seclusive	Combinative	Creative	Practical	Speculative	Dynamic	Controlled
EMOTION		IMAGINATION		INTELLECT		ACTIVITY	

Subject O

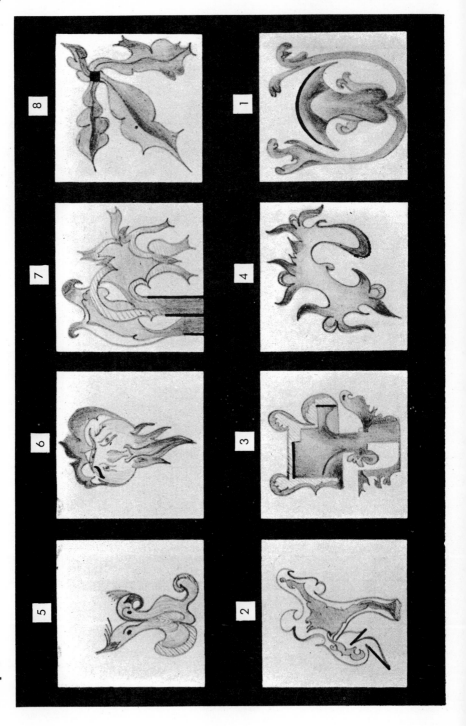

CRITERIA		Total Score	Drawings								CRITERIA	
			1	2	3	4	5	6	7	8		
NATURE	Animate	2	X	X							Fancy	FAN-TASY
	Physiognomy	1		X							Phantasm	
	Inanimate										Symbolism	
	Atmosphere										Original	
OB-JECTS	Utility										Symmetric	AB-STRACT
	Ornaments										Asymetric	
	Style										Technical	
COVERAGE	Movement	8	/	X/	X	X	X		XX	X	Careful	
	Full	5	/	/	X	X		X	X	X	Casual	
	Empty										Light	SHADING
	Expanded		/								Dark	
	Constricted										Orientation	
LINES	Organization	5	X	X	/	/	/	/		X	Closure	
	Detail			X	X						Parts	
	Curved	23	XXX	XXX	XXX	XXX	XXX	XX	XXX	XXX	Scribbles	
	Straight	4	/	/	/	/	/	X	X	/	Duplication	
	Strong	5	/		X/			XXX		/	Repetition	
	Soft										Schematism	

CRITERIA		Total Score	Drawings								
			1	2	3	4	5	6	7	8	
	Fancy		X								FAN-TASY
	Phantasm	3	X	XX							
	Symbolism	1									
	Original										
	Symmetric				XX	XX	XX	XX	XX	XX	AB-STRACT
	Asymetric	12			XX	XX	XX	XX	XX	XX	
	Technical	24	XXX	XXX	XXX	XXX	XXX	XXX	XXX	XXX	
	Careful										
	Casual										
	Light	16	XX	XX/	XXX	X	XX	XX	XX	XX	SHADING
	Dark	9	/	X/	/	XX		X	X	XX	
	Orientation	1					/			/	
	Closure										
	Parts										
	Scribbles	3			/	/	/	/	/	/	
	Duplication								X		
	Repetition	3			/	/	/	/	/	/	
	Schematism										

	OBJECTS			IMAGINATION		INTELLECT			ACTIVITY	
Anim. Phys.	Ina. Atm. Sof.	Phys. Orna.	Expo. FAN.	Orig. Asy.	Organized	Aim. Mov.	Emp.Con.Strai.			
Expan. Curv.	Sy.As.SHA.Pa	Styl. Organ.		Detail	Technical	Ful. Strong	Stra.Clo. Rep.			
Casual 26	Scri. Sche. 41	Symmetr. 16	Dark 24	1	5	Dark,Orie. 28	Duplic.Cas.34			
Open	Seclusive	Combinative	Creative	Practical	Speculative	Dynamic	Controlled			
EMOTION		IMAGINATION		INTELLECT		ACTIVITY				

Subject P

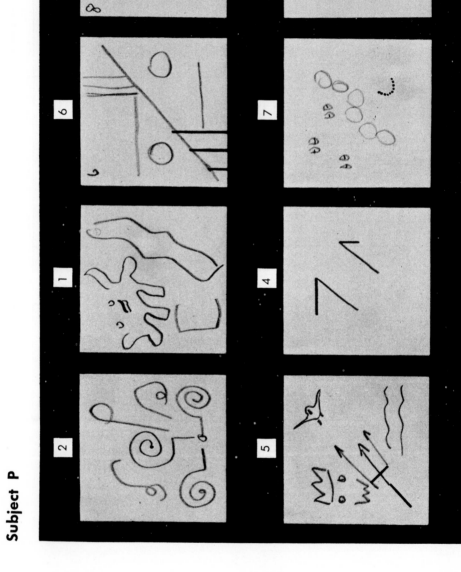

Subject Q

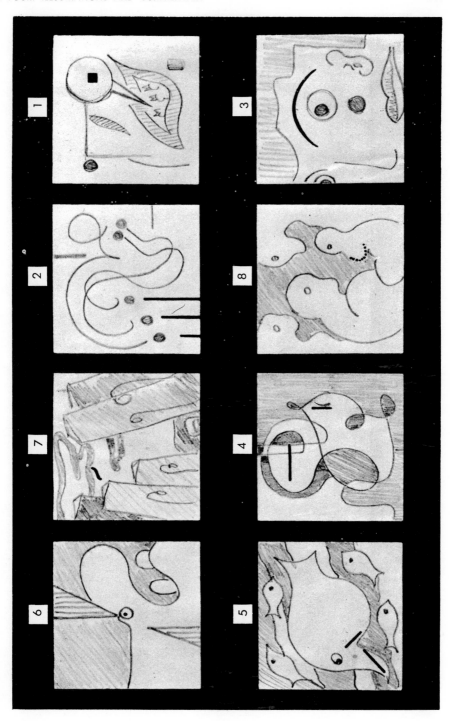

Subject R

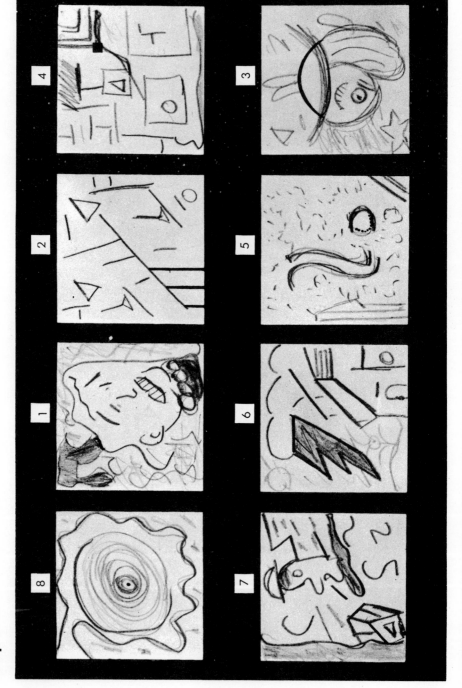

CRITERIA		Total Score	Drawings 1	2	3	4	5	6	7	8
NATURE	Animate / Physiognomy	2	X	X			/			/
	Inanimate	1		/				/	X	
	Atmosphere							/		
OB-JECTS	Utility / Ornaments	1			/	/	/	/		
	Style									
	Movement	7	X	/			XX	XX	X /	/
COVERAGE	Full	15	XX	XX	X	XY	XY	XY	XY	XX
	Empty									
	Expanded	2					/	X	X	
	Constricted									
	Organization	1		/			/	/		/
	Detail						/	/	/	X
LINES	Curved	4	X	X	X /	X /	/		X	X
	Straight	6			/	/	X	XX	/	/
	Strong	8	X /	X	/	X	X	X	X	X
	Soft	1								/

Total Score	CRITERIA		Drawings 1	2	3	4	5	6	7	8
	Fancy	FAN-TASY								
1	Phantasm						X			
	Symbolism								X	
	Original									
	Symmetric					/	/			
1	Asymetric	AB-STRACT			/					
	Technical									
	Careful									
	Casual									
	Light	SHADING	/							
5	Dark			X /		/	X	X /	X	/
	Orientation						.			
	Closure		X							
1	Parts									
10	Scribbles		X /	/	X /	X /	X /	X	XX	X
	Duplication									
2	Repetition			/	/	/	/	/	/	/
	Schematism		/							/

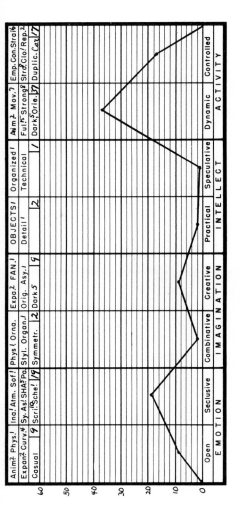

Subject S

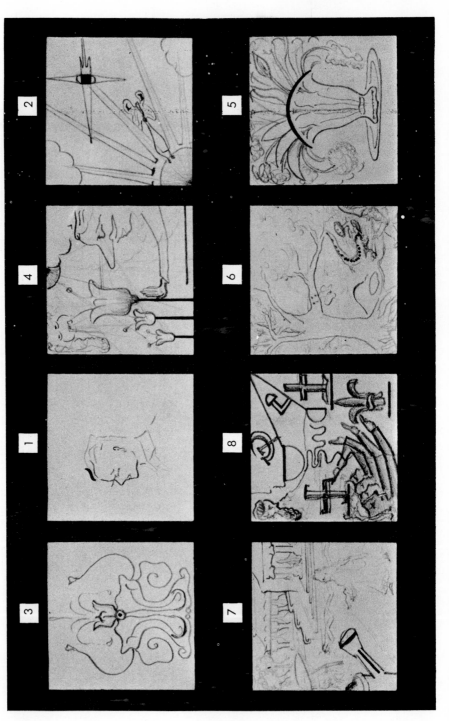

CRITERIA		Total Score	Drawings 1	2	3	4	5	6	7	8
NATURE	Animate	8	X	X	X/	/	X	XX	XX	
	Physiognomy	7		X/	X/	X	XX	XX	X/	
	Inanimate	6	X		X	X	/		XX	X
OB-JECTS	Utility	2			X	X	/		XX	X
	Ornaments	2					X			YY
	Style	2					X/			/
COVERAGE	Movement	8	X		XY		X	XX	XX	
	Full	16	/		XX	X/	XXX	XXX	XXX	XXX
	Empty	4		/						
	Expanded				X	X	X	X/	X/	
	Constricted							/		
	Organization	16	XX	X	XXX	X/	XXX	XX	XXX	XX
Detail		11	X	X	X	X	XX	XX	XX	X
		16	XX	X	XXX	X/	XX	XX	XXX	YX
LINES	Curved	5			/	XX	X	X/		
	Straight	2					/	XX		
	Strong		X	XX	XXX	XX	XX/	/	XXX	XX
	Soft	16	X	XX	XXX	XX	XX/	/	XXX	XX

CRITERIA		Total Score	Drawings 1	2	3	4	5	6	7	8
	Fancy	6			XX		X	XX	X	
FAN-TASY	Phantasm								X/	
	Symbolism	5			XX			XXX		
	Original	4	/			/			XXX	
AB-STRACT	Symmetric	1	X			X				
	Asymetric	1								
	Technical									
	Careful	15	XXX	X/	XX	XX/	XX	X	X/	XX
	Casual	2			/	/	/		/	/
SHADING	Light				X	X		X/		/
	Dark	1						/		
	Orientation									
	Closure	/	X							
	Parts									
	Scribbles									
	Duplication	/			/			/		
	Repetition									
	Schematism									

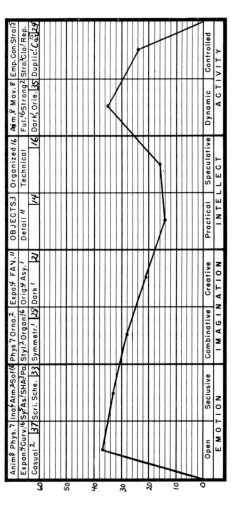

Anim.8 Phys.7 Ina.6 Atm.2 Sof.16 Phys.7 Orna.2 Expa.4 FAN.11 Anm.8 Mov.8 Emp.Con.Stra.5
Expan.4 Curv.16 Sy.2 As.1 SHA.3 Pa. Styl.2 Organ.16 Orig.4 Asy.1 Ful.16 Strong.2 Stro.2 Clo./ Rep.
Casual.2 37 Scri.Sche. 33 Symmetr.1 29 Dark.1 21 OBJECTS.3 Organized.16 Detail.11 14 Technical 16 Dark.Orie.35 Duplic.Car.24

Subject T

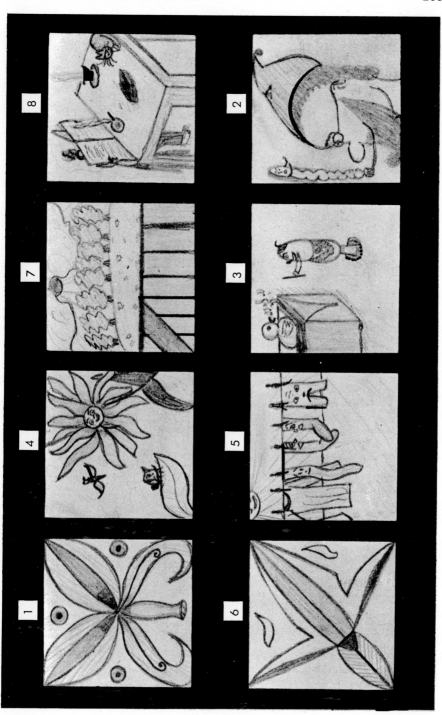

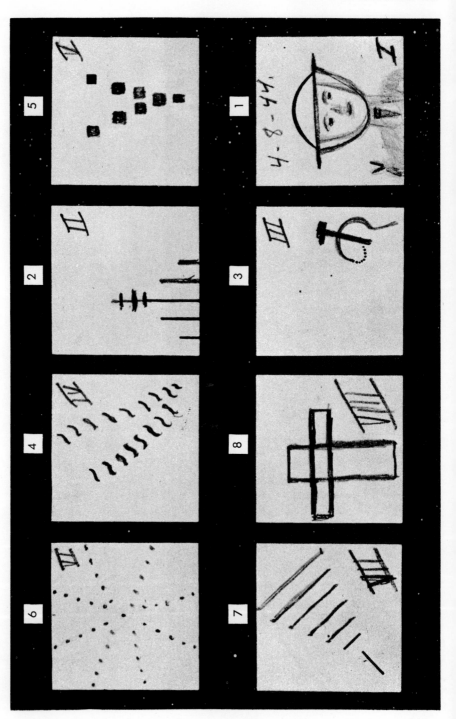

Subject U

CRITERIA	Total Score	1	2	3	4	5	6	7	8	
Fancy										FAN-TASY
Phantasm										
Symbolism	4	/	/	/	/	/	/	X		
Original										
Symmetric	1	/	/	/	/	/				AB-STRACT
Asymetric										
Technical										
Careful	6	/		X	X	X	X	X	/	
Casual										
Light									X	SHADING
Dark	2				X			/	/	
Orientation						/			/	
Closure										
Parts	/						/		/	
Scribbles										
Duplication										
Repetition	3	/	/	/	/	/	/	/		
Schematism										

CRITERIA	Total Score	1	2	3	4	5	6	7	8
NATURE Animate	1								X/
Physiognomy	1	X	X	XX	X	/	X	X	X
Inanimate									
Atmosphere							X		
OB-JECTS Utility	1	X	/	/	X	/	X	X	
Ornaments									
Style			/						/
Movement									
COVERAGE Full									
Empty	8	X/	X	XX	X	/	/	XX	
Expanded									
Constricted									
Organization	6	X	/	/	X	/	X	X	X
Detail	1	/	/					/	X
LINES Curved	2				X/	X/	X/	/	X
Straight	6	/	XX	XX	X	X	X/	X/	X
Strong	13	X/	X/	/		X		X/	XY
Soft									

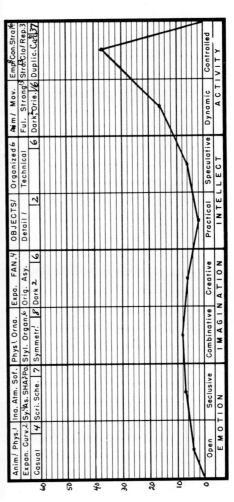

	Anim./ Phys.¹	Ina. Atm. Sof.	Phys¹. Orna.	Expo. FAN.⁴	OBJECTS/ Organized⁶	Anim./ Mov.	Emp.⁸Con.Stra.⁶
	Expan. Curv.²	Sy.⁴As. SHA.³Po.	Styl. Organ.⁶	Orig. Asy.	Detail Technical	Ful. Strong¹³	Str.⁶Clo./Rep.³
	Casual 4	Scri. Sche. 7	Symmetr.¹	8 Dark 2	Detail 1	6 Dark Orie./6	Dupic.Ca.²Ca.³7

Subject V

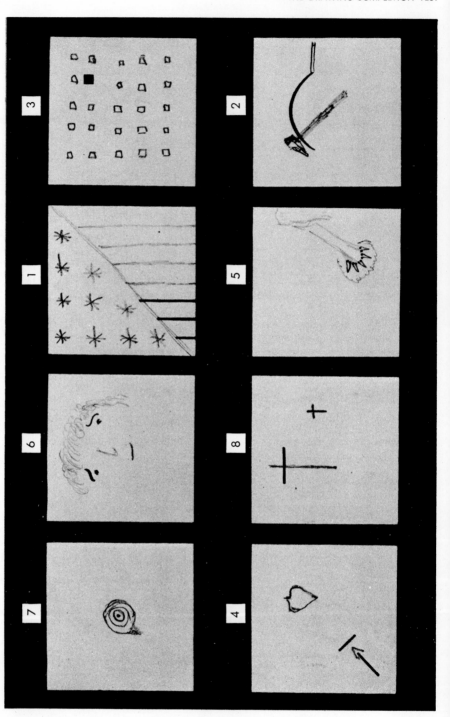

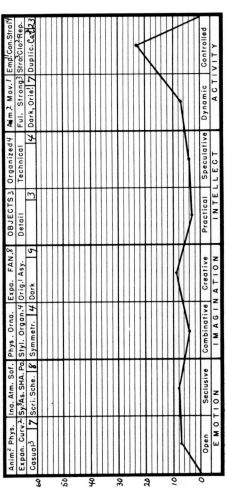

Subject W

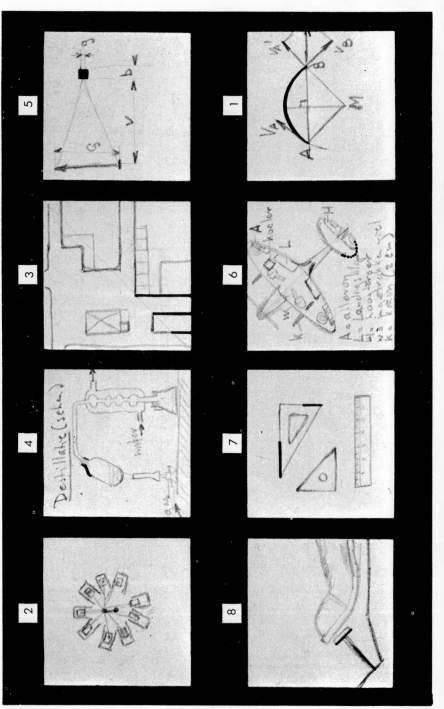

Subject X

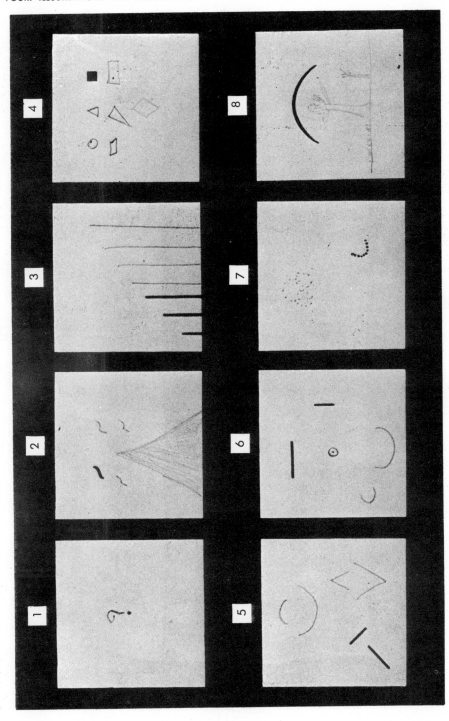

Subject Y

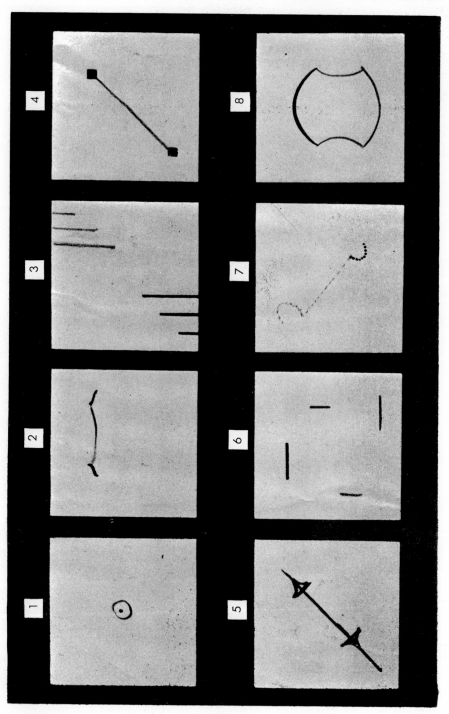

Subject Z

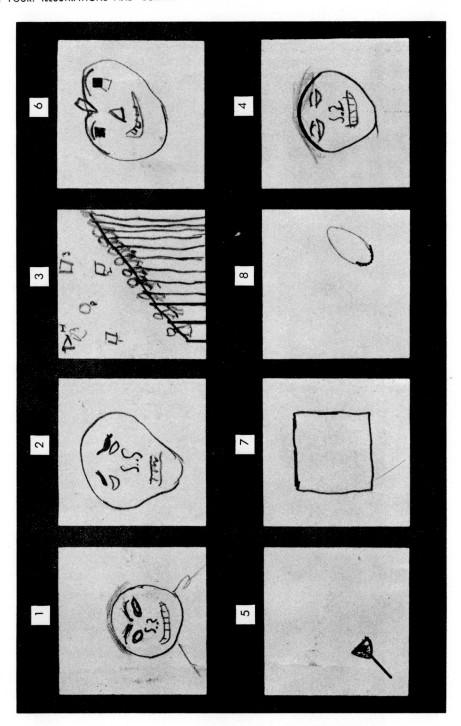

I. Scribblings

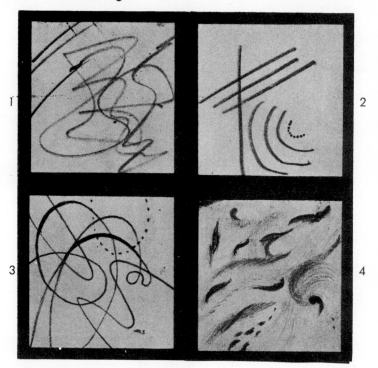

II. Abstractions
Asymmetrical Decorative Abstractions

Technical Abstractions

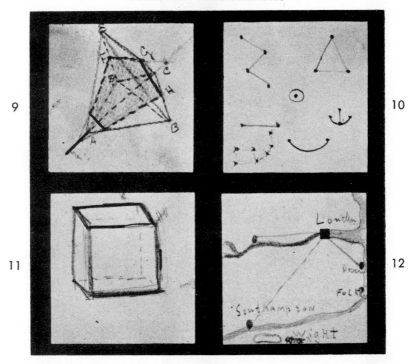

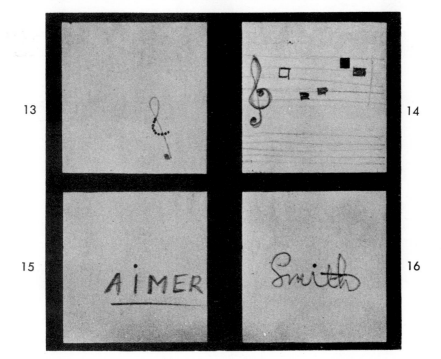

Symmetrical Decorative Abstractions

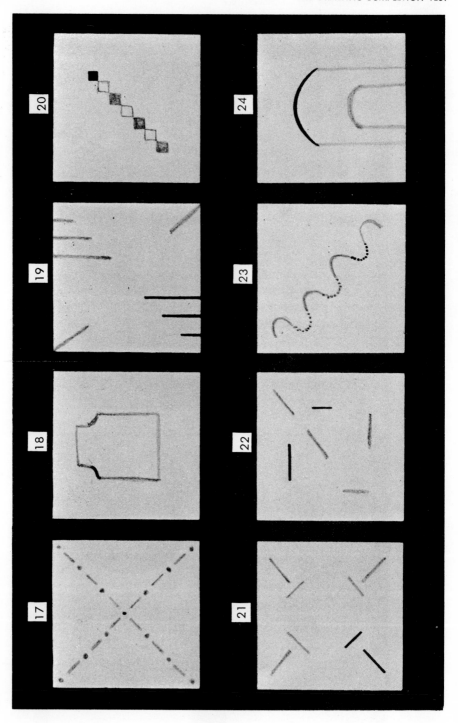

Symmetrical Decorative Abstractions

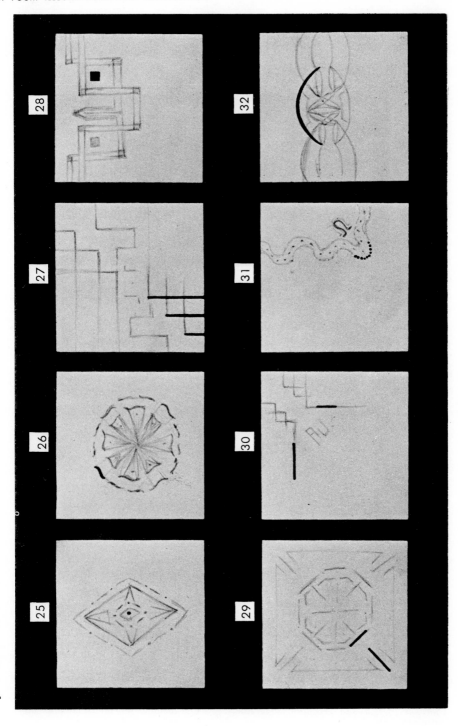

III. Pictures

Physiognomic Expression

In Faces

33. Fresh and youthful.
Dainty appearance: unaccentuated features, neat hairdo, modest clothing.
Friendly and bright expression.
Softly curved lines.
Strong, consistent pressure.
Firm and supple stroke.
Careful organization and execution.
Conventional style.

34. Alluring and artificial.
Slightly caricatured poster-type of representation.
Aggressive and sensual expression: wide-open eyes, strongly made-up lashes, full lips, disorderly hairdo, cap and bow.
Bold stroke.
Strong pressure.
Casual playful execution.

35. Fine and energetic features.
Willful expression: lifted posture of the head; strongly marked chin; muscle-structured face and neck.
Intellectually characterized representation: little indication of facial features and of hair.
Delicate pressure; short strokes.
Particularly sure, fluent and continuous line of the profile.
Unity of content and execution suggesting self-portraiture

36. Wretched and apathetic appearance.
Weak and depressed expression: drooping features; morbidly lean and elongated face; head supported by hand.
High form level of the execution: perfect organization, proportioned and balanced.
Addition of bottle suggesting need to communicate exact meaning of the picture.
Contrast between deteriorated character of the content and high quality of the execution calling for interpretations other than the self portrait.

37. Tense, vehement and unhappy.
Excessive emphasis on eyes, and taut lines of nose and mouth suggesting bitterness and anger.
Dishevelled, coarse straight hair.
Sharp, nervous strokes.
Scrawled execution.
Unity between tormented content and execution.

38. Schematic and bright.
Intellectualized representation: mouth featured by single line, nose by small v, no brows, lashes or hair.
Large and strongly marked pupils, together with faint smile, expressing keen attention and curiosity.
No indications of sex or age.
Cut-off head.
Unity between unemotional content and sober representation.

39. Rough and sluggish.
Prominent nose, large nostrils, marked-over ears, unshaven face, abundant hair growth, and smoking.
Completion of the delicately structured stimulus into a stubble beard, accentuating the unrefined sensuous character of the picture.

40. Sensual and inept.
Gross features and broad grin; absence of eyes and forehead emphasizing the unintelligent character of this face.
Low form level.
Cut-off representation and broken outline of the head.
Faintness of the pressure contrasting with grossness of content.

In Faces

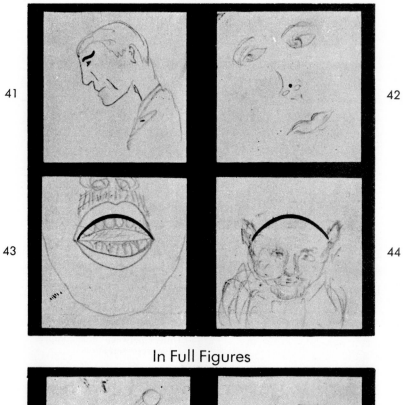

In Full Figures

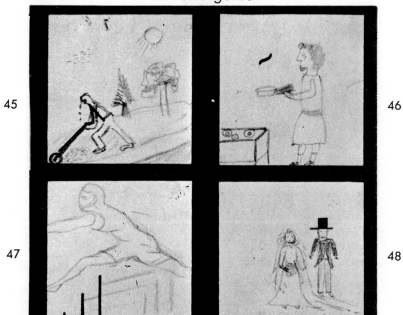

In Animals

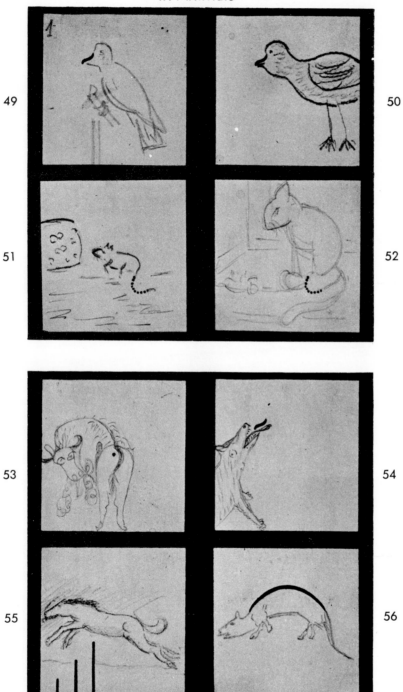

Schematism

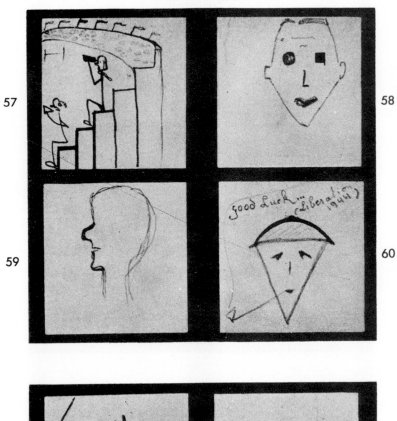

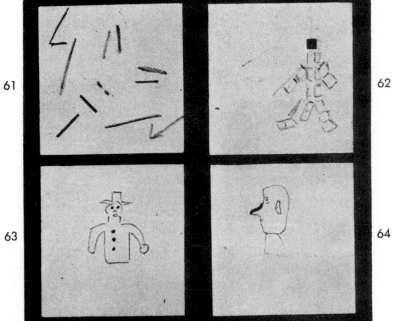

Movement

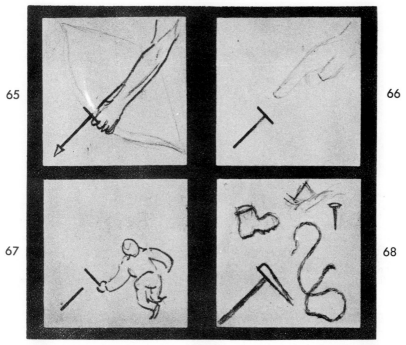

Inanimate Nature

73. Small, pretty, simple.
Gently rounded petals closely grouped; supple stem shooting directly from the earth; tiny leaves and surrounding grass.
Appropriate touch of shading.
Delicate, consistent pressure.
Softly curved fluent lines.
Adequate proportion between stimulus and size of the flower.

74. Meager and pale.
Elongated, irregular petals, widely separated; slightly disjointed structure.
Bare stalk.
Extremely poor form level; awkwardly bent lines.
Weak pressure
Continuous long strokes.
Dull and unharmonious appearance.

75. Full, open, strong.
Regularly arranged and equally shaped petals; large, rich center; leaf bearing stem, strong but not rigid.
Varied intensity of pressure, with predominance of the strong nuances.
Appropriate use of shading, radiating regularly from the center.
Slightly pointed petals, sharply pointed leaf.
Short, cautious strokes.
Unoriginal, but open and colorful representation.

76. Broadly expanding but weak and pale.
Disproportion between large stem, small calyx, flower heart, and wide petals.
Extremely faint pressure.
Shaky discontinuous lines repeatedly marked over.
Carefully closed contour of flower center.
Fragile, unharmonious composition.

77. Simple, fresh, and in a bouquet.
Straight, yet supple stems; firm flowers;
smoothly and equally shaped petals.
Fairly strong, consistent pressure.
Continuous, fluent lines.
Careful execution.
Closed contours.
Moderately expanding, well balanced composition.
Conventional, somewhat naive style.

78. Variegated, small, and close to earth.
Commonplace kinds of flowers.
Bent toward each other.
Composition kept down to level of stimulus;
structure and form of stimulus repeatedly
used in the picture.
Effect of balance, in spite of spare coverage of the square.

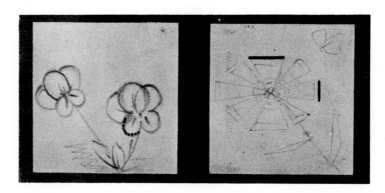

79. Graceful and strong.
Softly curved petals and leaves.
High quality combination of fluency and
firmness of the lines.
Broad intensity range of the pressure producing colorful effect.
Stimulus used only in its roundness, not in
its complex quality.
Careful and sure execution.
Conventional composition.

80. Abstract, rigid, and fragile.
Extremely delicate and painstaking execution.
Refined but cold appearance.
Sharp, needle-like leaves.
Thin, almost invisible stem.
Decorative effect impaired by weakness of
the pressure.
Top form level; rigorous exactness and regularity.
Harmonious composition in spite of inadequate use of stimulus.
Butterfly bringing a favorable note of life
and movement in the over-all artificial character of this picture.

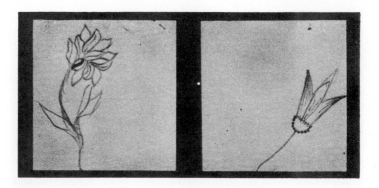

81. Full and tight.
Twisted flame-like petals.
Irregularly shaped stem, heavy in the middle, thin at the base; broken and strongly reinforced lines.
Slightly irregular pressure.
Inconsistent stroke: short strokes firm, long ones unsteady.
Curves lacking fluency.
Somewhat negligent execution; poorly balanced composition.

82. Sharp, frail, unnatural.
Rigid, somewhat overnice.
Unsupportive, floating, threadlike stem.
Leafless.
Fairly varied pressure.
Fluent but slightly inconsistent stroke.
Meticulous execution.
Spare use of space producing unbalanced awkward effect.

83. Heavy and solid.
Budlike, not blossoming; somewhat compact and stiff.
Fairly fluent lines.
Careful execution.
Varied intensity of pressure.
Appropriate use of delicate shading.
Unharmonious over-all effect due to inappropriate use of mechanical dynamic stimulus for representation of organic content, unduly large size, and disproportion between heavy flower and thin stem.

84. Supple and undulating.
Semi-abstract representation more decorative than realistic.
Remarkably fluent and firm execution of the flower contrasting sharply with casual treatment of sun and cloud.
Same disparity appearing in pressure and stroke of both parts.
Open contours of flower.
Rather inadequate use of the stimulus.

85. Full and round.
Bunched and surrounded by verdure.
Attracting birds.
Close to a house (human life implied).
Rich variety of pressure producing a colorful effect.
Naive need for embellishment appearing in the disproportionately large flowers under the trees.
Conventional representation.

86. Fruit-bearing.
Sturdy trunk.
Flowered meadow.
Basket (implying human presence).
Adequately varied pressure: vigorous for trunk, delicate for leaves and grass.
Slightly combination of fruits and flowers.

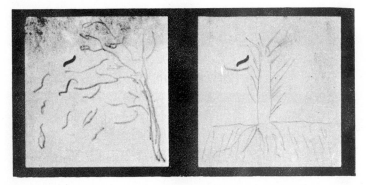

87. Windshaken and stripped.
Falling leaves.
Weak, bent trunk; double break in middle of trunk lines.
Cut-off crest.
Poor form level: lines neither straight nor curved.
Orientation of the picture from right to left, contrary to the usual direction of organization.

88. Barren and dead.
Atrophied, cut-off branches contrasting with massive trunk and huge roots.
Rigid lines.
Dull and weak pressure.
Groundline cut off toward the left and fading toward the right.
Mutilated appearance.

Atmosphere

In Landscapes

In Sea Views

In Sky Views

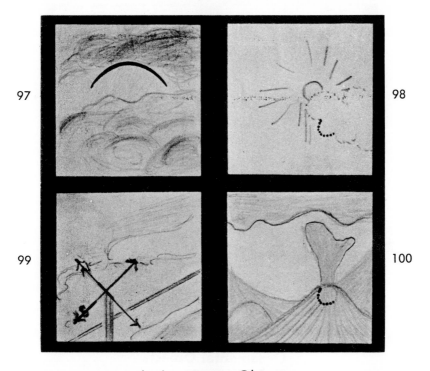

In Inanimate Objects

Utility Objects

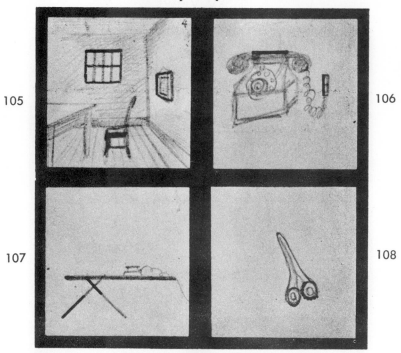

105

106

107

108

Ornamental Objects

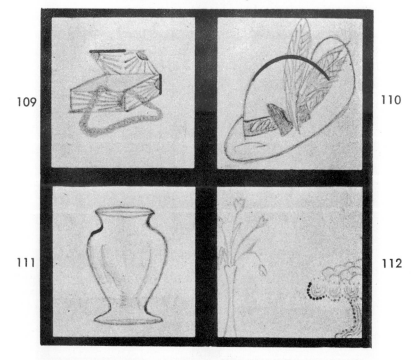

109

110

111

112

Style

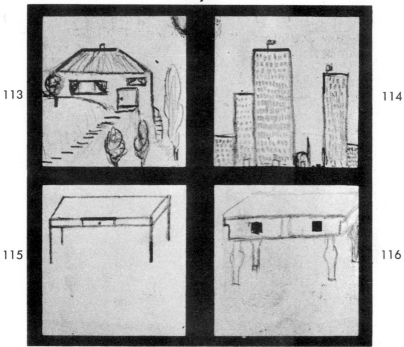

Fancy

121   122

123   124

Phantasm

125   126

127   128

Symbolism

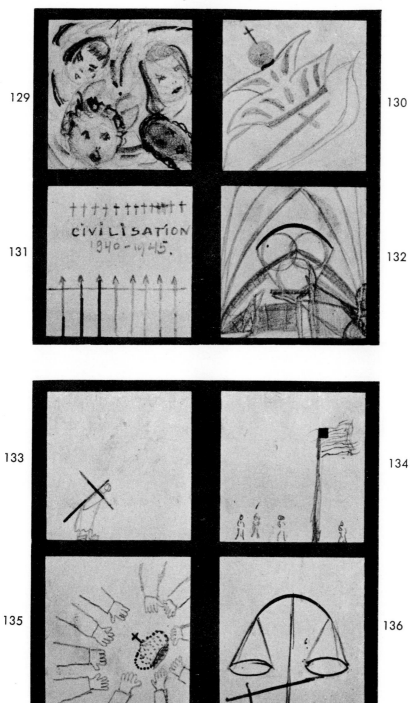

Index